SCHOOL LIBRARIANSHIP SERIES

Edited by Diane de Cordova Biesel

Reference Work in School Library Media Centers: A Book of Case Studies, by Amy G. Job and MaryKay Schnare, 1996.

The School Library Media Specialist as Manager: A Book of Case Studies, by Amy G. Job and MaryKay Schnare, 1997.

Forecasting the Future: School Media Programs in an Age of Change, by Kieth C. Wright and Judith F. Davie, 1999.

Forecasting the Future:
School Media Programs in an Age of Change

Kieth C. Wright
and
Judith F. Davie

School Librarianship Series, No. 3

The Scarecrow Press, Inc.
Lanham, Maryland, and London
1999

SCARECROW PRESS, INC.

Published in the United States of America
by Scarecrow Press, Inc.
4720 Boston Way, Lanham, Maryland 20706
http://www.scarecrowpress.com

4 Pleydell Gardens, Folkestone
Kent CT 20 2DN, England

British Library Cataloguing in Publication Information Available

Library of Congress Cataloging-in-Publication Data

Wright, Kieth C., 1933–
    Forecasting the future : school media programs in an age of change
/ Kieth C. Wright and Judith F. Davie.
        p. cm. — (School librarianship series : no. 3)
    Includes bibliographical references and index.
    ISBN 0-8108-3697-1 (cloth : alk. paper)
        1. School libraries—United States.   2. Instructional materials centers—
United States.   I. Davie, Judith F., 1942–   . II. Title. III. Series.
Z675.S3W96   1999
027.8'0973—dc21   99-28473
                                                                            CIP

⊗™ The paper used in this publication meets the minimum requirements of
American National Standard for Information Sciences—Permanence of Paper for
Printed Library Materials, ANSI/NISO Z39.48–1992.
Manufactured in the United States of America.

Contents

Editor's Foreword

The works in the School Librarianship Series are directed toward the library school professor, the library school student, and the district supervisor. The role of the school library media specialist as an agent of change within the educational system will be examined. The series will explore the philosophical basis of school librarianship yesterday, today, and tomorrow.

In *Forecasting the Future*, Wright and Davie have provided an analysis of the societal and economic changes that will affect school libraries of the future. They state that library media programs need to be viewed as going on everywhere in the school and its related community and as assisting everyone—students, teachers, administrators, and the community—in connecting to information resources anywhere in the world. There should be no separate library media program because everything that happens in the library media center must be related to the instructional program of the school.

It will become customary, I feel, to refer to this book as the primary work in its field against which all others will be measured.

Diane de Cordova Biesel
Series Editor

Preface

This book focuses on the library media specialist as instructor and instructional consultant. Library media specialists have been viewed in a number of different roles—as bookkeepers, as storytellers, as people who keep things organized. However, in the context of education, the school library media specialist is an *instructor*. He/she is trained to select appropriate materials for individual or group instruction and to support instruction by being a planner of instruction and a co-instructor with other teachers.

If the library media specialist is viewed as a teacher among teachers, then the library media center is viewed as a major support and resource for the instructional program of the school. In this context we see the information-finding tools of that center as resources that point teachers and students to resources in the school, the neighborhood, the community, and the world. The library media specialist works cooperatively with others to create a teaching/learning environment and collection that brings out all of the most positive capabilities that students have. The goal of instruction is to tap the learning styles and intelligences of students and teachers in ways that communicate high learning expectations to everyone.

Although these principles are presented as recommendations, the authors do not mean to imply that library media programs can continue to do whatever the library media specialist or the administration thinks is a good idea. We are far beyond that point in the knowledge base about effective school library media programs. Not just anyone's idea of what is effective will do. Education is beyond the stage of "everyone's opinions have the same weight."

It is time for library media programs to be operated under standard operating procedures adapted to the needs of the particular school and its students and staff. Library media specialists need to make good use of the research that has already been done and contribute to that research through planning, implementation, and evaluation of their programs on a continuing basis.

As the authors began thinking about the media program in the context of the future of education, it became increasingly clear that another narrative on how to run a school library media program well would not be helpful. Therefore, this book is organized on the basis of selected principles for the media program and then these principles are applied in the context of the future of education.

The book begins with several chapters to set the context for discussion of library media principles. Chapter 1 discusses the state of current school library media programs; chapter 2 presents a vision of future library media programs; chapter 3 details the obstacles to future library media program development; and chapter 4 outlines a new vision for these programs.

The remaining chapters of the book explore specific principles for media programs in the context of current and anticipated school reform. Chapter 5 discusses people principles; chapter 6 introduces instructional and collection development principles; chapter 7 presents scheduling principles; chapter 8 details planning and evaluation principles; chapter 9 discusses budgeting principles; chapter 10 outlines facilities principles; chapter 11 presents technology principles; and chapter 12 introduces high reliability principles as they apply to school library media programs.

Many educators, including the authors, have become convinced that the school cannot ignore the total life of the student and his/her family. Students bring the rest of their lives into the school setting. In our emerging information society, it is not acceptable to have any students who do not learn the basic skills necessary for functioning in the society. Society cannot afford to have partial learners, non-learners, or students who drop out.

The authors suggest that the school of the future should take as its overarching goal becoming a full-service school in which many different cultural, educational, health, and social services programs are available to students, families, and the larger community. It is important to remember that for many children the teacher, the assistant, or the library specialist may be the only caring adult in the child's life. The library media center and its collaborative instructional programs can provide a wonderful environment for resilience factors to grow. Creating numerous opportunities for students and teachers to talk with each other, imagining and delivering programs that celebrate the delight we find in one another's company, highlighting the family and life experiences of authors, illustrators, and storytellers who celebrate together—all such activities contribute to resilience.

Within these chapters the authors have used the experiences of library media specialists and supervisors who work on a day-to-day basis in the midst of the rapid changes in schools. Position statements from professional organizations and research on schools, schooling, school reform, and best practices in library media services have been highlighted at appropriate points.

Acknowledgments

This book could not have been written without the assistance of many library media specialists in North Carolina and the American Library Association. The authors want to give special thanks to the teachers, staff, and principal of Hampton Year Round School in the Guilford County School System of North Carolina for their assistance in helping the authors develop a sharper philosophy of school library media programs in the context of year-round public education.

1

Current School Library
Media Programs

Introduction

In order to take some measure of the future of school library media programs, we need to know something about the current state of those programs. A review of the literature reveals some specifics about the current state of affairs: (1) wide disparity exists among the library media programs available in schools and school systems; (2) among all the roles of the library media specialist, the teaching role is the one most widely understood, and the instructional consultant role the least well understood; (3) the quality and nature of a library media program and the varied roles of the library media specialist do have an impact on student outcomes; (4) flexible scheduling is essential as a means of integrating library/information skills into curricular areas; (5) information and communication technologies are changing library media programs and all the roles of the library media specialist; (6) emerging alternatives to traditional schooling will have a considerable effect on library media services.

Wide Disparity Exists among
Library Media Programs

The disparity in funding, staffing, and programs found in American public education is reflected in its school library media programs. Early in the 1990s the Schools and Staffing Survey (SASS) conducted by the National Center for Education Statistics provided estimates of library/media center resources. Data from the 1990–91 SASS show that most public and private schools in the nation had libraries/media centers, but these programs were understaffed in many cases, particularly in small schools.

When library/media center facilities and staff are available, between one-quarter and one-third of the teachers strongly agree that they work with library/media center staff in planning instruction.[1] More specifically, 96 percent of public and 87 percent of private elementary and secondary schools in the United States had a library or library media center. The expansion in the number of library media specialists seen between 1960 and 1980 has slowed, and in the early 1990s school library media center staffing levels have not kept pace with increases in student enrollment.

In the public sector, only 3 percent of schools with library media centers did not employ some kind of media center staff, but over half of the smaller, elementary, and non-Catholic religious private schools had neither a librarian/media specialist nor a library aide. Few school principals reported that the school librarian or media specialist had much influence over curriculum decisions, although private school librarians were more likely to be acknowledged as influential.[2]

In 1993, the American Library Association and the National Commission on Libraries and Information Science concluded that up-to-date statistics about school library media centers were needed in light of current state and local reform efforts and pending federal legislation related to the National Education Goals.[3] A questionnaire was sent to school libraries in twelve states to obtain information for a "snapshot" of the current status of library media centers. This report highlights the following: (1) many library media programs are poorly equipped to support instruction; (2) half of the elementary school libraries buy less than one book per student per year; and (3) almost no library media centers have access to the Internet.

The Miller and Shontz studies of school library media program funding clearly indicate a wide disparity in funding for school libraries. The most disturbing thing about their study is the fact that we have numerous schools with almost no resources and a few schools with a vast array of resources.[4] In their most recent study, published in 1996, Miller and Shontz illustrate the wide disparity among school library media programs.[5] When comparing high-technology schools (schools with both online circulation and an online catalog system) they found that high-technology schools spend twice as much money on technology as the low-technology schools (which do not have online circulation or catalog systems). The high-technology schools also spend more funds on books and their library media staff is more involved in staff development and in collaboration with teachers.

Thus it becomes difficult to generalize about school library media programs because of the wide disparity in funding, personnel, and programs. Common sense tells us that library media programs that are better funded, better staffed, and have better programs should make a difference in the education of children; however, looking across the nation, it is obvious that this commonsense opinion is not shared by the public that funds schools and libraries. In 1996, the Benton Foundation published *Buildings, Books, and Bytes*. In their survey of library leaders and library users, they found that:

A focus group of frequent library users affirmed much of the polling data, endorsing America's trust in libraries and sounding warnings about the need to remain relevant. In many respects, focus group participants saw libraries as playing an important role in their communities. . . . They also warmly endorsed the concept of the library as a place that provided equal and free access to information, especially to the information have-nots.

Yet, in other important ways, the focus group participants placed libraries at the fringes of modern life, especially in relation to the technological revolution. Most telling, they did not see libraries leading the way in the digital revolution. In fact, they thought libraries should take a reactive role, adapting to new technologies. Libraries "should stay just behind the curve. We don't need them to be on the curve because most people aren't," as one participant put it. . . . When asked to think about the role of libraries in the future, they placed libraries firmly in the past. In 30 years, they said, libraries would be relegated to a "kind of museum where people can go and look up stuff from way back when." Thus, the library of the future, far from being a technology leader, would function as an information archive.[6]

The Teaching Role of Media Specialists Is Understood

Information Power: Guidelines for School Library Media Programs outlines three major roles for the library media specialist: teacher, information specialist, and instructional consultant.[7] *Information Power:*

Building Partnerships for Learning discusses the library media specialist's role in terms of teacher, instructional partner, information specialist, and program administrator.[8] The teaching role, especially
focused on library and/or information skills, is widely familiar to
library media specialists, teachers, and administrators.[9]

Despite being discussed at length in the literature, the information
specialist and instructional consultant roles are less well understood or
implemented, although they are clearly important to curriculum development and the delivery of instruction in schools. There is considerable variability in the definitions and descriptions of these curriculum-related roles. The earlier national guidelines, *Media Programs:
District and School,* stated that the media specialist's involvement in curriculum lies in initiating and participating in curriculum development
and implementation.[10] With respect to the library media specialist as
an instructional consultant, *Information Power* listed four major responsibilities: (1) participating in curriculum design and assessment;
(2) helping teachers develop instructional activities; (3) providing expertise in materials and technology; and (4) translating curricular
needs into library media program goals and objectives.[11] These responsibilities are further refined into specific activities for the library
media specialist who is expected to: (1) participate in building, district,
department, and grade-level curriculum development and assessment
projects on a regular basis; (2) offer teachers assistance in using information resources, acquiring and assessing instructional materials, and
incorporating information skills into the classroom curriculum; (3) use
a systematic instructional development process in working with
teachers to improve instructional activities; and (4) provide leadership
in the assessment, evaluation, and implementation of information and
instructional technologies.[12]

The new standards attempt to clarify the interrelationships
between collaboration, leadership, and technology as integral aspects
of the library media program.[13] The central focus of all library media
specialist roles is *student learning.* Collaboration is defined as "working with others" (p. 50) and the documents stress the importance of
collaboration as defined by the following:

> Collaboration is a symbiotic process that requires active, genuine
> effort and commitment by all members of the instructional team. It
> may take considerable time and energy to establish truly collaborative
> relationships, but developing effective collaborative strategies is
> crucial to the library media program. Collaborating with the full
> range of school personnel to identify and solve information problems

presents a model of the approach that students and other must take to survive in the information age.[14]

Even the subtitle of the new edition of *Information Power* focuses on "building partnerships for learning." The role of the library media specialist is to "encourage a culture of collaboration throughout the school."[15] Such a culture is not part of the traditional model of schooling in America, which has tended to treat classroom activities, areas of study, and extracurricular events as isolated and unrelated to each other.

In 1977, Barron noted that many teachers and administrators still had negative attitudes toward school library media specialists as colleagues in curriculum development.[16] The literature underscores the difference between library media specialists' potential as curriculum consultants and the actual extent of their involvement in curriculum planning with teachers and school-wide curriculum committees. Ely saw the potential for library media specialists to become involved in curriculum design because of their ability to relate instructional media to stated instructional objectives in the teaching/learning process.[17] The more confident and competent the library media specialist is in using specific instructional media for instructional purposes, the greater the possibility of a role in curriculum planning and integration.

Loertscher developed an eleven-level taxonomy for measuring the school library media specialists' involvement with curriculum and instruction. He divided these levels into three broad categories: warehousing services, direct services to teachers and students, and resource-based teaching. In his view, the highest level of involvement was happening in the resource-based teaching category and in curriculum development, where the library media specialist was an integrally involved curriculum consultant.[18] Turner identified these global curriculum-related activities performed by library media specialists: (1) promoting reading and viewing by children and young adults; (2) providing library instruction and reference services; and (3) helping teachers in the design, implementation, and evaluation of instruction. He saw the difficulties in implementing these activities and placed the responsibility on library media personnel who were reluctant to assume new roles as they faced increasingly complex expectations.[19] In addressing the "reinvention" of the school library Loertscher has noted that part of the difficulty may also lie in the lack of understanding about the roles of the library media specialist on the part of administrators, school boards, and teachers. His 1998 book, *Reinvent Your School's Library in the Age of Technology*, is addressed to principals and superintendents as they supervise the rapidly changing learning environment of students and teachers.[20]

Eisenberg and Berkowitz have stressed several factors forcing a redefinition of the library media specialists' roles. Among them are technological change, the information explosion, a renewed emphasis on lifelong learning skills, and an increasing acceptance of additional responsibilities by library media specialists. They see five emerging roles for library media specialists: (1) collection management based on a unified media concept; (2) promotion of literature and guidance in the use of media; (3) teaching information skills through integration with classroom curriculum; (4) acting as a catalyst or agent of change through awareness of technology and consultation on curriculum and instructional design; and (5) assuming information management responsibilities beyond the centralized library media center facility. Based on these activities, they give a broad definition of the curricular role of the library media specialist.[21]

In spite of these efforts, the instructional consultant role of the library media specialist remains unclear to many of the professionals in the school scene. Eisenberg and Berkowitz offer the following explanation for the disparity between theory and practice: (1) the curriculum role is undefined; (2) resources are limited; (3) incentives for greater involvement are lacking; and (4) teachers and administrators do not frequently use school library media specialists as curriculum consultants. If they are consulted at all, library media specialists are often looked upon as supplementary participants when curriculum concerns are addressed by teachers, administrators, and boards of education.[22]

The roles that the library media specialist assumes in developing a library media program vary greatly depending on the view of those roles held by principals, system-level administrators, state department staff, teachers, and the public. Often the media specialist will need to educate other professionals as to the instructional importance and appropriateness of information specialist and consultant roles.

Media Programs Have an Impact on Student Outcomes

Library media specialists and their professional associations have always contended that high-quality, well-funded library media pro-

grams with sufficient staff, adequate materials, appropriate scheduling, and integration with the curriculum have positive outcomes in
terms of student learning. Lance's 1994 Colorado study points out
that most studies of this relationship were conducted between 1959
and 1979 and were limited in scope, and they usually used a small
number of subjects in a limited geographical area.[23] His carefully designed study provides evidence to support several conclusions about
the impact of school library media centers and academic
achievement:

1. *There is a relationship between expenditures on library media programs
   and test performance, particularly when social and economic differences
   between communities and schools are controlled.*
   Lance found that students at schools with better funded library
   media programs tend to achieve higher average reading scores,
   whether their schools and communities are rich or poor and
   whether adults in the community are well or poorly educated.
   Thus funding library media centers is more significant in student
   outcomes than the general wealth of the community and the education level of adults in that community.

2. *The number of library media program staff and the size and variety of
   collections are the intervening characteristics of those programs which
   help to explain the relationship of funding to reading scores.*
   Lance found that the size of the library media program's total staff
   and the size and variety of its collection are important characteristics of library media programs that can intervene between expenditures and test performance. The specific purposes of library
   funding are to ensure adequate levels of staffing in relation to the
   school's enrollment and a local collection that offers students a
   large number of materials in a variety of formats.

3. *The performance of an instructional role by library media specialists
   helps predict test performance.*
   Lance found that students whose library media specialists played
   such a role tended to achieve higher average test scores. In planning for the future, the authors of this book argue that we do
   not need to prove the value of library media programs in the
   teaching–learning process; we need to implement programs that
   demonstrate that value.[24] The future of school library media
   programs is tied to making these findings have realistic meaning
   for those who make political and funding decisions. If school libraries are to survive and flourish in the future, the school library

media personnel are going to have to convince a large number of people that, in fact, school library media programs *do* make a significant difference in student outcomes—measured in whatever way they wish to assess them.

In a 1998 follow-up to the Lance studies, the Colorado Library Research Service reports that library media specialists and technology are linked to higher test scores. Specifically, students are likely to earn higher reading scores on the Colorado Student Assessment program provided that their schools have state-endorsed library media specialists, that those specialists are supported by aides, and that the media specialists play a vital instructional role. They also report that higher student scores are positively linked to library media programs that incorporate the latest information technologies.[25]

Integrating Information Skills Demands Flexible Scheduling

The idea of moving away from rigid, once-a-week scheduling of students into libraries has been around for a long time. It is true that scheduling every class into the library media center does ensure that all students will have access to resources. The problem is that they may have access at times when they do not have any real reason for that access. Even primary grade students know how to judge the relevance of an activity to their lives. If teachers and students have the flexibility of using the library media center and its varied resources in ways and at times that are related to what they are doing in their classrooms, then the resources are more likely to be used effectively and better learning will take place.

Simply scheduling students into the library does not ensure that any learning will take place, nor that what is learned will be related in any way to their classroom experiences. Naturally, the principal, lead teacher, and library media specialist will need to keep records and note in the lesson planning materials which teachers are not making full use of the library media center. Once noted, these teachers and their instructional activities can become the target of collaborative efforts to encourage relevant use of the library media center resources and programs.

Flexible scheduling in the library media center began in 1910 when Ayres and McKinnie wrote that students should be able to visit the library "in leisure at different times during the day instead of going in haste at one time."[26] Fargo said that as schools move away from rigid scheduling "there is evident an inclination to send individuals or committees from the classroom to the library at any time as the need arises."[27] Douglas endorsed the regular scheduling of classes in the library media center, but went on to say that "schedule should include periods when no class or group is scheduled to be in the room. This arrangement permits individuals and small groups to use the library without interruption."[28]

Flexible scheduling in library media programs is dependent on a more general flexibility in the total instructional program of the school. All school schedules affect the schedule of the library media program. When an instructional program recognizes differences in the ways students learn and teachers teach, there will be flexibility in instructional scheduling. That flexibility should extend into when and how the library media center and the instructional skills of the library media specialist are utilized. Rather than having identically scheduled times for all classes in the school library media center, a schedule that recognizes differences among learners is based on consultation with each classroom teacher so that library media activities are correlated with classroom instruction and time is allowed for different rates and styles of student learning as well as difference in content.

Future library media programs cannot afford to have programs or other activities in the library media center that do not have this obvious correlation. Such flexibility is the exact opposite of the factory model of education, which tended to treat all students as identical units to be pushed through a series of identical processes at the same rate—very much like a production line. In the context of library media programs, this kind of flexible scheduling allows the school library media specialist and teachers to plan extended periods during the day for specific instructional uses; it can also include the daily scheduling of a particular class or group of students for up to a week or more. In fact, many flexible schedules include regular scheduling of specific groups of children *if that schedule meets the learning needs of the students.*

Substantial benefits result from flexible scheduling in the library media center. Van Deusen studied fifth graders and found convincing evidence that media specialists were more closely involved with the curriculum, and that there was an increase in the information skills integration into the curriculum in circumstances of flexible scheduling.[29] Toor states that with flexible scheduling there are improvements in access to resources, information analysis skills, and critical thinking skills.[30] Lankford cites *Prisoners of Time*, the report of the National Education Commission on Time and Learning, which begins by stressing that American education has held the amount of time allotted for education constant for the past one hundred fifty years. The theme has been "learn what you can in the time we give you." She criticizes fixed schedules because they limit the access of students, teachers, and media specialists to the "teachable moment" and points out that fixed schedules also severely limit the amount of time teachers and media specialists have for cooperative planning.[31]

Lankford goes on to describe a district-wide project to provide elementary schoolchildren with flexible library access, including such elements as factors leading to the project's success; people's attitudes as the greatest obstacle to change; how the project was sold to librarians and principals; project problem solving; and lessons learned during the project's first year. For media specialists the overriding concern seemed to be, "What happens if I give up *my* control in the library?"

Here is her summary of what the school system learned about flexible access:

1. It is beneficial to the learner in terms of enhancing information-gathering skills, increasing an appreciation of literature, and conducting activities which foster lifelong learning and library use.

2. What is taught and learned in the library media center cannot be separated from what is taught and learned in the classrooms.

3. Multiple activities and multiple grade levels can function in the library media center at the same time.

4. Flexible access results in no loss of control by the library media specialist, but enhances her/his role in the teaching/learning process.

5. Flexible access helps create students who are excited about learning and who become self-motivated learners eager to conduct and complete research projects.

6. Children in kindergarten and first grade can find their own way to the library for checkout of materials and can acquire basic skills necessary to later success in information research.

7. Flexible access and multiple usage increase noise levels and produce some disorder.

8. Flexible access gives full visibility to the creative capacities of the library media specialist.

All of the roles—teacher, organizer, leader, resource specialist, reading consultant, and curriculum wizard—become obvious in planning sessions with teachers and students. In 1991 the American Association of School Librarians issued a position statement on flexible scheduling[32] that encouraged planning between library media specialists and classroom teachers as well as both scheduled and unscheduled visits by students. The statement went on to affirm that "an open schedule must be maintained. Classes cannot be scheduled in the library media center to provide teacher release or preparation time."[33]

Emerging Technologies Are Changing Programs and Media Specialists' Roles

Information 2000 sets the stage for rapid technological change in this way:

> The Information Age is well underway. It has forever transformed the working world. As an indication, in some fields the half-life of technical information can be as short as three months. . . . Governments, companies, educational institutions, and people struggle to keep pace. . . . The now identifiable developing trend challenges the former national economic cornerstone of reliance on manufacturing productivity with the need to enhance literacy, increase productivity, and strengthen democracy to meet the requirements of an information-dependent world. The pivotal need for libraries and information services has been defined.[34]

In discussing the vision for school library media programs, *Information Power* (1988) notes that "today's student lives and learns in a world that has been radically altered by the ready availability of vast stores of information in a variety of formats. Innovations in traditional printing techniques have joined with advances in electronic technologies to transform the ways we seek and gain information."[35]

Business, government, and social institutions (including schools) are part of an "information society" in which the ability to find, interpret, and use appropriate information is critical.[36] Such higher order thinking abilities, also called "critical thinking skills," are proposed as necessary for all children in our society so that they can function in the emerging information society. Many argue that we are in the midst of a revolution based on computer-related technologies. Peter Drucker calls this society the "knowledge society," made up of large organizations—government and business—which operate on the flow of information. He goes on to note specific skills needed in that society, including "the ability to present ideas orally and in writing; the ability to work with people; the ability to shape and direct one's own work, contribution and career."[37] In passing, the author notes that none of these skills is particularly dependent on computer-related technologies.

As the use of such technologies transforms the way in which society operates, the pace of change has been astonishing. Even a decade ago, Toong and Gupta could claim that, "if [aircraft technology] had evolved as spectacularly as the computer industry over the last 25 years, a Boeing 767 would cost $500 today and it would circle the globe in 20 minutes on 5 gallons of fuel."[38] Or, as Reddy puts it, "If automotive technology changed at the same rate [as information technologies], a Rolls-Royce would cost less than 10 dollars, get over 100 thousand miles per gallon, and go at a speed of over one million miles an hour."[39] Business and industry use computer-related technologies for two reasons: (1) the sharp decline in computer costs contrasted with the sharp increase in human costs, and (2) the dramatic increase in the capacity of this technology to create, manipulate and communicate needed information. The lowering of equipment costs has kept pace with the huge expansion in the computing power and storage capacity of personal computer systems. If computing capacity (central processing capacity, memory capacity, and disk storage capacity) is held constant, costs have declined dramatically. Anderla and Dunning have estimated that computer costs will continue to decline at about 25 percent per year (without adjustment for inflation).[40]

By 1992 it was possible for the personal computer user to buy a machine that had far greater capacity in computing speed, memory, and storage than many previous mainframe computers—at a much lower cost. These costs have continued to decline as the capabilities of computers have increased. The ability to manipulate information successfully has become critical in our time. These information management abilities have been called "information literacy." Todd defines information literacy as:

The ability to use information purposefully and effectively. It is a holistic, interactive learning process encompassing the skills-based phases of defining, locating, selecting, organizing, presenting, and evaluating information from sources that include books and other media, experiences, and people; being able to consider information in light of knowledge; adding information to current knowledge; and applying this knowledge to solve information needs.[41]

Information Power (1998) calls information literacy "the term being applied to the skills of information problem-solving. . . . Many aspects of both the school restructuring movement and library media programs relate directly to information literacy and its impact on student learning."[42]

Its position statement goes on to point out that the Association of Supervision and Curriculum Development (ASCD) adopted the following statements:

Information literacy equips individuals to take advantage of the opportunities inherent in the global information society. Information literacy should be a part of every student's educational experience. ASCD urges schools, colleges, and universities to integrate information literacy programs into learning programs for all students.

ASCD is one of sixty educational associations that have formed the National Forum on Information Literacy (NFIL). *Information Power's* simple definition of information literacy is "the ability to find and use information."[43]

The changing concept of information literacy has had an effect on the restructuring of schools with calls for teachers to assume the role of coaches and students to become active learners who build their own knowledge frameworks in the process of interacting with a variety of information sources and formats (also called resource-based learning). The verbs most often used to describe information literacy include: locating, interpreting, analyzing, synthesizing, evaluating, and communicating information. As an example, the Maryland State Department of Education incorporates information literacy in seven outcomes: (1) students will demonstrate the ability to locate and use materials and equipment; (2) they will demonstrate the ability to review, evaluate, and select media for an identified information need; (3) they will demonstrate the ability to learn and apply study, research, reference, and critical thinking skills to organize information; (4) they will demonstrate the ability to comprehend content in various types of media; (5) they will demonstrate the ability to retrieve and manage information; (6) they will demonstrate an appreciation of books and other media as sources of information and recreation; and (7) they will demonstrate the ability to create print and nonprint media.[44]

Another example focusing on the restructuring of library media programs is the National Library Power Program. The DeWitt Wallace-Reader's Digest Fund started the program in 1988 in New York City public schools. In the first three years of the program, more than one hundred school library media centers were renovated and improved. Based on that success, the fund expanded the program nationally and made grants to local education funds throughout the country. By 1996 the National Library Power Program was implemented in nineteen sites nationwide and the fund's investment in the 463,000 children in Library Power schools totaled more than $40 million. The goals of this national program are: (1) to create a national vision and new expectations for public elementary and middle school library programs and to encourage new and innovative uses of the library's physical and human resources; (2) to create exemplary models of library media programs that are an integral part of the educational process; (3) to strengthen the role of the librarian as a teacher, information specialist, and learning facilitator who assists teachers and students in becoming effective users of ideas and information; (4) to encourage collaboration among teachers, administrators, and librarians that results in significant improvement in teaching and learning processes; (5) to demonstrate the significant contributions that library programs can make to school reform and restructuring efforts; and (6) to encourage the creation of partnerships among leaders in school districts, public libraries, community agencies, business communities, academic institutions, and parent groups to improve and support school library programs.[45]

Readers of this book will not take seriously the proposal that libraries will all become virtual places and the traditional library media center will disappear. Yet school library media programs have been greatly impacted by the emergence of new technologies since the introduction of audiovisual education in the post–World War II era. The computer-related technologies now emerging will clearly affect the ways in which teachers, students, and parents access information, and will require searching, evaluation, and production skills not required in a previous age. Teaching students and teachers to be effective users of these emerging information technologies will be a major task.

Library Media Services Are
Affected by Alternative Programs

Alternatives to public education have existed since prerevolutionary days in the United States. Many private and religious agencies have established tuition-based schools with specific educational, cultural, and religious objectives. Currently, alternatives include private schools, schools of choice, charter schools, and home schooling. Each of these alternatives is discussed below together with implications for school library media services.

Private Schools

It is a widely held public perception that the private schools in this country are superior to public schools. The National Education Longitudinal Study (NELS) completed by the U.S. Department of Education's National Center for Education Statistics in 1988 describes the public's opinion of private schools. According to NELS, students in nonpublic schools do more homework, watch less TV, and have higher educational goals than their public school counterparts. Other statistical reports document that 44.6 percent of parents with children in public schools say they would enroll their children in a private school if there were no financial obstacle. Also, public school parents are four times more likely to be dissatisfied with their child's school.[46] On the other hand, in a survey for the University of Florida's Bureau of Economic and Business Research, Keen found that many Florida parents prefer the diversity and quality of public schools and would not send their children to private schools even if tuition were paid.[47]

The bureau asked about Florida schools during its monthly consumer surveys of Floridians in August, September, and February of 1995. Conway has examined two of the characteristics contributing to the positive assessment of private educational programs: (1) the smallness factor, and (2) the school culture factor. These two factors are examined in more detail below.[48]

First, consider the smallness factor. Research on the impact of reducing class size is mixed, but the public's perception is that private school classes are smaller than public education classes and that this smaller class size has an impact on the quality of life in the school.[49] The average public school is about twice as large as the average private school. Large school size compounds the difficulties that confront children and youth—from poor attitudes about school, to substance abuse, to achievement levels.[50] We may not understand how private schools improve the quality of life, although it is clear that being able to select (and deselect) student applications does have an impact.[51]

Second, consider the school culture factor. One major aspect of school culture is the presence or absence of shared goals among teachers, students, parents, and the community. Large public schools often serve widely diverse groups residing within a single enrollment district. The school population—students, parents, and teachers— rarely comes together as a single community to discuss the purposes or goals of the school to which they all are committed. There are often no shared goals related to educational outcomes. Because of this lack of shared purposes, public schools tend to be most account- able for goals set by their local school districts or state departments of education. Often these goals are expressed in concrete, quanti- tative terms: academic achievement scores, attendance rates, and dropout statistics. Technical solutions are sought to raise achieve- ment scores, compel children to come to school, and keep them coming until they graduate. Private schools tend to have a shared commitment to specific educational, religious, or philosophical goals, many of which can not be measured in quantitative terms, but lie in the arena of the quality of life and its purposes.

A major aspect of school culture is found in the personal loyalties of those involved in the schools. In public education such loyalties are very often found centered around cocurricular activities such as athletic programs, band, and various clubs. Occasionally, such loyalty will be found among teachers and parents of specifically identified and tracked groups in the public schools such as the gifted, the men- tally or physically challenged, and so on. Personal loyalty seems to be at the heart of many private schools. Such personal loyalties or feel- ings of connectedness are not limited to private education; often they are formed in small schools, public or private.[52]

When students and parents feel they know the teachers and school leaders, and are known by them, and feel that teachers care about the students, the students perform better.[53] Studies of the teaching conditions in private schools suggest that the culture of pri- vate schools might arise from the interactions of teachers—who are empowered and highly valued by the institution—with the parents, students, and the school's leadership.

School culture is strengthened by common commitments. Shared commitments to cultural goals, religious ideals, or philosophical positions always create a strong cultural base. Public schools are asked (or mandated) to reflect the diversity of the community's sentiment; private schools are free to establish their own sentiments and actively profess them to those who enroll. Private schools transmit what they consider worthy to new teachers, parents, and students through institutional rituals and traditions (e.g., chapel services, honor codes, assemblies, rituals, dress codes, etc.). Most private school teachers report that they have a sense of shared institutional values and they believe their colleagues share them as well.[54] The well-established private school usually enjoys the support of the parents and alumni for maintaining its institutional beliefs and customs despite the vicissitudes of public sentiments.

There is a kind of tacit understanding present among the school staff and the parents that because they have chosen the private school and are paying tuition, the people who enroll their children in private schools embrace, or at least accept, the school's values. In contrast, public schools are often required to respond to changing public opinion and diverse sentiments; thus, they may be perceived, fairly or unfairly, as committed only to accepting the diversity of their students' cultural backgrounds and standing for no specific set of traditions.

One of the most curious phenomena in private schools is that although teacher pay in private schools lags significantly behind that of their public school colleagues, the quality of the private school faculty is believed to be very high. Why should private schools seem to "pay less and get more" instead of "getting what they pay for?" The answer may lie in how the school impresses on the teacher common sentiments about teaching. Research shows that most teachers upon entering the profession do not fundamentally differ in purpose; however, the culture of the private school apparently helps shape the individual teacher professionally and makes good teaching not only possible "but more likely."[55]

Private schools programs have implications for library media programs both in those schools and in public schools. Private schools often operate on very limited budgets and have widely varying funding and staffing patterns for library media services, ranging from volunteer staffing of library programs based on information resources received as gifts all the way to professional staffing and outstanding resource and technology funding. If, indeed, private schools are popular with parents and the rest of the community, then public sentiment to provide adequate tax-based funding to public school library services will diminish. If public funding for private education through vouchers or schools of choice becomes a reality, both private and public education may not be able to afford adequate library media services.

Schools of Choice, Vouchers, and Charter Schools

Two basic types of programs could potentially receive governmental funding at the federal or state levels: those in which families choose among various options within a public school or district, and those in which vouchers are used. Voucher systems establish a grant to parents and allow them to select school programs, using the vouchers to pay for public and/or private education. Many advocates of public education fear that voucher systems will undermine both funding for and participation in public education. If private educational programs can exclude students through their application procedures, public schools could increasingly become racially and economically segregated. Raywid argues that "to assign parents full and unfettered responsibility for choosing their children's education in an open market is to telegraph the message that the matter is solely their affair and not the community's concern."[56]

She contends that the perception of education as a public as well as a private good is crucial to the survival of public education. She points out that a voucher system could create a situation where private schools serve the affluent and public schools serve the poor. Lobbyists and special interest groups would then establish themselves around the private schools, thus making the voucher system impossible to reverse.

Fear of the resegregation of schools into rich and poor populations has caused some educational reformers to suggest keeping choice within the boundaries of the public school systems through alternative school programs. Alternative schools consist of a distinct administrative unit, voluntary student and staff participation, responsiveness to particular needs or interests not served in the public core school, a structural design strongly influenced or established by local constituents, and a developmental format that encourages a broad range of student personal and academic skills. Power tends to be more evenly distributed among students, teachers, and administrators. Curriculum is often characterized by independent study and experiential learning.

Many alternative programs offer greater autonomy, especially the freedom to withdraw from the program, which creates a relaxed, congenial environment and gives students a sense of control over and responsibility for their learning. Magnet schools, as an example, are often organized around a theme, with all subjects revolving in relation to the core emphasis. Brought together by common goals, constituents then work on developing an appropriate curriculum. Some school systems attempt to create magnet or specialty schools within other schools; however, the most common pattern is for magnet schools to be located in areas with high minority enrollment with the hope that the program of the school will attract parents and their children to enroll in that school thereby improving racial balance.

Charter Schools

Dunn reports that as of October 1995, seventeen states had adopted charter-school legislation. The strength and scope of charter-school laws vary greatly among states. Charter laws were passed in 1995 by the states of Alaska, Arkansas, Louisiana, North Carolina, Rhode Island, and Wyoming. There are also older charter schools in California, Colorado, Georgia, Hawaii, Kansas, Massachusetts, Michigan, Minnesota, New Mexico, and Wisconsin.[57]

Proponents argue that charter schools offer flexibility, decentralized decision making, performance accountability, school choice, and increased pressure for change. Opponents charge that charter schools are expensive and that they may reduce teacher salaries and disrupt existing desegregation plans. Some critics have stated that charter schools may very well herald the beginning of the end of public education as it now exists. Those sounding this alarm claim that these schools will compete with public schools for much-needed financial resources while refusing to accept students with special needs. Others fear that the schools will serve as a Trojan horse for extremists who, for religious or political reasons, would use public funds to finance schools whose primary purpose would be to indoctrinate students rather than educate them.

Generally, charter schools arise in a climate of reform and are the result of an increasing public demand for accountability, quality, and choice in public schools. In response to these demands, the Texas legislature created a new category of public schools and freed them from many of the mandated constraints that some critics claim inhibit regular public schools from implementing truly innovative programs.

In most states where such legislation has been passed, any interested group, including parents, students, teachers, or local leaders, may form a charter school by incorporating as an educational foundation and filing an application with the state board of education or the local educational agency (often the school board). The applications are then reviewed and competitively awarded. Once the group has been granted a charter, it can enroll students and bill the state for the "average daily attendance" of those students, depending on the state's per-pupil allocation. In many areas charter schools must submit to some state accountability measures as well as statewide evaluation; for the most part, however, these schools are free to enact rules and practices which they think will improve the quality of education for their students.

Although charter schools are still too new for much empirical evaluation, it seems that charter schools are more conventional, less selective, less elitist, and more accepting of the hard-to-educate students than many would have predicted. Primarily as a result of federal regulation, special education students are potentially the most difficult and expensive students to serve, particularly for schools struggling to open their doors. There have been some fears that charter schools will limit the enrollment of such students. However, in their 1996 study of the first twenty charter schools in Texas, Llanes and Marchbanks found that twelve schools (60 percent) anticipated that fewer than 5 percent of their enrollment would be special education students, which is approximately the same percentage of special education students who were enrolled in the local public schools in 1995. Yet five schools (22 percent of the total) expected their special education population to be about 10 percent or slightly higher than the local rate and one school anticipated that about 25 percent of its enrollment would qualify for special education services, or twice the local school system's rate.[58]

It appears, therefore, that charter schools are ready and willing to accept the challenge of educating handicapped students and perhaps even specializing in serving their needs. Llanes and Marchbanks found that far from being exclusive and elitist, the average charter school is, in fact, addressing basic educational needs. For example, eleven schools expected between 40 and 95 percent of their students to come from economically disadvantaged homes. Furthermore, some schools (about 15 percent of those state-authorized) specialize in serving students who have dropped out of the public schools system. These students, labeled by the state as "recovered dropouts," are expected to constitute over 50 percent of the students of three of the state's charter schools. Two additional schools anticipate receiving from 18 to 36 percent of their enrollment from this category.[59]

One expectation of policymakers was that the charter schools would be harbingers of innovation and would force public schools into a quality improvement model. Most charter schools proposed are very traditional in their overall educational plan. The organization of these schools is also quite traditional and mirrors the public school model of governance. Some charter schools have community-based boards, larger in size than the local school board. These schools are like private schools in that they must solicit their enrollment from those currently enrolled in the local schools, appealing to parents who must often fill in for services provided by public schools, such as driving children to the school or committing to more volunteer participation in the child's schooling than a public school requires.

The early evidence is that charter schools view themselves as more like community service organizations, or even public schools, than the uniquely new form of organization they really are. In order to attract and retain students, charter schools must truly become market- and customer-oriented and provide more, not fewer, services than public schools. The small size of these schools, too, has serious financial drawbacks. Charter schools receive from $3,000 to $4,200 a year for each student who attends a minimum number of days during the school year. They do not receive local funds from property taxes nor do they get federal funds for special needs students. In some cases this means that these schools receive 25 percent less than public schools, which have local tax funds and federal monies added to the state contribution. Charter schools cannot charge tuition, cannot freely engage in fund-raising, and are limited in where they can go for additional funds.

Compounding the problem is the fact that fewer than 25 percent of the charter schools have space available to them that they own. The majority of these schools intend to rent space that they must also remodel, make handicapped-accessible, and equip with communications, computers, books, athletic equipment, and other expensive capital investment needs. Renting space, leasing equipment, and purchasing instructional materials is an expensive proposition for a nonprofit organization. To get under way, charter schools must have capital funding. This need for start-up capital is shared by charter schools throughout the nation and was highlighted in a study by

Finn and and his colleagues at the Hudson Institute.[60] This should be of major concern to policymakers who want to promote future charter schools.

The emergence of charter schools will have a definite, but uncertain impact on library media programs. The future of the charter school movement is unclear. There is a great deal of promise and a lot of peril. Public educators should realize that there is a new, state-funded competitor for the public school system in many states—a competitor that can grow only by taking students away from public schools. Whether this competition will improve public, private, or charter education remains to be seen. Many charter schools will be operating with minimum budgets and minimum personnel. These schools may or may not want or need to meet regional school accreditation standards. Additionally, it is not clear that they need to meet state standards for specialized personnel in any area other than special education, which is mandated by federal regulations.

Given these factors, it is very likely that library media services and programs in charter schools will be limited, often staffed by volunteers, and that the quality and extent of library services will depend on the demands of the parent and teacher groups that charter the individual school. It can be anticipated that many of these groups will expect the local or regional public library and the nearby school library media centers to be the source of library media services and be reluctant to spend scarce charter school resources on providing school library media services.

Home Schooling

A growing number of school-age children will not routinely spend time in a school classroom this year. Instead, these children will be engaged in home schooling. Home schooling is typically conducted by parents or groups of parents in a home or private institutional setting. There is no one way to do it. One family may begin with opening ceremonies to signal the start of the daily routine and follow a scheduled curriculum. Another family may opt for child-led learning, where parents provide help as the child expresses interest in a topic. Parents usually provide supervision and help, but most children assume increasing responsibility for choosing and carrying out projects as they mature.

Lines points out that schooling at home was a necessity in an age when there were a limited number of schools. After schools became universally available, some traditional groups, including the Seventh Day Adventists and Mormons, still elected to teach their younger school-age children at home. The Amish kept their older children out of public schools, preferring to train them through life in the community. Beginning in the 1970s, other families opted for home schooling, despite easy access to schools. Early in this contemporary movement, most parents were pursuing a philosophy of child-led learning, as articulated by writers and educators such as John Holt. Later, many families with strong religious convictions also turned to home schooling.[61]

Lines estimates that roughly half a million school-age children are probably learning outside a school classroom. They make up about 1 percent of the total school-age population and almost 10 percent of the privately schooled population. This estimate assumes modest growth since the fall of 1990, when data were collected from three independent sources: those state education agencies that have data; distributors of popular curricular packages; and memberships of supportive associations. As each source represents only the tip of an iceberg, upward adjustments were made based on surveys of home-schooling groups.[62]

The legality of home schooling is no longer in question. Today, all state compulsory education laws explicitly make home schooling a valid option, or the state interprets compulsory school-attendance laws to include "attendance" at a "school" located at home.[63] Most states have also liberalized requirements for the home teacher. For example, parents do not need teaching certificates, and only Michigan requires the involvement of a certified teacher. Even in Michigan, however, court decisions have restricted the scope of this requirement. Almost all states require families to file basic information with either the state or local education agency. Many states have additional requirements, such as the submission of a curricular plan, testing of students, or, less frequently, education or testing requirements for parents.

There are problems in establishing the effectiveness of home schooling though tales of success are abundant. Reporting of test scores is not mandated in a number of states. When it is, there are numerous problems related to the collection of the data, whether standardized test scores are reported, how many parents actually report test scores, and the natural bias of home schooling association reports. Keeping these limitations in mind, most of the data show that groups of home-schooled children who are tested perform at above average rates. The pattern for children for whom data are available resembles that of children in private schools. There is also disagreement about whether home schooling helps or hinders a child's social development.

Children engaged in home schooling spend less time with same-age children and more time with people of different ages. Most spend time with other children through support and networking groups, scouting, churches, and other associations. Many spend time with adults other than their parents through community volunteer work, running their own businesses, tutoring or mentoring arrangements, or other activities. Also, there is no conclusive research suggesting that additional time spent with same-age peers is preferable to more time with individuals of varying ages. Limited testing of a self-selected group of home-schooled children suggested above-average social and psychological development.

There is some literature on libraries and home schooling. Brostrom has published a guide to providing library resources and services that support home schooling.[64] He envisions the future role of the library as a "home school laboratory," in which there would be cooperation between libraries, home schoolers, and school districts, as well as online home education. For the most part, public school library services have not been made available to home schooling families or groups.

The major resource for home school is like-minded families who have more experience and resources. Local support groups form whenever there is more than a handful of families pursuing home schooling in a particular locale. There is at least one state-level association in every state, and in some states there are a dozen or more regional associations. Other resources include libraries, museums, colleges, extension courses, parks departments, churches, local businesses, mentors, private schools, and, in some states, public schools. Books and other educational materials are also important. Many private educational institutions offer curricular packages, books, and other materials for use in home schooling. Some districts have organized education centers where families may obtain resources, find instructional support, and/or sign up for scheduled classes. Other states or districts also allow part-time enrollment, "shared schooling," "dual enrollment," or similar forms of part-time school attendance.

As home schooling grows, local and state education agencies will be forced to consider that library and information services are going to be offered to these parents and home-schooling groups. Critics of home schooling have long argued that, as home schooling grows, the ability of public schools to offer a full range of services, including library media services, will be cut because home schooling will drain off public support, leaving public education with only those students who are at risk, in ethnic minorities, or in special education. The authors feel that proponents of home schooling are not necessarily enemies of public education and that their involvement in library activities could strengthen the support for both public libraries and school library services.

Taking a more positive view, the authors would argue that public libraries and school library media centers should cooperate to provide access to information resources, online services, and programs by including home-schooling families in the planning, selection, and service provision of these libraries. Many parents starting out in home schooling need advice about sources of curricular materials, home-schooling organizations, World Wide Web sites, and the importance of libraries in the lifelong learning process. There is no better way to ensure their children's success than to provide these services to the parents and to include them in all possible programs and services of public and school libraries.

Summary

As with all education, library media programs are in a transitional state. These programs face major obstacles in their efforts to prepare students and teachers for the world of the twenty-first century. These obstacles can only be overcome if there is a clear vision of what the future of library media programs might be. Chapter 2 presents guideposts for possible future school library media programs.

Notes

1. Eileen O'Brien et al., *Libraries/Media Centers in Schools: Are There Sufficient Resources?* (Washington, D.C.: National Center for Educational Statistics, 1994, ERIC Document Reproduction Service No. ED 385 293).

2. Richard M. Ingersoll and Mei Han, *School Library Media Centers in the United States: 1990–91 Survey Report* (Washington, D.C.: American Institutes for Research in the Behavioral Sciences, 1994, ERIC Document Reproduction Service No. ED 377 858).

3. Janet V. Rogers, "Real Information Power: Why We Need Statistical Data about School Library Media Centers," *School Library Journal* 39, no. 3 (March 1993), 113–17.

4. Marilyn L. Miller and Marilyn L. Shontz, "Expenditures for Resources in School Library Media Centers, FY '88–'89," *School Library Journal* 35, no. 10 (June 1989), 31–40. Marilyn L. Miller and Marilyn L. Shontz, "Expenditures for Resources in School Library Media Centers, FY 1991–92," *School Library Journal* 39, no. 10 (October 1993), 26–36. Idem, "Inside High-Tech School Library Media Centers Problems and Possibilities," *School Library Journal* 40, no. 4 (April 1994), 24–29.

5. Marilyn L. Miller and Marilyn L. Shontz, "Live Wires: High Tech Media Specialists Get Connected," *School Library Journal* 42 (October 1996), 26–32.

6. Benton Foundation, *Buildings, Books, and Bytes: Libraries and Communities in the Digital Age* (Chicago, Ill.: Benton Foundation, 1996). The quote is from a section called "Warning Bells." URL source: http://www.benton.org/library/kellogg/buildings.html.

7. American Association of School Librarians and Association for Educational Communications and Technology, *Information Power: Guidelines for School Library Media Programs* (Chicago, Ill.: American Library Association, 1988), 2.

8. American Association of School Librarians and Association for Educational Communications and Technology, *Information Power: Building Partnerships for Learning* (Chicago, Ill.: American Library Association, 1998), 4–5.

9. Thomas Walker and Paula Montgomery, *Teaching Media Skills* (Littleton, Colo.: Libraries Unlimited, 1983), 7. Carol Kuhlthau, *Information Skills for an Information Society: A Review of the Research* (Syracuse, N.Y.: ERIC Clearinghouse on Information Resources, 1987, ERIC Document Reproduction Service No. ED 327 216).

10. American Association of School Librarians, *Media Programs: District and School* (Chicago, Ill.: American Library Association, 1975), 19–21.

11. *Information Power* (1988), 35.

12. *Information Power* (1988), 39.

13. *Information Power* (1998), chap. 3.

14. *Information Power* (1998), 50.

15. *Information Power* (1998), 51.

16. Dan D. Barron, "A Review of Selected Research in School Librarianship: 1972–1976," *School Media Quarterly* 5, no. 4 (1977), 271–89.

17. V. Gerlach and Donald P. Ely, *Teaching and Media: A Systematic Approach*, 2nd ed. (Englewood Cliffs, N.J.: Prentice-Hall, 1980), 45. Margaret E. Chisholm and Donald P. Ely, *Instructional Design and the Library Media Specialist* (Chicago, Ill.: American Library Association, 1979), 38.

18. David V. Loertscher, *Taxonomies of the School Library Media Program* (Englewood, Colo.: Libraries Unlimited, 1988), 336.

19. Phil P. Turner, *Helping Teachers Teach* (Littleton, Colo.: Libraries Unlimited, 1985), 22–24.

20. David V. Loertscher, *Reinvent Your School's Library in the Age of Technology: A Guide for Principals and Superintendents* (San Jose, Calif.: Hi Willow Research and Publishing, 1998), 64.

21. Michael B. Eisenberg and Robert E. Berkowitz, *Curriculum Initiative: An Agenda and Strategy for Library Media Programs* (Norwood, N.J.: Ablex Publishing, 1988), 5–7.

22. Michael B. Eisenberg and Robert E. Berkowitz, *Resource Companion for Curriculum Initiative: An Agenda and Strategy for Library Media Programs* (Norwood, N.J.: Ablex Publishing, 1988), 15.

23. Keith C. Lance, *The Impact of School Library Media Centers on Academic Achievement* (Denver, Colo.: Colorado State Department of Education, Library Research Service, State Library & Adult Education Office, 1994), 167–70. Lance cites Shirley L. Aaron, "A Review of Selected Research Studies in School Librarianship 1967–1971: Part I," *School Libraries* 21, no. 2 (Summer 1972), 29–46. Keith C. Lance, "A Review of Selected Research Studies in School Librarianship, 1967–1971: Part II," *School Library Media Quarterly* 21, no. 1 (Spring 1972), 41–48. Len Ainsworth, "An Objective Measure of the Impact of a Library Learning Center," *School Libraries* 18, no. 4 (Winter 1969), 33–35. Patricia S. Breivik, "The Role of Libraries in the Search for Educational Excellence," *School Library Media Quarterly* 16, no. 1 (March 1987), 45–46. Evelyn H. Daniel and Donald P. Ely, *Assessing the Competencies of Media Professionals: A Model for Determining Costs and Effectiveness*, 1979 (ERIC Document Reproduction Service No. ED 179 250). Elaine K. Didier, *Research on the Impact of School Library Media Programs on Student Achievement* (Paper presented at the annual meeting of the American Association of School Librarians, Atlanta, Ga., November 2, 1984 (ERIC Document Reproduction Service No. ED 279 340).

24. Loertscher, *Reinvent Your School's Library*, 3.

25. Colorado Library Research Service, *The Impact of School Library Media Centers on Academic Achievement* (Denver, Colo.: Colorado State Department of Education, Library Research Service, State Library & Adult Education Office, 1998), 4.

26. L. P. Ayres and A. McKimmie, *The Public Library and the Public Schools* (Cleveland, Ohio: Survey Committee of the Cleveland Foundation, 1916), 13.

27. Lucille F. Fargo, *The Program for Elementary School Library Service* (Chicago, Ill.: American Library Association, 1930), 100.

28. M. P. Douglas, *The Primary School and Its Services. New York* (New York: UNESCO, 1960), 63.

29. Jean D. van Deusen, "The Effects of Fixed Versus Flexible Scheduling on Curriculum Involvement and Skills Integration in Elementary School Library Media Programs," *School Library Media Quarterly* 21, no. 1 (Spring 1993), 175–77.

30. Ruth Toor, "Focus on Flexible Scheduling," *School Library Media Quarterly* 19, no. 3 (Fall 1990), 36–37.

31. Mary D. Lankford, "Flexible Access: Foundation for Student Achievement," *School Library Journal* 40, no. 8 (August 1994), 21–23. Lankford cites the report, National Education Commission on Time and Learning, *Prisoners of Time* Report of the National Education Commission on Time and Learning (ERIC Document Reproduction Service No. 378 686).

32. American Association of School Librarians, *Position Statement on Flexible Scheduling* (Chicago, Ill.: The Association, 1991). URL source: http://www.ala.org/aasl/positions/PS_flexible.html.

33. *Position Statement*, para. 2.

34. *Information 2000: Library and Information Services for the 21st Century. The Summary Report of the White House Conference on Library and Information Services Position Statement (Washington, D.C., July 9–13, 1991)*, (Washington, D.C.: The White House Conference on Library and Information Services, 1991), 3.

35. *Information Power* (1998), 1.

36. Jane L. David, "Restructuring and Technology: Partners in Change," *Phi Delta Kappan* 73, no. 1 (September 1991), 37–40, 78–82.

37. Peter F. Drucker, *Managing for the Future; The 1990s and Beyond* (New York: Truman Talley Books, Dutton, 1992), 5.

38. Hoo-min D. Toong and Amar Gupta, "Personal Computers," *Scientific American* 247, no. 6 (1982), 86–107. Quote is from p. 87.

39. R. Reddy, "A Technological Perspective on New Forms of Organization," in *Technology and Organization*, ed. P. S. Goodman, L. E. Sprovill, and Associates (San Francisco: Jossey-Bass, 1990), 232–53.

40. G. Anderla and A. Dunning, *Computer Strategies 1990–9: Technologies Costs Markets* (Chichester, England: John Wiley & Sons, 1987).

41. Ross J. Todd, *The Power of Information Literacy: Unity of Education and Resources for the 21st Century.* Paper presented at the 21st Annual Meeting of the International Association of School Librarianship, Belfast, Northern Ireland, July 19–24, 1992 (ERIC Document Reproduction Service No. ED 354 916). Quote is from the abstract.

42. *Information Power* (1988), 15.

43. *Information Power* (1998), 1.

44. Maryland State Department of Education, *Learning Outcomes in Library Media Skills* (Baltimore, Md.: Maryland State Department of Education, 1992 (ERIC Document Reproduction Service No. ED 349 005).

45. American Association of School Librarians, *National Library Power Program* (Chicago, Ill.: American Library Association, 1996). URL source: http://www.ala.org/aasl/libpower.html.

46. Peter Benson and Marilyn M. McMillen, *Private Schools in the United States: A Statistical Profile, with Comparisons to Public Schools* (Washington, D.C.: National Center for Educational Statistics, 1991 (ERIC Document Reproduction Service No. 331 847).

47. C. Keen, *Many Floridians Prefer Public to Private Schools* (Gainesville, Fla.: University of Florida, 1996), 22.

48. George E. Conway, *Small Scale and School Culture: The Experience of Private Schools. ERIC Digest*, 1994 (ERIC Document Reproduction Service No. ED 376 996).

49. Robert E. Slavin, "Class Size and Student Achievement: Is Smaller Better?" *Contemporary Education* 62, no. 1 (Fall 1990), 6–12.

50. William J. Fowler, Jr., *What Do We Know about School Size: What Should We Know?* Paper presented at the annual meeting of the American Educational Research Association, San Francisco, April 22, 1992 (ERIC Document Reproduction Service No. ED 347 675). Paul Lindsay, "High School Size, Participation in Activities, and Young Adult Social Participation: Some Enduring Effects of Schooling," *Educational Evaluation and Policy Analysis* 6, no. 1 (spring 1984), 73–83.

51. Arthur G. Powell, "A Glimpse at Teaching Conditions in Top Private Schools." *American Educator* 14, no. 4 (Winter 1990), 30.

52. Allen C. Ornstein, "Private and Public School Comparisons: Size, Organization, and Effectiveness," *Education and Urban Society* 21, no. 2 (February 1989), 192–206.

53. Barney M. Berlin and Robert C. Cienkus, "Size: The Ultimate Educational Issue?" *Education and Urban Society* 21, no. 2 (February 1989), 228–31.

54. Marilyn M. McMillen et al., *Detailed Characteristics of Private Schools and Staff: 1987–88* (Washington, D.C.: National Center for Educational Statistics, 1991 (ERIC Document Reproduction Service No. ED 341 724).

55. S. M. Johnson, *Teachers at Work: Achieving Success in Our Schools*, 1990 (ERIC Document Reproduction Service No. 336 387).

56. Mary Anne Raywid, "Public Choice, Yes: Vouchers, No!" *Phi Delta Kappan* 68, no. 10 (June 1987), 762–69. Quote is from p. 762. Mary Anne Raywid, "The

Mounting Case for Schools of Choice," in *Public Schools by Choice*, ed. Joe Nathan (St. Paul, Minn.: The Institute for Learning and Teaching, 1988), 13–40.

57. Donald Dunn, *Charter Schools: Experiments in Reform. An Update* (Austin, Tex.: Texas State Legislative Budget Board, 1995 (ERIC Document Reproduction Service No. ED 394 199). Information on charter school legislation can be found in John Dornan, *Chartering for Excellence; Developing & Implementing Charter School Legislation* (Greensboro, N.C.: SouthEastern Regional Vision for Education, 1998).

58. Jose R. Llanes and M. Marchbanks, *The First Twenty Texas Open-Enrollment Charter Schools* (Austin, Tex.: CARE, University of Texas–Pan American, 1996), 14.

59. Llanes and Marchbanks, *First Twenty*, 14.

60. Chester E. Finn, Jr., et al., *Charter Schools in Action: What Have We Learned?* (Indianapolis, Ind.: Hudson Institute, 1996, ERIC Document Reproduction Service No. ED 399 671).

61. Patricia M. Lines, *Estimating the Home Schooled Population. Working Paper* (Washington, D.C.: U.S. Department of Education, Office of Research and Improvement, 1991 (ERIC Document Reproduction Service No. ED 337 903).

62. Patricia M. Lines, *Home Schooling. ERIC Digest* (Eugene, Ore.: ERIC Clearinghouse on Educational Management, 1995, ERIC Document Reproduction Service No. ED 381 849).

63. Martha McCarthy, *Home Schooling and the Law. Policy Bulletin No. PB-B15* (Bloomington, Ind.: Education Policy Center, Indiana University, 1992, ERIC Document Reproduction Service No. ED 349 702).

64. D. C. Brostrom, *A Guide to Homeschooling for Librarians; Highsmith Press Handbook Series* (Fort Atkinson, Wis.: Highsmith Press, 1995).

2

A Vision of Library
Media Programs

Introduction

The schools of the future are being formed today by current school reform efforts. Quellmalz and colleagues describe this reform movement as follows:

> Increasingly, over the past decade, educational reformers have called for fundamental shifts in what takes place in classrooms and schools. These arguments follow from the now common conclusion that our nation's schools are failing to provide many students with the high-quality education needed to become responsible citizens and productive workers. To address this problem, reformers urge reconsideration of traditional notions of schools as institutions with isolated classrooms where students spend fixed periods of time studying rigidly differentiated subjects. Instead, new institutions need to be designed, from the bottom up, limited by neither previous practice nor burdensome regulations. Doing so, the argument continues, entails deregulating the educational system and transferring authority from the federal, state, and even district levels to schools—in return for accountability for student results.[1]

Most organizations tend to persist in what they are now doing in spite of exterior or interior efforts to change what the organization does. Schools are no exception to this rule because so many people are invested in continuing operations as they are now. Schools have been described as organizations with "loosely coupled systems."[2] Such systems maintain a high degree of consistency and resistance to change because they readily take to changes at the outer edge of system activity, but reject any influence of those changes on the core of the system.[3] As institutions, schools have been able to ignore, absorb, and modify many revolutionary factors without much change in what actually happens in classrooms.

Models for Changing the Schools

Changing the organization of schools and school systems is a top priority in the educational reform movement. In discussing organizational responses to technology in schools, Wright[4] has outlined several organizational models currently operating in education:

The "Fad" Model: Change as an End in Itself

Computer-based technology is a widely accepted example of this model in operation. Much has been written in educational journals and communicated at national conferences about the wonders of computer-based technologies as solutions to almost all education problems. Webb notes that "where recalcitrant problems remain, the progress view of science readily transfers into the field of educational technology in exhortations to take up the latest technology as an answer to all problems."[5] School organizations following the "fad" model do not just focus on technology, but also on new and innovative ways of planning, management, and teaching reading, mathematics, or any other subject. Often one finds a fad school involved in multiple fads at the same time—sometimes fads that contradict one another.

The fad model often overlooks the social and technical complexity of computer-related technologies and the diversity of problems associated with human interaction. Further, the fad model is without mission and goals; it is adopted without thought to consequences for students, teachers, or the larger community. Fads in education come and go with regularity. Beware of the latest fad unless you can find research that actually supports its positive effects.

The Avoidance Model: Change Is to Be Avoided

An exact opposite of the "fad" model is the model that opposes the introduction of any change into the schools or, once changes have been introduced, would limit their uses. Such critics argue that every change alters the culture that adopts it, suggesting that we are being controlled by the changes imposed by technologies (television, computers, mass communications) rather than exerting control over them. The danger is that we tend to define ourselves in terms of technologies. We tend to trivialize our religious and aesthetic heritages.[6]

This avoidance model and its proponents may cause teachers, library media specialists, and administrators to raise questions about the whole sphere of students' and teachers' lives. If so, the model serves a purpose; we are forced to take seriously the amazing variety of learning styles and interests, which may or may not be enhanced by a particular change or innovation. Some less philosophical proponents of this model begin their conversations with, "Well, when we tried something like this in 19__ , it did not work because...." Often there is a realistic skepticism about fads in education and society; the latest thing is often just the old thing in new clothes and will have no more effect than other fads. When such an attitude brings up questions about the relationship of change to the school's goals for students and the goals of the whole educational process, it can be a healthy corrective. But when such criticisms are simply used as ways to enforce "tradition" and resist change, they are suspect.

Sometimes those who adopt this model base their opinion on an assessment of the current budget limits in public education. All schools face the "zero-sum budget" situation so that any new activity, program, or purchase means that something else will need to be cut. If a technological application is adopted, what will be sacrificed? Will it be books, periodicals, curricular materials? Here, the fear is that successful resources and procedures known to work, and often beloved by teachers and students, will be replaced by new applications whose efficacy is unknown and whose adoption will require major adjustments of teachers, students, and parents. Every institution in the world is in a zero-sum budget situation and that situation is not likely to change. Administrators, teachers, and library media specialists must repeatedly evaluate everything they are doing to see what is pushing the school toward its goals, what is irrelevant, and what really needs to be changed.

The Status Quo Model:
Change as More of the Same

All too often, innovations have been part of one more cycle of reform typically calling for the introduction of new kinds of curricula, new teaching methods, new, more rigid standards, new tests, or new machines. Writing about the limited impact of technology in schools, David notes:

> The primary reason technology has failed to live up to its promise lies in the fact that it has been viewed as an answer to the wrong question. Decisions about technology purchases and uses are typically driven by the question of how to improve the effectiveness of what schools are already doing—not how to transform what schools do. Consequently, choices about instructional hardware and software are based on whether they are likely to increase standardized test scores. Choices about administrative technology are made to facilitate existing financial and record-keeping systems. Moreover, as has been typical with innovations of the past, scant attention has been paid to preparing teachers and administrators to use new technology well and even less to their preferences about hardware and software. Instead, the acquisition of technology has been viewed as an end in itself, and the more "teacher-proof" the better.[7]

The status quo model operates on a set of educational assumptions that have been remarkably hard to change. The same model was used in the industrial revolution: standardize, then process in an assembly-line way to achieve a standard of functioning. Education became universal on a mass production model. The implications of this model for school activities are information retention, rote memorization, standardized procedures, and standardized testing. Everyone is to have the same set of basic skills learned in exactly the same ways. Where innovations, including computer-related technologies, are helpful in this process, as in drill and practice, memorization, or standardization, they are eagerly adopted. Students who do not work in this model are dropped out of the system or "tracked" into other programs with different outcomes.

The critics of the educational process and its institutions often recommend a readoption of this model. These recommendations are usually coupled with harsh criticisms of other models that are now claimed to be "not working"—for example, "Back to Basics!", "End of Course Testing," and "National Examinations for All Students in All Subjects." Findley and Wyer identify the assumptions underlying much education in schools and industry: (1) all learners are alike; (2) learners are passive recipients of all messages; (3) learners are not themselves engaged in an active process of making sense of their lives; (4) learners need to be standardized; and (5) such an approach brings success.[8]

In such a production model of education, it is little wonder that administrators, teachers, and library media specialists all work hard "just to get to 3 P.M. and end my shift on the assembly line." The status quo model is hard to change, especially in nonprofit agencies like schools. Businesses and industries that do not change find negative outcomes in the profit-and-loss columns, as witness several American automobile companies and department stores. But the changes are coming in the workplace, in government, and in the political process, and that is where our students are going. Schools must change or the community will find alternatives so that workers and citizens can function in the emerging information society.

The Educational Change Model: Change as Educational Reform

Braun, in the final report on Vision: TEST, sees the information-age model of the school as follows:

> We recognize that students learn in different ways, and we celebrate the diversity they bring to the learning process. In this model, teachers have many roles—facilitators, resource allocators, collaborators, researchers, etc.—as they help students not only acquire facts but also gather data, form and test hypotheses, do research, develop problem solving skills, and learn to work together. In this model, students—individually and in cooperative groups—are actively engaged in the learning process.[9]

David, too, stresses the great difference between the educational reform movement of the 1990s and previous reform efforts:

> The systemic reform agenda of the 1990s no longer aims to improve what schools are already doing. National and state policymakers, including governors as well as education and business leaders, now imagine a restructured education system that qualitatively increases the performance of all students. The language of this reform communicates a very different image of teaching and learning from the traditional one in which teachers "deliver" knowledge and assign seat work. The new image captures a much more dynamic view of schooling in which teachers guide students through individual and collaborative activities that encourage inquiry and the construction of knowledge.[10]

In discussing the potential impact of computers on schooling, Becker states that "for computers to make a difference in how students experience schooling will require teachers and administrators to modify their concepts of appropriate and inappropriate teaching behaviors, to reprioritize the value of different types of instructional content, and to change habits and assumptions that guide their classroom and school management strategies."[11]

How society, the local community, parents, and educators define the goals of education will ultimately determine the goals and the program in school library media centers. The authors favor an educational change model for setting goals and objectives in education and in the library media center. We do not support just going on as usual or flip-flopping among a variety of fads.

In the process of school reform, we still face a number of persistent questions:

1. What are the cost benefits resulting from the application of new educational processes including information technologies to education?

2. Can we find ways of being more effective and efficient in what we do?

3. What is the most effective way to introduce change in the schools so that our students learn more and better?

4. How will we manage reform to make that happen?

5. What is the potential for making changes, given the existing budgets of schools?

6. As current budgets are not adequate, how do we seek additional funding?

7. What is the impact of *not* making essential changes?

8. Do we simply abandon some students who are at risk, and create additional advantages for those children and teachers who are already successful in the system?

9. How can we provide better teacher training in using innovations effectively in their classes, and how will we pay for this training?

10. How does needed research that might address these questions get funded, reported, and utilized?

11. As the scarce resources for education are spread across home schooling, charter schools, and private education, will there be sufficient resources to fund the continuation of public education as we have known it or as we hope to see it change?

The school reform movement has gone on long enough for some trends to emerge. Among them are radical changes in the concept of what goes on in teaching/learning; a movement toward site-based management at local school sites; and increasing demands for radical change in teacher training programs.

Changing Concepts of the Teaching/Learning Process

The school reform movement has suggested specific changes in traditional forms of teaching and learning. In general, these instructional strategies move away from the passive "teacher-lecture/ student-listen" mode of instruction to a more active arrangement of learning activities. Instruction is viewed as taking place both within and outside the classroom, and in both settings a personal connection with a "teacher" can make a difference in whether a student succeeds or fails. Specific instructional strategies include nontraditional forms of learning from mentors or others who act as role models in issues of race or gender, adult and cross-grade peer tutoring, and the integration of technology as a tool for instruction.

Reform advocates suggest using adult volunteers from the community as mentors or advocates.[12] Mentoring is defined as a one-to-one relationship between an adult volunteer and a student who needs support in reaching academic or personal achievement goals.

Advocacy is defined as a continuing set of relationships between an adult (volunteer or paid) and members of a group of students, in which the adult provides support and services by intervening on a student's behalf, monitoring participation in programs, or brokering additional services.[13] A major problem with these suggestions has been the difficulty of recruiting and training enough appropriate volunteers to make the programs work. Instructional changes of such magnitude have to do with restructuring what happens in the classroom, with changing the ways in which teachers work with other teachers, with changing the ways in which students work with other students in schools and in other places, and with changing the ways in which student performance is evaluated. What has been called the constructionist view of education in schools is drastically different from the view of an industrial-age assembly line. To the constructionist, the process of education operates on the following assumptions:

1. The learner is active—we must capture his/her imagination so that he/she can see that what is offered has relevance and merit.

2. "How-we-do-it" is taught conceptually, not by rote memorization, so that learners can place what is learned in their own context of meaning.

3. Learning is complemented through real-world applications or simulations, and hypotheses are tested by actual experience.

4. There is more dialogue and mutual conversation than teacher-controlled instruction.

5. Control is negotiated and the learner is respected.

6. Several learning styles are recognized and encouraged, not just the analytical process.

7. Cognitive strategies that include learning how to think, problem solving, and decision making are viewed as skills that can be both learned and improved.

8. Higher-level cognitive skills are the goals of teaching and learning activities.

9. The learner's personal state of development is recognized and accommodated in the educational process.

10. What we teach must be interesting and be taught in an interesting way.[14]

When the constructionist model works successfully, the student moves from the role of passive receiver to that of active learner; the teacher can move from the role of lecturer to that of counselor, mentor, and adviser; and the library media specialist can move from the role of resource provider to that of team teacher, cooperative planner, and instructional developer. The curriculum becomes increasingly interdisciplinary and the subject specialties of the staff begin to blur. Standard scheduling of classes becomes a barrier to learning and is replaced with block or flexible scheduling. The wider community becomes a site for educational experience and a source of valued information for research and evaluation. Administratively, the staff, students, and parents of the school become involved in decision making, assessment of outcomes, and site-based management.

Another major change advocated in the school reform movement is site-based management. The concept is borrowed from the business community where it has been found that those who do the work most often know most about how it should be done. The notion of participatory management has been around a long time, and is regularly brought back into fashion when organizations find that they cannot effectively manage their institutions from a distance. In the field of education, site-based management tries to transform schools into communities where the appropriate people participate constructively in major decisions affecting their lives and their work.

There are obstacles to such collaboration. Collaborative relationships between teachers and school leaders are problematic when teachers' duties and performance appraisals are hierarchically decided by principals or central administrators.[15] Black points out that little uniformity exists among school districts concerning the implementation of site-based management. Principals and teachers are managing schools through trial and error. Many principals are paranoid about their changing roles, and teachers are struggling with budgeting and other management responsibilities. A major obstacle to the implementation of site-based programs is the amount of time it takes to get the programs actually working.[16] Meriwether estimates that it takes from five to ten years to make such programs operational.[17] Effective site councils have a well-designed community structure, which in turn facilitates leadership, student and adult learning focus, and a school-wide perspective. Few school administrators, teachers, or library media specialists have the background and training to make such efforts successful.

There have also been a number of criticisms of the move toward site-based management. Critics argue that this management style appears to be primarily concerned with dismantling the centralized education systems that traditionally have supported the work of teachers, students, and parents and replacing them with a free-market ideology of competition and choice. It is argued that this separates elite policy makers and interest groups from those who must implement policy. What has actually occurred, the critics say, is a justification of the state's avoidance of its social responsibility to provide an equitable quality education for all. It promotes greater inequality, detracts from educational issues, may lower teacher quality, and cuts resources for education.[18] Site-based management will become real when the local school leadership team actually has some program and funding flexibility so that it can adapt the school teaching and learning environment to the needs of the students in that local school.

In response to the calls for reform, general teacher education programs have acted to raise admission standards and exit requirements. They have also revised curricula to reflect multiculturalism and new K–12 standards; paid more attention to pedagogy, teaching practice, and relevance; included clinical experiences in the learning environment, in public schools and elsewhere; and proposed new model standards and principles for licensing beginning teachers.[19] Many of these educational program changes have three characteristics in common:

1. They require all teachers to know subject content.

2. They teach pedagogy in the context of academic content.

3. They offer prospective teachers many varied school-based experiences.

Another radical change in teacher education has been the emergence of professional development schools in the mid-1980s, as a promising approach to simultaneously improving both teacher education and K–12 schooling. The primary missions of these local schools are to maximize student achievement; to provide a rigorous clinical setting for the professional development of preservice and inservice teachers; and to develop, test, and refine effective practices through applied research. These school/university partnerships are known by several names: professional development schools (Holmes Group), professional practice schools (American Federation of Teachers), clinical schools (Carnegie Report), and partner schools (National Network for Educational Renewal).

In *Tomorrow's School* the Holmes Group put forth the idea of focusing their six goals through what they called professional development schools in which a university-based teacher education program would work intensively with the professional staff of the school so that preservice teacher education, clinical experience, teacher staff development, and research would be collaborative efforts to the benefit of all.[20] One mark of professional development schools is collaboration between university and school personnel, enabling elementary and secondary schools to connect with higher education in more direct ways than currently exist.[21]

These "structured partnerships" provide opportunities for teachers and administrators to influence the development of their profession and for university faculty to increase the professional relevance of their work through (1) mutual study of problems with student learning and their possible solutions; (2) shared teaching in the university and the schools; (3) collaborative research on the problems of educational practice; and (4) cooperative supervision of prospective teachers and administrators.[22]

In addition to the training role, these schools also strengthen knowledge and practice in schools by providing exemplary sites for research, experimentation, inquiry, evaluation, and eventual dissemination of innovative programs and effective practices. Such schools are designed to contribute to the "ongoing refinement and codification of successful teaching and schooling,"[23] thus adding to the knowledge base for teaching. These schools would serve as actual demonstration sites where recent scholarship could be consistently reviewed and selectively incorporated into operating policy and practices.

A third goal of professional development schools is to strengthen the profession by serving as models of promising and productive structural relations among school personnel. New patterns of decision making and shared authority between teachers and administrators can be tested. In this way such schools can contribute to ongoing efforts to restructure schools to facilitate pupil learning by utilizing the expertise of practicing teachers.[24] Because professional development schools require the melding of two very different educational cultures, each with its own history and expectations, there have been some problems. A number of these have been as: time constraints, conflicting demands, logistics, lack of commitment, lack of shared vision, mistrust, funding problems, external factors, differing reward structures, and existing traditions.[25]

There are lots of sources for ideas about new practices in teacher education. Groups such as the National Commission on Teaching and America's Future, Goodlad's National Network for Educational Renewal, and the Holmes Group partnerships as well as many pilot programs can provide guidance. While reform groups in education are moving in positive directions, their efforts betray the painfully slow pace of academic change.

The National Commission on Teaching and America's Future studied teacher education and issued a report, *What Matters Most: Teaching For America's Future*.[26] They state their teacher education premises and strategy as follows:

This Commission starts from three simple premises:

1. What teachers know and can do is the most important influence on what students learn.

2. Recruiting, preparing, and retaining good teachers is the central strategy for improving our schools.

3. School reform cannot succeed unless it focuses on creating the conditions in which teachers can teach, and teach well.

We propose an audacious goal for America's future. Within a decade—by the year 2006—we will provide every student in America with what should be his or her educational birthright: access to competent, caring, qualified teaching in schools, . . . The single most important strategy for achieving America's education goals is to recruit, prepare, and support excellent teachers for every school.

Financed by the Rockefeller Foundation and the Carnegie Corporation of New York, the 151-page report offers a scathing indictment of current barriers to good teacher education and good teaching, which it defines as:

1. Low expectations for student performance and unenforced standards for teachers.

2. Major flaws in teacher preparation and painfully slipshod teacher recruitment.

3. Inadequate induction for beginning teachers; and a lack of professional development and rewards for knowledge and skill.

4. Schools that are structured for failure rather than success.

In *Teachers for Our Nation's Schools*, Goodlad proposed a number of postulates designed to address the four dimensions of teaching: facilitating critical enculturation, providing access to knowledge, building an effective teacher-student connection, and practicing good stewardship.[27] His efforts are continued through the National Network for Educational Renewal. This network at the University of Washington comprises school-university partnerships committed to the simultaneous renewal of schooling and of the education of educators. John Goodlad's Center for Educational Renewal serves as the hub of the network. Approximately twenty-five colleges and universities, one hundred school districts, and 250 partner schools in fourteen states are linked to the National Network for Educational Renewal. The network emphasizes forming partnerships, strengthening liberal arts and professional curricula, and developing a system of rewards and incentives for faculty members. Goodlad's nineteen postulates are:

Postulate One. Programs for the education of the nation's educators must be viewed by institutions offering them as a major responsibility to society and be adequately supported and promoted and vigorously advanced by the institution's top leadership.

Postulate Two. Programs for the education of educators must enjoy parity with other campus programs as a legitimate college or university commitment and field of study and service, worthy of rewards for faculty geared to the nature of the field.

Postulate Three. Programs for the education of educators must be autonomous and secure in their borders, with clear organizational identity, constancy of budget and personnel, and decision making authority similar to that enjoyed by the major professional schools.

Postulate Four. There must exist a clearly identifiable group of academic and clinical faculty members for whom teacher education is the top priority; the group must be responsible and accountable for selecting students and monitoring their progress, planning and maintaining the full scope and sequence of the curriculum, continuously evaluating and improving programs, and facilitating the entry of graduates into teaching careers.

Postulate Five. The responsible group of academic and clinical faculty members described above must have a comprehensive understanding of the aims of education and the role of schools in our society and be fully committed to selecting and preparing teachers to assume the full range of educational responsibilities required.

Postulate Six. The responsible group of academic and clinical faculty members must seek out and select for a predetermined number of student places in the program those candidates who reveal an initial commitment to the moral, ethical, and enculturating responsibilities to be assumed.

Postulate Seven. Programs for the education of educators, whether elementary or secondary, must carry the responsibility to ensure that all candidates progressing through them possess or acquire the literacy and critical thinking abilities associated with the concept of an educated person.

Postulate Eight. Programs for the education of educators must provide extensive opportunities for future teachers to move beyond being students of organized knowledge to become teachers who inquire into both knowledge and its teaching.

Postulate Nine. Programs for the education of educators must be characterized by a socialization process through which candidates transcend their self oriented student preoccupations to become more other oriented in identifying with a culture of teaching.

Postulate Ten. Programs for the education of educators must be characterized in all respects by the conditions for learning that future teachers are to establish in their own schools and classrooms.

Postulate Eleven. Programs for the education of educators must be conducted in such a way that future teachers inquire into the nature of teaching and schooling and assume that they will do so as a natural aspect of their careers.

Postulate Twelve. Programs for the education of educators must involve future teachers in the issues and dilemmas that emerge out of the never ending tension between the rights and interests of individual parents and special interest groups, on one hand, and the role of schools in transcending parochialism, on the other.

Postulate Thirteen. Programs for the education of educators must be infused with understanding of and commitment to the moral obligation of teachers to ensure equitable access to and engagement in the best possible K–12 education for all children and youths.

Postulate Fourteen. Programs for the education of educators must involve future teachers not only in understanding schools as they are but in alternatives, the assumptions underlying alternatives, and how to effect needed changes in school organization, pupil grouping, curriculum, and more.

Postulate Fifteen. Programs for the education of educators must assure for each candidate the availability of a wide array of laboratory settings for observation, hands-on experiences, and exemplary schools for internships and residencies; they must admit no more students to their programs than can be assured these quality experiences.

Postulate Sixteen. Programs for the education of educators must engage future teachers in the problems and dilemmas arising out of the inevitable conflicts and incongruities between what works or is accepted in practice and the research and theory supporting other options.

Postulate Seventeen. Programs for educating educators must establish linkages with graduates for purposes of both evaluating and revising these programs and easing the critical early years of transition into teaching.

Postulate Eighteen. Programs for the education of educators, in order to be vital and renewing, must be free from curricular specifications by licensing agencies and restrained only by enlightened, professionally driven requirements for accreditation.

Postulate Nineteen. Programs for the education of educators must be protected from the vagaries of supply and demand by state policies that allow neither backdoor "emergency" programs nor temporary teaching licenses.[28]

The foundation of the Holmes Partnership is a set of goals issued by the Holmes Group over a decade from 1986 to 1995. These goals are presented in three volumes: *Tomorrow's Teachers* (1987), *Tomorrow's Schools* (1990), and *Tomorrow's Schools of Education* (1995).[29] The strategic agenda of the Holmes Partnership is formulated in six strategic goal areas:

Goal 1: High Quality Professional Preparation. Provide exemplary professional preparation programs for public school educators. These programs must demonstrate rigor, innovation, and attention to the needs of diverse children and youth. Their design, content, and delivery must reflect research and best practice.

Goal 2: Simultaneous Renewal. Engage in simultaneous renewal of public K–12 schools and the education of beginning and experienced educators by establishing strong partnerships of universities, schools, and professional organizations and associations.

Goal 3: Equity, Diversity, and Cultural Competence. Actively work on equity, diversity, and cultural competence in the programs of K–12 schools, higher education, and the education profession by recruiting, preparing, and sustaining faculty and students who reflect the rich diversity of cultural perspectives in this country and our global community.

Goal 4: Scholarly Inquiry and Programs of Research. Conduct and disseminate educational research and engage in other scholarly activities that advance knowledge, improve teaching and learning for all children and youth, inform the preparation and development of educators, and influence educational policy and practice.

Goal 5: Faculty Development. Provide high quality doctoral programs for the future education professorate and for advanced professional development of school-based educators. Redesign the work of both university and school faculty to enable accomplishments of the Holmes Partnership goals—better preparing educators in improving learning for children and youth. Promote conditions that recognize and reward educational professionals who better serve the needs of all learners.

Goal 6: Policy Initiation. Engage in policy analysis and development related to public schools and the preparation of educators. Advocate policies that improve teaching and learning for all students, promote school improvement and enhance the preparation and continuing professional development of all educators.[30]

There has also been a effort toward creating national certification for teachers through portfolio or examination procedures. Wise contended that an important trend supporting the professionalization of teaching is the nationalization of education policy.[31] *Goals 2000* places a strong emphasis on professional development, maintaining that high standards for teachers can be a powerful means to achieve goals for students.

There are several national organizations involved in the effort to professionalize teaching by strengthening its quality-assurance mechanisms.[32] They are the National Board for Professional Teaching Standards (NBPTS), which is developing advanced standards for teacher performance; the Council of Chief State School Officers (CCSSO), through its task force on licensing standards; the Interstate New Teachers Assessment and Support Consortium (INTASC); and the National Council for Accreditation of Teacher Education (NCATE). These groups have cooperatively proposed a continuum of policy areas for action: accreditation, licensing, and advanced certification. The CCSSO has developed a flowchart that begins with the adoption of standards and leads to assessment in three areas: (1) preparation, (2) induction/support, and (3) professional development. Acknowledging induction as a phase of teacher preparation demonstrates a recognition that all beginning teachers need support and that teacher preparation is ongoing and must be connected to practice. The impact of these standards will depend on how states implement them.

The National Board for Professional Teaching Standards has worked with teachers and national teacher organizations to develop standards and assessment procedures for recognition of exemplary teachers. It is hoped that this voluntary certification will reward master teachers for their expertise and help promote these teachers to positions of greater responsibility. Teachers who have engaged in this intense teacher assessment process claim that they learned more by going through the process than by partaking in any other professional development activity in their entire career, because it requires them to document their practice and reflect on their strengths and weaknesses.[33]

Established in 1927, the Council of Chief State School Officers is a nationwide nonprofit organization of the fifty-seven public officials who head departments of education in the fifty states, the District of Columbia, and other U.S. jurisdictions. The CCSSO expresses its members' views to civic and professional organizations, federal agencies, Congress, and the public. Through its structure of committees and task forces, the council responds to a broad range of concerns about education and provides leadership on major educational issues. The CCSSO forms coalitions with many other organizations and works on a variety of policy concerns that affect elementary and secondary education.

The Interstate School Leaders Licensure Consortium (ISLLC), organized by the Council of Chief State School Officers in partnership with the National Policy Board for Educational Administration, is a consortium of states and associations formed for the purpose of developing model standards and assessments for school leaders. ISLLC's primary constituency is the state education agencies responsible for administrator licensing. The consortium includes representatives of state agencies/departments of education, professional standards boards, and the major educational leadership associations.

The National Board for Professional Teaching Standards was established in 1987 as a central recommendation of the Carnegie Corporation's report, *A Nation Prepared, Teachers for the 21st Century*.[34] NBPTS was designed as an independent, nongovernmental teacher majority board to improve student learning by setting clear, high, and rigorous standards for what accomplished teachers should know and be able to do. It develops performance-based assessments for certifying experienced teachers who voluntarily seek recognition for demonstrating achievement of those high standards.[35] National Board certification represents professional recognition of achievement of the highest standards for teaching. The National Board standards also provide a strong, sound, teacher-developed framework for the organization and implementation of professional development and improvements in teaching and learning.

A teacher must successfully complete a two-part assessment designed to examine talent, skills, and knowledge. The first part requires the compilation of a school-site portfolio reflecting various facets of teaching, including student work with teachers' written comments, lesson plans, and videotape(s) of interaction(s) with a class. The second part requires a teacher to participate in one day of performance-based activities at an assessment center, including simulations, structured interviews and collegial discussions.

The National Board certification is analogous to board certification for other professionals, for example, physicians, accountants, and so on. It represents the achievement of the highest standards of the profession, in contrast to basic state licensure or certification, which represents the achievement of entry-level standards that permit a candidate to practice in that profession. The National Board holds to five core propositions concerning certifiable teachers:

1. Teachers are committed to students and their learning.

2. Teachers know the subjects they teach and how to teach those subjects to all students.

3. Teachers are responsible for managing and monitoring student learning.

4. Teachers think systematically about their practice and learn from experience.

5. Teachers are members of learning communities.

National Council for Accreditation of Teacher Education is a voluntary accrediting body made up of colleges and universities, state departments of education, school boards, teachers, and other professionals who are devoted to the evaluation and accreditation of institutions for preparation of elementary and secondary teachers, schools service personnel, and other school-oriented specialists. The idea of teacher growth and development as a continuum spanning a teaching career guides the National Council for Accreditation for Teacher Education's emerging standards. The 1995 NCATE standards revision emphasizes performance and performance-based assessments, professional collaboration and community, technology, and diversity of curriculum, student body, and faculty.

NCATE has published twenty standards and sixty-nine indicators against which professional education units (schools, colleges, or departments of education) are evaluated to determine their accreditation status.[36] The standards are divided into four unit areas: design of professional education, candidates in professional education, professional education faculty, and the unit for professional education. The standards mandate that the design, delivery, and content of the curriculum reflect national concerns about the knowledge bases for professional education. In subject areas, NCATE has cooperated with other professional education associations in developing subject-specific standards and indicators. The standards are:

Standard I.A: Conceptual Framework(s). The unit has high quality professional education programs that are derived from a conceptual framework(s) that is knowledge-based, articulated, shared, coherent, consistent with the unit and/or institutional mission, and continuously evaluated.

Standard I.B: General Studies for Initial Teacher Preparation. The unit ensures that candidates have completed general studies courses and experiences in the liberal arts and sciences and have developed theoretical and practical knowledge.

Standard I.C: Content Studies for Initial Teacher Preparation. The unit ensures that teacher candidates attain academic competence in the content that they plan to teach.

Standard I.D: Professional and Pedagogical Studies for Initial Teacher Preparation. The unit ensures that teacher candidates acquire and learn to apply the professional and pedagogical knowledge and skills to become competent to work with all students.

Standard I.E: Integrative Studies for Initial Teacher Preparation. The unit ensures that teacher candidates can integrate general, content, and professional and pedagogical knowledge to create meaningful learning experiences for all students.

Standard I.F: Advanced Professional Studies. The unit ensures that candidates become more competent as teachers or develop competencies for other professional roles (e.g., school library media specialist, school psychologist, or principal).[37]

Standard I.G: Quality of Instruction. Teaching in the unit is consistent with the conceptual framework(s), reflects knowledge derived from research and sound professional practice, and is of high quality.

Standard I.H: Quality of Field Experiences. The unit ensures that field experiences are consistent with the conceptual framework(s), are well-planned and sequenced, and are of high quality.

Standard 1.I: Professional Community. The unit collaborates with higher education faculty, school personnel, and other members of the professional community to design, deliver, and renew effective programs for the preparation of school personnel and to improve the quality of education in schools.

Standard II.A: Qualifications of Candidates. The unit recruits, admits, and retains candidates who demonstrate potential for professional success in schools.

Standard II.B: Composition of Candidates. The unit recruits, admits, and retains a diverse student body.

Standard II.C: Monitoring and Advising the Progress of Candidates. The unit systematically monitors and assesses the progress of candidates and ensures that they receive appropriate academic and professional advisement from admission through completion of their professional education programs.

Standard II.D: Ensuring the Competence of Candidates. The unit ensures that a candidate's competency to begin his or her professional role in schools is assessed prior to completion of the program and/or recommendation for licensure.

Standard III.A: Faculty Qualifications. The unit ensures that the professional education faculty are teacher scholars who are qualified for their assignments and actively engaged in the professional community.

Standard III.B Composition of Faculty. The unit recruits, hires, and retains a diverse faculty.

Standard III.C: Professional Assignments of Faculty. The unit ensures that policies and assignments allow faculty to be involved effectively in teaching, scholarship, and service.

Standard III.D: Professional Development of Faculty. The unit ensures that there are systematic and comprehensive activities to enhance competence and intellectual vitality of the faculty.

Standard IV.A: Governance and Accountability of the Unit. The unit is clearly identified, operates as a professional community, and has the responsibility, authority, and personnel to develop, administer, evaluate, and revise all professional education programs.

Standard IV.B: Resources for Teaching and Scholarship. The unit has adequate resources to support teaching and scholarship by faculty and candidates.

Standard IV.C: Resources for Operating the Unit. The unit has sufficient facilities, equipment, and budgetary resources to fulfill its mission and offer quality programs.

A more detailed description of the standards and the sixty-nine indicators can be found at URL source: http://www.usca.sc.edu/

ncate/ncate.html. A number of state departments of education and
professional associations are working with NCATE to modify and
improve the cooperative teacher education evaluation processes.
More information about NCATE and its new publication, *Making a
Difference*, will be found at URL source: http://www.ncate.org/.

Summary

Doiron and Davies have summed up the changes in education:

1. A more balanced emphasis on process and product has become
   increasingly important. Educators focus more on developing concepts and skills than simply mastering a specific content.

2. Tied to this influence is the fact that subject area teachers recognize that the content of their courses is too vast and changes
   too quickly to be mastered in one textbook.

3. Instruction and learning are far more holistic and student-
   centered, with increased opportunities for the integration of skills
   in information processing, critical thinking, and problem solving.

4. Collaborative learning has become much more common in our
   classrooms in response to the fact that the future workplace will
   require teamwork and problem solving. This creates new demands for using a wide range of resources in more flexible facilities for more purposeful activities.

5. Technology is no longer an "extra" added to the educational
   agenda. It is an integral part of all new curriculum initiatives and
   a pervasive influence across the system.[38]

The American Library Association's *Information Literacy; Final Report by the American Library Association Presidential Committee on Information Literacy* paints a picture of the information-age school:

> The school would be more interactive, because students, pursuing
> questions of personal interest, would be interacting with other
> students, with teachers, with a vast array of information resources, and
> the community at large to a far greater extent than they do today. . . .
> Students' quests would involve not only searching print, electronic,
> and video data, but also interviewing people inside and outside of
> school. As a result learning would be more self-initiated. . . . Both
> students and teachers would be familiar with the intellectual and emo-

tional demands of asking productive questions, gathering data of all kinds, reducing and synthesizing information, and analyzing, interpreting, and evaluating information in all its forms.[39]

Institutions are very difficult to change. The school reform movement still may falter. Obviously, library media specialists cannot reform education alone; but this book suggests strategies that the library media specialist can employ in collaboration with others to bring about needed changes. The role envisioned for the school library media specialist is that of a competent change agent who will devise strategies for taking appropriate action so that innovations will have a positive impact on teachers, students, and school administration. The library media specialist can help everyone through this time by assisting in finding, evaluating, and integrating change into the life of the school. The role of *instructional collaborator* becomes increasingly important and the need for a clear understanding of how instructional design interacts with student/teacher learning styles becomes critical. A list of school reform agencies is included at the end of this book. Chapter 3 presents some of the obstacles faced by library media specialists in their efforts to realize the potential of library media programs. Chapter 4 outlines some of the radical paradigm shifts essential to a new vision of library media programming.

Notes

1. Edys Quellmalz et al., *School-Based Reform: Lessons from a National Study. A Guide for School Reform Teams* (Menlo Park, Calif.: SRI International, 1995, ERIC Document Reproduction Service No. ED 395 384), 2.

2. Karl E. Weick, "Technology as Equivoque: Sensemaking in New Technologies," in *Technology and Organization*, ed. P. S. Goodman, L. E. Sprovill, and Associates (San Francisco: Jossey-Bass, 1990), 1–44. Quote is from p. 31.

3. Karl E. Weick, "Educational Organizations as Loosely Coupled Systems," *Administrative Science Quarterly* 21, no. 1 (March 1976), 1–19.

4. Kieth C. Wright, *The Challenge of Technology: Action Strategies for the School Library Media Specialist. School Library Media Programs: Focus on Trends and Issues; No. 13* (Chicago, Ill.: American Library Association, 1993), 3.

5. G. Webb, "Epistemology, Learning and Educational Technology," *Educational and Training Technology International* 28, no. 2 (May 1991), 120–28.

6. N. Postman, *Technology* (New York: Knopf, 1992).

7. J. L. David, "Realizing the Promise of Technology: The Need for Systemic Education Reform," in *Systemic Reform: Perspectives on Personalizing Education— September 1994* (Washington, D.C.: U.S. Department of Education, 1994), 1. J. L. David, "The Who, What, and Why of Site-based Management," *Educational Leadership* 53, no. 4 (December–January 1996), 4–9.

8. Charles A. Findley and Jo-Anne Wyer, "Learning in the Information Age," in *Proceedings of the International Conference on Computer Assisted Learning in Post-Secondary Education, May 5–7 1987* (Calgary: School of Education, University of Calgary, 1987), 9–16.

9. Ludwig Braun, *Vision: TEST (Technologically Enriched Schools of Tomorrow). Final Report: Recommendations for American Educational Decision Makers* (Eugene, Ore.: International Society for Technology in Education, October 1990, ERIC Document Reproduction Service No. ED 327 173), 1.

10. David, *Systemic Reform*, 3.

11. Henry J. Becker, *When Powerful Tools Meet Conventional Beliefs and Institutional Constraints: National Survey Findings on Computer Use by American Teachers. Report No. 49* (Baltimore, Md.: Center for Research on Elementary and Middle Schools, The Johns Hopkins University, October 1990, ERIC Document Reproduction Service No. ED 337 112), 8.

12. Erwin Flaxman and Carol Ascher, *Mentoring in Action: The Efforts of Programs in New York City* (New York: Columbia University, Institute for Urban and Minority Education, April 1992, ERIC Document Reproduction Service No. ED 354 291). Marc Freedman, *The Kindness of Strangers: Adult Mentors, Urban Youth, and the New Voluntarism* (San Francisco: Jossey-Bass, 1993).

13. James M. McPartland and Saundra Murray Nettles, "Using Community Adults as Advocates or Mentors for At-Risk Middle School Students: A Two-Year Evaluation of Project RAISE," *American Journal of Education* 99, no. 4 (August 1991), 568–86.

14. Findley and Wyer, "Learning," 12, paraphrased.

15. Oneida L. Martin and John F. Heflin, *Redefining Leadership Roles for Site-Based Management Systems.* Paper presented at the annual meeting of the Mid-South Educational Research Association, Biloxi, Miss., November 8–10, 1995 (ERIC Document Reproduction Service No. ED 403 640).

16. Susan Black, "Share the Power," *Executive Educator* 18, no. 2 (February 1996), 24–26.

17. Charlene O. Meriwether, "Site-based Management in Secondary Schools," *NASSP Practitioner* 22, no. 3 (February 1996),14–19.

18. John Smyth, ed., *A Socially Critical View of the "Self Managing School* (Bristol, Pa.: Falmer Press, Taylor & Francis, 1993), chap. 1.

19. Richard L. Lynch, *Designing Vocational and Technical Teacher Education for the 21st Century: Implications from the Reform Literature; Information Series No. 368* (Columbus, Ohio: ERIC Clearinghouse on Adult, Career, and Vocational Education, 1997).

20. Holmes Group, *Tomorrow's Schools* (East Lansing, Mich.: Holmes Group, 1990).

21. Carnegie Forum on Education and the Economy's Task Force on Teaching as a Profession, *A Nation Prepared: Teachers for the 21st Century. The Report of the Task Force on Teaching as a Profession* (New York: Carnegie Corporation, 1986, ERIC Document Reproduction Service No. ED 268 120).

22. Holmes Group, *Tomorrow's Teachers* (East Lansing, Mich.: Holmes Group, 1986).

23. Holmes Group, *Tomorrow's Teachers*.

24. Holmes Group, *Tomorrow's Teachers*.

25. F. L. Kochen, *Problems, Solutions, and Benefits of Professional Development Schools as Perceived by University Faculty.* Paper presented at the annual meeting of the Mid-

South Regional Education Research Association, Tuscaloosa, Ala., November 6–8, 1996 (ERIC Document Reproduction Service No. ED 404 937).

26. National Commission on Teaching and America's Future, *What Matters Most: Teaching for America's Future* (New York: Columbia University, 1996. URL source: http://www.tc.columbia.edu/~teachcomm/what.html.

27. John I. Goodlad, *Teachers for Our Nation's Schools* (San Francisco: Jossey-Bass, 1990).

28. Goodland, *Teachers*, 54, 63.

29. Holmes Group, *Tomorrow's Teachers*. Holmes Group, *Tomorrow's Schools* (East Lansing, Mich.: Holmes Group, 1990). *Tomorrow's Schools of Education* (East Lansing, Mich.: Holmes Group, 1995. URL source: http://www.udel.edu/holmes/.

30. See http://www.udel.edu/holmes.

31. Arthur E. Wise, "The Coming Revolution in Teacher Licensure: Redefining Teacher Preparation," *Action in Teacher Education* 16, no. 4 (summer 1994), 1–13.

32. Arthur E. Wise and Jane Leibrand, "Accreditation and the Creation of a Profession of Teaching," *Phi Delta Kappan* 75, no. 2 (October 1993), 133–57.

33. A. Bradley, "Pioneers in Professionalism," *Education Week* (April 20, 1994), 19–27.

34. Carnegie, *A National Prepared.*

35. National Board for Professional Teaching Standards, *National Board for Professional Teaching Standards Report, December 31, 1991. The U.S. Senate Committee on Labor and Human Resources and U.S. House of Representatives Committee on Education and Labor* (Detroit, Mich.: National Board, 1991). National Board for Professional Teaching Standards, *Toward High and Rigorous Standards for the Teaching Profession. Initial Policies and Perspectives of the National Board for Professional Teaching Standards,* 3rd ed. (Detroit, Mich.: National Board, 1991, ERIC Document Reproduction Service No. ED 337 440). Note: Further information on NBPTS is found at URL source: http://www.nbpts.org/.

36. National Council for Accreditation of Teacher Education, *Standards, Procedures, and Policies for the Accreditation of Professional Education Units* (Washington, D.C.: National Council, 1995, ERIC Document Reproduction Service No. ED 385 532).

37. The American Library Association has an agreement (ALA Policy 54.2.2) on accreditation of school library media programs at NCATE-approved institutions.

38. Ray Doiron and Judy Davies, *The Impact of the Prince Edward Island School Library Policy on the Development of School Library Programs across Prince Edward Island,* 1998 (ERIC Document Reproduction Service No. ED 412 964), 3.

39. American Library Association, *Information Literacy; Final Report by the American Library Association* (Chicago, Ill.: Presidential Committee on Information Literacy, 1989), 74.

3

Obstacles to Future Library
Media Program Development

Today's student lives and learns in a world that has been radically altered by the ready availability of vast stores of information in a variety of formats. The learning process and the information search process mirror each other; students actively seek to construct meaning from the sources they encounter and to create products that shape and communicate that meaning effectively. Developing expertise in accessing, evaluating, and using information is in fact the authentic learning that modern education seeks to promote.[1]

Introduction

The authors believe that there is incredible potential for school library media programs and services if these programs become a means by which teachers, students, and administrators learn to find, evaluate, transform, and utilize information from a wide variety of sources and places. We also realize that there are a number of obstacles to reaching that potential. This chapter highlights five of these: obstacles in the pace of change, in funding, in the planning process, in staff development, and in technical development and standards. This chapter discusses these obstacles in detail, and suggests some strategies for the library media specialist to use to overcome them.

Pace of Change Obstacles

The incredible pace of change in our society makes planning and evaluating educational efforts very difficult. It is not just that there is change, because there is always change. Rather, it is that the pace of change is very fast and the amount of change is very extensive. People have difficulty not only in understanding the changes, but in understanding how those changes are affecting their lives. Anderson describes the topography of a rapidly changing global society, noting the following shifts in educational systems:

Shifts *away* from (1) learning based on time spent in the classroom; (2) teaching done mainly via information delivery; (3) a hierarchical, control-oriented organizational structure; and (4) a system operating separately from other youth services. Shifts *toward* systems dominated by (1) learning determined by demonstrable skills, knowledge, and habits focused on higher order thinking skills including understanding, communication, problem solving, decision making, and teamwork; (2) an instructional approach that actively engages students and employs teachers as coaches, critics, and learning facilitators; (3) an organizational structure stressing participative decision making and supportive leadership; and (4) an education system more connected with other youth-serving systems. She notes that the change goes through several stages, including maintenance and defense of the old system, awareness of the need for change, exploration of options, transition toward new models, development of an new infrastructure, and, finally, the emergence of a new system.[2]

In the new information society, the major issue is the management of rapid and pervasive change. *Information Power* sees change as the single most important characteristic of life in the twentieth century. The new technologies are rapidly introducing new equipment, new processes and methods, new relationships, and new work assignments into our society and into our school library media programs.[3] Again, *Information 2000: Library and Information Services for the 21st Century* focuses attention on the change problem:

> The abundance of technologies and associated information places new demands on people in the work force who must adapt to those changes. The velocity and rapid turnover of information has created today's 'knowledge worker' who must be prepared for lifelong learning habits, access to relevant information, and analytical skills to remain productive in his/her chosen field. Some estimates indicate that today's worker will have to update skills every three years.[4]

Much of the reaction to change is based on previous experience with change, relationships with the individual proposing a change, and reactions of the peer group. Many changes in society and education are based on the introduction of computer-related technologies. People may fear that they cannot keep up with the computer-based changes, that they do not have the ability to learn how to use the technologies effectively, that they may lose their jobs, and that the computer-related systems will not function as promised. On the positive side, when computer-related technologies work, and when people have time to learn how to use them, these technologies offer people the chance to do work that they could not do before. They can, for example, contact persons at remote sites, retrieve information from electronic files in many locations, order by computer, create and manage complex databases, develop attractive publications with graphics, and browse the World Wide Web.

The first step in overcoming these change obstacles is to realize that they exist. Simply urging teachers and library media specialists to adapt to change will not work. People like routine and stability. They like to know what is going to happen next. Reading aloud to children, we note that they enjoy the same story over and over because they can predict what will happen. People are confused about the future and their place in it. They do not have time to understand what is happening now before what is happening changes.

Because the school library media specialist is positioned in the school to have contact with all teachers, students, and staff, he/she is in a unique position to assist the school in dealing with change problems. Take note that we are discussing a *process* for dealing with change, not a one-person task. Even if your library is small and there is only one professional staff person, you cannot do the job alone.

Involving all of the school staff and related groups can be a time-consuming process, but such involvement is unavoidable. The only way in which the school staff will deal successfully with change is through a process of total staff involvement in which everyone takes some responsibility for what is happening now and what is going to happen in the future. Because change will affect the work of all staff and students, it is important that all members of the staff be involved in the decision-making process. Having uninvolved staff can only bring about misunderstandings, rumors, and increased resistance to change when change comes. Everyone should be encouraged to ask questions—yes, even the questions that are dumb ones. This process of staff involvement in discussion of change and change planning is a basic form of training.

In her 1993 surveys, Winstead found that library staff members overwhelmingly believed (100 percent in 1987, 99 percent in 1993) that good staff communication skills were essential for library administrators. Qualities desired in administrators included being patient, accepting staff suggestions, allowing time for staff to learn, having realistic expectations, and being sensitive to staff needs.[5] Several steps are essential in this staff involvement change process. The media specialist and other leaders of the school should:

1. *Demonstrate knowledge and concern about the work of all the staff.*
   The school leadership must demonstrate that it knows the jobs that people do and cares about the work the rest of the staff is doing. Often the question is: "Do they know and care about what I do?" Effective staff involvement begins when the top administration takes everyone's job seriously and shows that ideas and changes suggested by the staff are important. The staff will then want to become involved in learning more about change and its positive effects. Everyone needs to know that school leadership is concerned about the impact of change on the lives of staff and students, and is seeking to work with everyone on finding solutions. The media specialist needs to know and care about the work that everyone on the staff does. Knowing what people do, what frustrations they face, and how they work leads to being able to provide the information resources that people need to do their jobs.

2. *Emphasize the positive aspects of change.*
   Some of the coming changes will allow people to do work that was impossible before. They will be able to be in contact with persons at remote sites, order by computer, provide access to resources at remote sites, and easily provide information in graphic form. People will spend less time on tedious writing of reports, or accounting details, or hand drawing of graphs and charts. The school leadership needs to help staff explore ways in which change can make their jobs easier, faster, more effective, and maybe more fun. If the library media center becomes a place where people have access to information in a variety of formats from a wide variety of places, then the positive aspects of change become more apparent.

3. *Allow for the denial processes at work in any social setting.*
   Given a rapidly changing situation, one reaction is to deny that the change is happening or that the change is threatening. People

who have had positive experiences with changes in the past assume that such experience is normal and that everyone will naturally want to become involved. Some people will deny that there is a problem and resist their need for training.

Denial also influences staff who will deny to themselves and others how they really feel about changes in operations, new equipment, different report forms, and so on. Some steps can be taken to deal with these denial phenomena: encouraging discussion of the proposed changes, giving illustrations of how people might feel in meetings, and allowing time for free discussion and experimentation with hardware and software. Often, the ability to have time to experiment *alone* without being observed is essential. For the library media specialist, it is important not to oversell a particular technology or information resource. Concentrate on knowing how people think, and how they like to work and plan. Introduce new information ideas and technologies in the most appropriate way possible. Avoid the "one size fits all" mentality.

4. *Find out how people really feel about their work situation and about the resources, equipment, and technology they are currently using.*

   Often the staff, assistants, students, and others who use materials, media equipment, typewriters, files, and telephones have excellent insights as to the usefulness and limitations of these tools. Their ideas about improvements in instructional functions and needed equipment capabilities can be helpful in deciding what types of computer-assisted technologies are needed. When the library media specialist encourages the staff and students to participate in the planning of change and in assisting with the selection of appropriate technological programs and standards, it offers a way of enriching work life and communications. People can get information from other individuals working at their peer level in other institutions and people can acquire new and more complex skills. People make good decisions about which application to use for what purpose and people can be rewarded.

5. *View the development and use of computer-assisted technologies as a long-term planning and evaluation project involving people as the opportunity arises.*

   Not everyone will support change. The school leadership can identify those work groups who are either most interested or most in need of the changes coming. Few organizations can make massive changes all at once. If the school leadership makes a careful analysis of current instruction and administration in the school, it can identify areas where current functions are in trouble and areas where the department or work group is eager to get involved. Neither capital nor staff development funds are limitless, so beginning with areas of critical need or eagerness makes sense. The school leadership can involve several groups in detailed planning, pilot operations, training seminars, and so on.

This staff involvement is critical because, as Drucker emphasizes, "the only way to bring costs down is to restructure the work."[6] The only way to restructure effectively is to involve those who do the work. When groups do a good job using the technologies, or solve vexing problems, the leadership team needs to be sure that everyone (staff, supervisors, the public) knows about how well they are doing. This "island culture" idea has been successfully used in many institutions and is celebrated in Peters and Austin's *A Passion for Excellence.*[7] If the people who are making changes can make it work for them in their jobs and are enjoying it, other staff groups may want to get into the act. Many agencies use an electronic newsletter on the local area network to announce new applications, to praise effective uses, and to share solutions to problems bothering everyone on the system.

Planning Process Obstacles

Schools and library media centers tend not to be involved in any planning process. The daily demands of educating children, meeting administrative directives, and filling out the correct forms often make any pretense at planning impossible. Everyone thinks that a planning process is important and that organizations should have goals and objectives, make plans to reach the objectives, and evaluate their progress. But the school library media center functions in the midst of an operating school, which in turn is part of a larger operating system, which means that all planning efforts are going to be rather messy. This messiness results from several factors:

1. *Everyone in the school and school system already has more to do than they can handle.*

   Typically, planning efforts are added on top of whatever else people have to do rather than having people released from day-to-day activities so that they can plan. We plan when we can get the right people together, snatching the time as it is available. In a more perfect world there would be time to sit down and plan co-operatively with teachers, parents, the instructional consultants, and community agencies with similar goals. Many school reform efforts have floundered because of a lack of time for planning and decision making. In our world we will have to do the best we can with the time we have.

2. *School systems are often organized from the top down in a traditional bureaucratic way.*
Even in situations where there is discussion of site-based management or "empowering the local school," the actual operation of budgets and time allocations clearly indicates the true sources of power in the system. All site-based planning must take this organizational fact of life into account. We do not plan in a vacuum, but must also consider the plans of the larger school system, the state educational agencies, and the planning trends in education at the national level. Our local plans will have to fit into the larger context.

3. *Plans have to be fitted into the realities of available budget and available facilities.*
In the planning process we need to have big program dreams; the messy part comes when we try to fit those dreams into the available space, or we hear from the associate superintendent for finance about the cost of adding additional doors or changing basic electrical wiring in the school to accommodate some of those dreams. Chapter 8 of this book focuses on the whole planning and evaluation process and makes specific suggestions about how to integrate the library media program's planning process into the planning process of the school. Do not believe that you are too busy to plan; you are too busy not to plan!

Funding Obstacles

Because so many library media centers have very limited budgets,[8] it is tempting to avoid a discussion of budget on the basis that "there is so little money to talk about!" There may be very little to talk about, but how that money is spent says a great deal about the real goals and objectives of the library media program. As Kingma notes:

> Economics is defined as the study of scarce resources. . . . Allocating
> these scarce resources means determining how to use, spend, or divide

the resources, in other words, how to spend the library's budget, how to allocate hard disk space to store computer files, how to schedule employee's time, . . . or how to manage personal time. In each case, choices have to be made to make the best use of limited resources.[9]

Any school or district has a limited amount of money to spend. There will be competition for these funds and a high probability that there will be mandates from state and federal authorities about what programs are to be funded. The budget is a fundamental control mechanism for management. It relates directly to strategic planning within an organization. Most school systems operate, like other public agencies, on a line budget in which specific funds are allocated for specific cost items such as personnel, supplies, equipment, or travel. Traditionally, such agencies had come to expect that each year there would be some increase in the line budget items. More recently some organizations have started a process of "zero-based" budgets in which every budget cycle represents a new beginning. Programs and services must be justified in terms of cost-benefit analysis. Chapter 9 of this book presents budget principles illustrating the process of relating planned objectives to actual budgets.

The long list of funding obstacles includes:

1. *Lack of support for public agencies*
   Weber notes that "following the recession of the early 1990s, American industry cut operations, keeping just enough staff to thrive at the bottom line. Likewise, most public schools, out of financial necessity, have had to reduce costs, while maintaining facilities and essential instructional programs and remaining accountable for student outcomes."[10] Such school downsizing can mean making painful decisions about program elimination and staff layoffs. Downsizing of schools can be used to some advantage—discovering and reducing programs of limited benefit, making instructional programs more focused and more defensible, gathering detailed information about district staff's efforts, and tapping into staff ideas for cost savings.

   However, the lack of public support has had a particularly devastating effect on school facilities.[11] Constitutionally, education is the state's responsibility, whereas school facilities are generally the local district's responsibility. State and federal mandates for educational programs and environmental safety are almost never accompanied by the funds needed to implement them. These mandates place a financial burden on local districts. In most cases, districts must rely on taxpayers' ability or willingness to help meet capital expenses. This results in glaring inequities in school environments among districts in the same state.[12]

States, facing their own budget shortfalls, have been unable to offset school districts' mounting financial needs. In 1991, thirty-seven states were affected by budget shortfalls. In times of austerity, maintenance costs are often slashed first. The consequences of electing to defer maintenance include premature building deterioration, indoor air problems, increased repair and replacement costs, and reduced operating efficiency of equipment. The price tag for deferring maintenance has quadrupled in eight years, from $25 billion in 1983 to $100 billion in 1991. Rising energy costs have also cut into the maintenance budget. When utility costs exceed the budgeted amount, 40 percent of districts in the nation report using funds earmarked for maintenance to meet energy-related expenses.[13] Even with the majority of states now reporting budget surpluses, it is not clear that the public is interested in restoring support to public education.

This lack of public and legislative support may mean going beyond the advantages of downsizing into the crippling or destruction of programs. Downsizing and rethinking budget program priorities means that the library media program must be justified as a program that is essential to the goals and objectives of the school. If the California experience is any indication, wherever this essential tie is not presented strongly the library media program stands a good chance of being eliminated.

2. *Lack of focus concerning budget planning, allocation, and expenditure*
Even if there is a lot of money, it is necessary to know where it should be allocated. School programs that lack focus can waste large amounts of money because it gets spent in multiple directions. One of the problems with site-based management has been the need to train local school personnel in making goal-driven budget decisions.[14] Money does matter, the Committee on Economic Development concludes, "but only if schools are organized to use it effectively to promote achievement. School boards and superintendents must ensure that sufficient funds get to the classroom to improve learning."[15]

3. *Groundless investment in technology*
Although states, school districts, and local schools have invested large sums in a variety of computer-related technologies, there is

no convincing evidence that the investment is based on sound educational research. Miller and Shontz (1995) have repeatedly noted that school library media programs are spending an increasingly large amount of their small budgets to support a variety of technologies.[16] All schools are in a zero-sum budget situation, which means that funds spent for one thing must be taken from funds that were to be spent for other things. In many library media programs funds for books, periodicals, and other print materials have been reallocated to purchase computer hardware and software. Trotter notes that:

Technology's stock is flying high in the nation's schools as it is on Wall Street. In poll after poll, parents say that technology is essential to a child's education. Many educators believe it's the missing linchpin of school reform. Business leaders consider it a mandatory part of a student's preparation for the workplace. And policymakers at every level of government are spending more money on it each year. With support for technology so strong, people might assume its value for schools has been proven beyond question. In fact, the dividends that educators can expect from this investment are not yet clear. There is no guarantee that technology improves student achievement. Research in this area has produced little hard evidence, and few studies have yet examined the kinds of technology use that experts believe are the most valuable to learning.[17]

Sometimes the investment of technology is state-mandated through special budget allocations requiring schools to create technology plans and to spend categorical funds for technology. These funds rarely continue over time, meaning that the schools are stuck with having to replace hardware and software from their own budgets. The situation is further complicated by state requirements for competency testing in the area of technology. For example, in North Carolina there is an eighth-grade technology test that must be passed before a student can graduate from high school. In addition, preservice teachers are now required to pass a state examination much like the student technology exam. The current test is based on specific hardware and software configurations, which means that schools must have these technologies in order for their students to take the test. There is no data to support the idea that technology testing in isolation from subject study is effective; yet the tests are mandated and school programs must not only fund the technology but also take precious instructional time to teach to the test.

Overcoming funding obstacles for the library media program will not be easy. The chapters on technology principles and budget principles in this book outline strategies for the library media specialist in dealing with technology so that appropriate technologies will be purchased and actually used in instruction. Unless such strategic technology planning is done, school and library media programs may find that technology is the beast that ate the whole school. The Committee for Economic Development recommends that those who govern schools do the following:

1. Make it clear to the community that the fundamental goal of schools is learning, and ensure that all policies support learning and achievement and are "well-coordinated and coherent."

2. Set goals for and monitor student achievement, using state and national standards. Ensure that adequate resources are provided to schools to meet such goals. Delegate responsibility and authority, as well as accountability, for making progress toward these achievement goals.

3. Provide incentives to teachers, students, and administrators for rewarding achievement.

4. Establish methods "for dealing with teachers and administrators who perform poorly.[18]

All funding decisions must be based on the goals and objectives of a particular school and school district. Further, once plans are implemented, the *outcomes* of these plans must be evaluated and the planning cycle started again. Library media programs that "just happen" or "only respond to demands" can be in danger of going out of existence.

Staff Development Obstacles

All schools have staff development in a wide variety of areas. In many cases such staff development is actually mandated and school staff members are required to develop professional development plans that must be approved and filed. Continuing teacher licensure or certification is often tied to having completed a number of staff development or graduate course hours or continuing education units. There is clearly a lot of activity and documentation, so what is wrong?

1. *Lack of time*

The basic obstacle to school-based staff development is *time*. Teachers and staff are often expected to participate in staff development activities on top of their responsibilities for teaching, planning, and administrative work. Staff development activities are scheduled at the end of long days. Teachers not only have commitments within the local school, but also at the district and state levels. The competing demands of profession and family make time a very scarce commodity.

2. *Irrelevant and conflicting staff development programs*

A major obstacle to effective staff development is lack of relation to the daily life and work of the teacher or staff member. Often staff development activities are not site-based or planned on the basis of instructional needs, but mandated by the state or school district. These activities may even be driven by grant funds that arise from grant applications requiring a certain number of requisite staff development hours to qualify for the grant. School systems sometimes adopt one program after another, and each new adoption mandates staff development activities. For staff development to be effective, it must be related to the perceived needs of the individual staff member and school, not merely a part of a larger institutional planning process.

3. *Lack of expertise*

As a part of the downsizing of public agencies many states have reduced the number of professional staff persons available at the state department of education level. Some areas that formerly had regional education centers offering professional staff development services have been closed. Other educational agencies already have their hands full dealing with their primary clients— their students. Often this leaves private organizations or professional educators with the task of promoting and offering a variety of staff development activities. Even if there are experts available, it is tempting for them to offer a "package" of staff development activities, which may or may not meet the needs of the local school staff.

Overcoming staff development obstacles is clearly not just a local school issue. However, even at the local school level, certain things can be said about effective staff development. Such staff development has two characteristics: (1) it is planned as part of a school's overall planning and evaluation process so that what happens in staff development is directly related to the goals, objectives, and programs of a particular school, and (2) it is offered at times of particular need—when the school staff faces a problem and wants help with its resolution.

Naturally, such staff development is more costly than the pre-planned, annually scheduled staff development activities offered by school districts, state agencies, or private consultants. It is more expensive because the local school staff must take time to define their own staff development needs and it is expensive because it cannot be packaged in the "large economy size" and offered when the consultant is available.

However, staff development that helps a school toward its goals and improves the teaching and learning environment is far more effective in the long run. People forget mandated workshop information; they discard the handouts; they go back to doing what they were doing before. For the library media specialist, staff development programs in the local school provide valuable opportunities to assist staff in integrating a variety of information resources and technology tools into their instructional programs.

Again, these staff development activities are not packaged at the beginning of the year and offered during mandated staff development days. Staff development arises out of the instructional consultant's work with individual teachers or small groups of staff members working on a project. Working with teachers as they plan and deliver instruction should provide opportunities to discover staff development needs and cooperatively define how to meet those needs. The library media specialist does not have to lead all such events, but may serve as the resource person who finds the right person or resource to do the job. The library media specialist needs to be alert to the "teachable moment" with all the staff and students, so that staff development may indeed be a daily occurrence.

Technology-Related Obstacles

Ever since the days of the National Defense Education Act, school libraries have been involved with technologies that deliver information resources.[19] Some of the older technologies had two characteristics that made them very useful. They were built to a standard, so that learning to operate and maintain one machine meant that the individual could work with other machines of the same type, and the machines remained the same over a long period of time. Examples of such technologies included overhead projectors, 16mm machines, cassette recorders, and, more recently, VHS playback equipment.

The current computer-related technologies lack both of these characteristics. There are several hardware platforms and a wide variety of operating systems and software application programs. Learning how to use a particular configuration does not mean that an individual will be able to operate another configuration. With networking, schools often have several technology systems operating at the same time. Instructional and utility software is upgraded on a regular basis and while files saved in older versions may automatically upgrade to the new system, the new systems do not produce files that can operated by the older systems. So schools are caught in the catch-22 situation of acquiring new software which requires new hardware which is incompatible with other configurations still operating in the school or school district.

These obstacles are further complicated by the fact that computer-related technologies change at a very fast rate. It used to be said that your computer system would be obsolete in a year. Now people are saying that it gets obsolete before you can get it home. Hardware and software vendors seem almost to compete to see who can most quickly introduce the most new things and new system requirements. On the hardware side, the cry is often heard, "The plug I have in my hand does not fit anything on the back of the computer!" On the software side, the complaints are, "My files won't work on this system!" Or "My machine at home does not understand this program!"

Chapter 11 on technology principles details some practical ways to overcome technological obstacles. The basic rule in this process is to change technologies only when that change is mandated by instructional needs, not whenever a new system, software, or product emerges. Text processing—putting words on the screen, making changes, and printing them out on a printer—can be done on a wide variety of systems, some of which are quite old. If the instructional objective has to do with keyboard skills, practice in writing skills, and producing an easy-to-read text, many of the older systems will work well.

Summary

There are many obstacles to establishing effective library media programs. Library media specialists in the future will discover still other obstacles and devise ways to overcome them and provide an instruction-based library media program. If library media specialists know where they are going, they can get around almost any obstacle. The next chapter outlines a new vision for school library media services.

Notes

1. American Association of School Librarians and Association for Educational Communications and Technology, National Guidelines Vision Committee, *Information Literacy Standards for Student Learning, Draft #5, October 7, 1996* (Chicago: American Library Association, 1996). URL source: http://www.ala.org/aasl/stndsdrft5.html.

2. B. L. Anderson, *A Framework for Understanding and Assessing Systemic Change* (Boulder, Colo.: InSites, Education Commission of the States, 1993, ERIC Document Reproduction Service No. ED 375 459), 5–9.

3. American Association of School Librarians and Association for Educational Communications and Technology, *Information Power: Guidelines for School Library Media Programs* (Chicago: American Library Association, 1988), 3. American Association of School Librarians and Association for Educational Communications and Technology, *Information Power: Building Partnerships for Learning* (Chicago: American Library Association, 1998), iv.

4. *Information 2000: Library and Information Services for the 21st Century. The Summary Report of the 1991 White House Conference on Library and Information Services*, 1991 (Washington, D.C.: The White House Conference on Library and Information Services, 1991), 5.

5. Elizabeth B. Winstead, "Staff Reactions to Automation," *Computers in Libraries* 14 (April 1994), 18–21.

6. Peter F. Drucker, *Managing for the Future: The 1990s and Beyond* (New York: Truman Talley Books, Dutton, 1992), 197.

7. Tom J. Peters and Nancy K. Austin, *A Passion for Excellence: The Leadership Difference* (New York: Random House, 1995).

8. Marilyn L. Miller and Marilyn L. Shontz, "The Race for the School Library Dollar (Expenditures for Resources in School Library Media Centers, FY 1993–94)," *School Library Journal* 41 (October 1995), 22–33.

9. B. R. Kingma, *The Economics of Information: A Guide to Economic and Cost-benefit Analysis for Information Professionals* (Englewood, Colo.: Libraries Unlimited, 1996), 3.

10. James Weber, *Can Cutbacks Leave School Programs Viable? ERIC Digest, No. 106*, June 1996 (ERIC Document Reproduction Service No. ED 406 717).

11. Linda M. Frazier, *Deteriorating School Facilities and Student Learning, ERIC Digest, No. 82*, May 1993 (ERIC Document Reproduction Service No. ED 356 564).

12. Anne Lewis et al., *Wolves at the Schoolhouse Door: An Investigation of the Condition of Public School Buildings* (Washington, D.C.: Education Writers Association, June 1989, ERIC Document Reproduction Service No. ED 306 660).

13. Shirley J. Hansen, *Schoolhouse in the Red. A Guidebook for Cutting Our Losses. Powerful Recommendations for Improving America's School Facilities* (Arlington, Va.:

American Association of School Administrators, June 1992, ERIC Document Reproduction Service No. ED 347 697).

14. David Peterson, *School-Based Budgeting, ERIC Digest, No. 64*, 1999 (Eugene, Ore.: ERIC Clearinghouse on Educational Management, ERIC Document Reproduction Service No. ED 336 865).

15. Committee for Economic Development, *Putting Learning First: Governing and Managing the Schools for High Achievement. Statement by the Research and Policy Committee of the CED*, 1994 (New York: Committee for Economic Development, ERIC Document Reproduction Service No. ED 377 561), 60.

16. Miller and Shontz, "The Race for the School Library Dollar."

17. Alan Trotter, "Taking Technology's Measure," *Education Week* 17, no. 11 (November 10, 1997), 6–11. Quote is from p. 6.

18. Committee for Economic Development, *Putting Learning First*, 60.

19. *Information Power* (1998), 54.

4

A New Vision for
Library Media Programs

Although changes in society, education, and technology have transformed many of the challenges facing library media programs during the past decade, the mission itself remains the same. Today, this mission focuses on offering programs and services that are centered on information literacy and that are designed around active, authentic student learning as described in the information literacy standards for student learning. The goals of today's library media program point to the development of a community of learners that is centered on the student and sustained by a creative, energetic library media program.[1]

Introduction

The future of school library media programs depends on a new vision of what the program can mean in instruction. What is called for is a paradigm shift in the way the program and the library media specialist is viewed. Barker defines a paradigm as "a set of rules and regulations (written or unwritten) that does two things: (1) it establishes or defines boundaries, (2) it tells you how to behave inside the boundaries in order to be successful.[2] He illustrates what happens when people or institutions are forced into situations that are not defined by their current boundaries and where their rules do not apply. When we see people frustrated by their inability to understand what is happening and unable to function effectively in the midst of change, we have a paradigm shift. This chapter proposes a number of changes in school library media programs based on a radically different paradigm of the goals of school library media services.

These shifts include: (1) the shift from centralized to distributed school library media programs and services; (2) the shift from the school librarian's role as media specialist to the role of an integrating connector; (3) the shift from library collections to access to information resources; (4) the shift to information technologies appropriate to library needs; (5) the shift from terminal education to education for a lifetime; and (6) the shift from local or national economies to a global economy.

The authors believe each of these major shifts are not only impacting library media programs, but also impacting all levels of education and society.

From Centralized to Distributed Library Media Programs

This paradigm shift is from a library media *center* to *distributed* library media programs. In the computer world there were once very large main-frame computers to which everyone was attached through terminals or telephone connections. Such operations required a computer center operated by a professional and support staff, where all of the real computing was done. Today, almost all computing is distributed among a number of file servers and desktop computers so that people have access to incredible computer power in their own offices. In the same way, library media programs need to be viewed as going on everywhere in the school and its related community and assisting everyone—students, teachers, administrators, and community—in connecting to information resources anywhere in the world.

Ask most people to define a library and they will begin by describing a place, or building, that contains books—usually for the use of patrons. People still apply to library education programs because of their love of books or libraries, referring to this old paradigm. Many libraries, including school library media centers, began with the old paradigm: create an attractive place, stock it with books and periodicals, and develop programs to assist people in the use of these materials.

The new paradigm means that library media programs will provide programs and access to information materials that may be located at a single site, distributed via computer network, or available through the Internet. Teachers, students, and parents may access information in classrooms, or on laptops located in lounges, at home, or in community centers. The format of the information available will vary from site to site. This shift will change the format and content of library media instruction, how budget and program planning are done, how the library media program supports instruction, the arrangement of the media facilities, and the ways in which the library media program cooperates with other agencies.

From Media Specialist to Integrating Connector

The paradigm shift for the role of the library media specialist is from being a *specialist*—someone who knows about books, audiovisuals, cable, technology, and how to fix things—to a role as *integrating connector*. This new role places major emphasis on connecting individuals to the information resources they need at the time they need them. The role includes providing the means and training so that connecting with appropriate information resources is as easy as possible for all individuals. The traditional paradigm for the library media specialist grew out of the traditional view of libraries. If the library was a place in which books were organized and shared with patrons, then the librarian was the selector, organizer, and sharer of books—the book person.

In a slight shift following Sputnik (1957), the role was changed to include audiovisual materials and the school librarian became the book person *and* the AV specialist. As new information technologies emerged (television, cable, personal computers) these roles were added to the current roles of the school librarian; often the title was also changed to reflect the institutional view that the new roles were more important than the continuing older roles. In all of these changes, the paradigm of library media specialist roles was not changed; functions and responsibilities were simply piled on top of one another without the addition of staff.

Obviously, library media specialists can not create a paradigm shift on their own. This book suggests actions the library media specialist can take in concert with others to bring about needed changes in the ways in which the role of the school library media specialist is viewed. The role advocated here is that of a *change agent*, who will devise strategies for taking appropriate action so that the library media program will have a positive impact on school administration and the instructional program.

Information Power (1988) suggests a paradigm shift by defining three roles for the library media specialist—information specialist, teacher, and instructional consultant.[3] As the role of instructional consultant becomes increasingly important, the need for a clear understanding of how instructional design interacts with student/teacher learning styles becomes critical.[4] The AASL/AECT National Guidelines Vision Committee focused on the instructional consultant role in this way:

> Learning is the primary goal of a student-centered library media program, and the library media specialist is key to achieving that goal. By fostering a culture of learning in partnership . . . the library media specialist sets the stage for the active, dynamic pursuit of knowledge within and beyond the formal curriculum. An effective program is one that models and promotes active, collaborative participation in this culture and supports the development of students' and others' potential as lifelong learners.[5]

Information Power (1998) highlights the value of the collaborative role of the library media specialist:

> Research and practice have established the school library media program's vital role in collaborative planning and curriculum development, serving all grade levels, ages, and abilities of all members of the school's learning community. That perspective makes the school library media program a natural hub for bringing teachers and library media specialists together to create exemplary and innovative curricula. The program also offers a model for weaving content-area goals and information literacy skills into active, authentic learning experiences.[6]

From Resource Collections to Access to Resources

This shift is from "our collection here" to access to resources without regard to location. Loertscher contrasts the traditional concept of library collections with the newer concept in this manner:

Traditional	**New**
Print rich	Information-rich in every format
Print and AV oriented	Multiple technologies
Centralized (one location)	Centralized and decentralized simultaneously
Rigidly scheduled	Flexibly scheduled
Single-person staff	Professional and technical staff
A quiet, almost empty place	A busy, bustling learning laboratory[7]

Most library collections developed during a era when librarians were concerned to own the resources that were essential to their patrons. Such ownership meant having the necessary materials for patrons on the shelves. When there was high demand, librarians created reserve collections or ordered multiple copies. The goal was availability through ownership. Early in twentieth-century library development it became obvious that every library could not own all of the resources essential to patrons. A variety of cooperative arrangements were created, of which interlibrary loans, the *Union List of Serials*, the *National Union Catalog*, common catalog copy formats, and MARC, are just a few.

The idea, if not the actual fact, of resource sharing emerged. Most resource-sharing ideas faltered on two basic characteristics of library patrons: the fact that patrons want what they want right now, and the principle of least effort. As any librarian can tell you, library patrons do not plan ahead. They show up when the term paper is due, or the reading has long been assigned, or they plan to plant the garden that day or have the party that night. Patrons expect that the library will have, on hand, the resources that they have just decided they need. Thus anticipation of patron demand and studies of user needs became important in librarianship. But no matter how much was anticipated, the long process of resource selection, purchasing, cataloging, processing, and putting on the shelf always caused delays.

The availability of online resources began to change this picture. In the early days of accessing computer files via telephone connections, the only information available was an online form of indexes and abstracts—with a heavy emphasis on science, technology, and business sources. When individuals actually wanted to read the referenced article, they had to go to a place where a printed full-text copy was available. Some vendors, including the National Library of Medicine and the Institute for Scientific Information, created easy ways for people to receive printed copies of articles through the mail. Slowly, certain sectors of the information users (business, law, medicine) began to demand, and be willing to pay for, full-text information online. Once a citation was found, the full text of the reference without graphics or color could be downloaded. With the coming of CD-ROM technology, some vendors of information began to put encyclopedias and other reference works into that format and to add graphics, color, and sound to their products. As the CD-ROM technology advanced, more and more information in more and more formats could be stored on a single CD.

As the Internet and World Wide Web began to emerge, the idea of sharing full-text, graphics, and other computer-based files grew in popularity and availability. Many resources once only available at one place and in one format now became available to anyone who had access to the communication systems of the Internet. The idea that the library media program serves to connect people to information in almost anyplace in the world is remaking the idea of library media collections. However, making lots of information widely available in different formats has both positive and negative implications. Fishman and Pea put it this way:

> The next five years will radically change the ways that schools relate to the world around them as global computer networks—long the exclusive domain of higher education and private industry—link up to primary and secondary schools. The Internet . . . represents a powerful educational resource unlike anything that precedes it. Its potential for education grows with the establishment of each new connection. For the first time, children have the means for simple, direct contact with millions of adults in a forum that masks their physical youth and presents them as virtual equals. However, just as the new kid in school has to learn new social codes and rituals to fit in, schools must learn some of the practices, dangers, and etiquette of the Internet. Of course, the established denizens of the Internet will soon have some adjusting to do as well, with thousands (or millions) of new kids knocking electronically at their doors. Since the Internet was not designed with children in mind, many potentially difficult issues must be discussed by both the education and the Internet communities.[8]

The American Library Association has issued an interpretation of the Library Bill of Rights concerning access to electronic information. That document states:

> Freedom of expression is an inalienable human right and the foundation for self-government. Freedom of expression encompasses the freedom of speech and the corollary right to receive information.

These rights extend to minors as well as adults. Libraries and librarians exist to facilitate the exercise of these rights by selecting, producing, providing access to, identifying, retrieving, organizing, providing instruction in the use of, and preserving recorded expression regardless of the format or technology. . . . [The] *Code of Ethics* and in the *Library Bill of Rights* and its interpretations . . . serve to guide librarians and library governing bodies in addressing issues of intellectual freedom that arise when the library provides access to electronic information, services, and networks. Issues arising from the still developing technology of computer-mediated information generation, distribution, and retrieval need to be approached and regularly reviewed from a context of constitutional principles and ALA policies so that fundamental and traditional tenets of librarianship are not swept away.[9]

Like it or not, the future school and library media program will be connected to a vast set of information resources that require careful evaluation, selection, organizing, and modifying for use in instruction.

The AASL/AECT National Guidelines Vision Committee's *Information Literacy Standards for Student Learning* places these skills in the student learning context:

Literacy Standards for Student Learning

Category I: Information Literacy
The student who is information literate:

Standard 1: Accesses information efficiently and effectively, as described by the following indicators: 1. recognizes the need for information; 2. recognizes that accurate and comprehensive information is the basis for intelligent decision making; 3. formulates questions based on information needs; 4. identifies a variety of potential sources of information; 5. develops and uses successful strategies for locating information.

Standard 2: Evaluates information critically and competently, as described by the following indicators: 1. determines accuracy, relevance, and comprehensiveness; 2. distinguishes among facts, point of view, and opinion; 3. identifies inaccurate and misleading information; 4. selects information appropriate to the problem or question at hand.

Standard 3: Uses information effectively and creatively, as described by the following indicators: 1. organizes information for practical application; 2. integrates new information into one's own knowledge; 3. applies information in critical thinking and problem solving; 4. produces and communicates information and ideas in appropriate formats.

Category II: Independent Learning

The student who is an independent learner is information literate and:

Standard 4: Pursues information related to personal interests, as described by the following indicators: 1. seeks information related to various dimensions of personal well-being, such as career interests, community involvement, health matters, and recreational pursuits; 2. designs, develops, and evaluates information products and solutions related to personal interests.

Standard 5: Appreciates and enjoys literature and other creative expressions of information, as described by the following indicators: 1. is a competent and self-motivated reader; 2. derives meaning from information presented creatively in a variety of formats; 3. develops creative products in a variety of formats.

Standard 6: Strives for excellence in information seeking and knowledge generation, as described by the following indicators: 1. assesses the quality of the process and products of one's own information seeking; 2. devises strategies for revising, improving, and updating self-generated knowledge.

Category III: Social Responsibility

The student who contributes positively to the learning community and to society is information literate and:

Standard 7: Recognizes the importance of information to a democratic society, as described by the following indicators: 1. seeks information from diverse sources, contexts, disciplines, and cultures; 2. respects the principle of equitable access to information.

Standard 8: Practices ethical behavior in regard to information and information technology, as described by the following indicators: 1. respects the principles of intellectual freedom; 2. respects intellectual property rights; 3. uses information technology responsibly.

Standard 9: Participates effectively in groups to pursue and generate information, as described by the following indicators: 1. shares knowledge and information with others; 2. respects others' ideas and background and acknowledges their contributions; 3. collaborates with others, both in person and through technologies, to identify information problems and to seek their solutions; 4. collaborates with others, both in person and through technologies, to design, develop, and evaluate information products and solutions.[10]

Library media collections have always been either a vast, bewildering array of very important information and junk, or, alternatively, a carefully selected, ordered, useful array of resources available to teachers and students at their point of need. The new paradigms will mean that library media specialists are required to do a lot more selecting, organizing, and instructing in the instructional programs if we are to avoid chaos. Future library media instruction must equip students and teachers to deal with this vast and bewildering array, or students and teachers will be overwhelmed. What happens will depend on the library media specialist and the program he/she designs and delivers. As *Information Power* (1998) notes:

> Authentic learning for today's student is not bound by the textbook, the classroom, the library media center, or the school. By linking students with the unlimited learning opportunities available throughout the learning community, the school library media program provides a bridge between formal, school-based learning and independent, lifelong learning. . . . The program's connections with the learning community increase the resources available to all learners in the school and build a base of community support for student learning and for continuous school improvement.[11]

From Any Technology to Appropriate Technologies for Learning Needs

The paradigm shift here is from adopting every new technology as it emerges to adopting technologies as they become appropriate to learning needs. Libraries were so late in the process of adopting computer-related technologies for administrative and public use that there was a tendency to play catch-up. Often libraries adopted technologies just because they were new or different. Little study was devoted to the training needs of staff or patrons. Patron and librarian work-study habits or interests were rarely considered in the particular technological applications adopted.

The typical pattern was to adapt current library operations to the technology—make the online catalog look like the card catalog—and then to train the library staff and patrons in the use of the adapted operation. Sometime formats from data processing or database management systems were adopted, thereby increasing the need to learn multiple new systems, on site and online. As more and more technology was adopted, the need for training became critical.

Hannigan points out "the curve of nonsatisfaction" as computer-related technologies continue to be introduced into libraries. This move toward dissatisfaction with the system(s) is usually made up of increased breakdown of hardware, increased software failures, increased data loss, voiced dissatisfaction with software, and reported system slowdowns. Also common are requests for additional and more complex data manipulation and reporting, suggestions for purchase of peripherals, increased requests for machine replacement, and for newer or enhanced versions of software, linked with reports of frustration because the system does not meet user needs and awareness that breakthrough technology is making current architecture obsolete.[12] Much of the dissatisfaction results from viewing technology in isolation from the rest of the school program.

Computer-related technologies in school library media operations will only be successfully integrated into instruction and library operations when the process of technology selection is driven by the goals and objectives of the local school. No matter what state or local educational agencies demand, computer-related technologies imposed on schools will not improve instructional outcomes or enhance the development of teachers and students. For such technologies to be meaningful in terms of outcomes, they must be adopted on the basis of local school instructional planning. The Benton Foundation's *The Learning Connection: Schools in the Information Age* stresses that appropriate use of technology can be a powerful force in educational (and library media) reform:

> But advocates say that new technologies can be used to do more than make school fun or help busy parents reach teachers. As they see it, teachers can use Internet-based explorations as part of an entirely new approach to education that is more appropriate to the world students will face as adults. Traditional classrooms—with their strong central authority, carefully prescribed curriculums, 55-minute classes, homogeneous student groupings, and emphasis on rote learning—may have trained children adequately for the old-style mass-production economy, analysts say. That was a world in which products changed relatively infrequently, work typically was organized according to a strict division of labor controlled by steep hierarchies, and individuals were expected only to master relatively discrete and simple tasks that they performed repeatedly. Often, they held such jobs for years.
>
> In the Information Age economy, however, businesses must innovate and customize their products constantly. Because hierarchical workplaces can't adapt to changing market conditions rapidly enough to survive, authority has increasingly devolved to self-directed, interdisciplinary teams. Frequent job changes have become much more common. This environment places a premium on workers who are

flexible, innovative, self-directed, and able to solve problems collaboratively.[13]

The library media specialist can play a key role in assisting educators and school administrators in selecting computer-related technologies that can help teachers and students develop the higher-order thinking and working skills essential to survival in the twenty-first century.

From Terminal Education
to Lifetime Education

The paradigm shift here is from a view of education that has an end—graduation from high school, college, or a graduate program—to a view of education as a lifelong process in which people will find the need to continually update their interests and skills through some institutional means. Because of the factory model of education, many segments of society still believe that one graduates from an education and is then finished with the process. An assembly line produces a particular finished product, and for education that product is the graduate. The school reform movement is seeking to move away from the factory model of identical programs for identical students toward programs that recognize and create educational programs for widely differing individuals.

Before making such a departure, however, several questions must be raised:

1. How should we organize education in space and time to make full use of information technology?

2. What should the location and schedule be for instruction and library media programs?

3. Where do we get the people, energies, and budgets to get this transformation up and running?

4. How should we manage the works and knowledge of our culture so that presentation of them through advanced information technologies will best support our educational efforts?

5. What instructional resources and formats will best enable students to explore, select, and appropriate the skills and ideas that the culture offers them?

6. How can we structure the activities of teaching so that they attract highly talented people and provide them with self-renewing and self-developing conditions of work?

These are complex, systemic questions and educators, parents, and librarians will be struggling to define them over the next few years. The ways in which our government and citizens answer these questions will determine the relevancy of the educational enterprise to the needs of people in the future.

From National Economies to a Global Economy

The new, information-based global economy is shifting us from a paradigm of the economics of scarcity to one of an economics of plenty. During the last twenty years three major revolutions have transformed world markets: globalization, new management thinking, and technology. These three forces have created vast new open deregulated markets, wired together by a converging information highway and dominated by new business organizations that are in the process of rewriting the rules of business. In traditional industrial economies the most important resources were raw materials, real estate, and cheap labor. All of these resources have limits, and because we can run out of them, such economics were known as the economics of scarcity and spawned the concept of the "haves" and the "have-nots." A nation state (and its businesses) either had access to these scarce resources or they didn't. Much of colonialism was based on this economic model: "Seize the resources you need wherever they are!"

The most competitive countries of the new, information-based economy do not have raw materials, real estate, or cheap labor. In fact, the world's top five most competitive countries also have some of the highest labor costs on the planet. These information skill areas form the new paradigm for an economy that is not based on scarcity or on natural resources. The new resources are increasingly available to anyone, and they are totally unlimited. The economic model has shifted from the economics of scarcity to the economics of plenty.[14]

Increasingly, consumer expectations for products and services (including library services) are based on innovative customer service and flexibility in providing better, cheaper products faster, which are tailored exactly to customer needs. The library patron is not limited to what is available locally, but can call up a vast menu of product choices and prices and choose instantly from a global Web-based menu. The world is rapidly becoming a global supermarket of products and services. Grulke sums up:

> Over the past decade we have begun to realize that the "old" Industrial Economy has entered the end of its life cycle. In the United States less than 30% of employment is now in the traditional industrial businesses, with the balance being in service and information businesses. Analysts estimate that more than 90% of the US GDP this year will come from information and service businesses. We see similar shifts world-wide.[15]

For schools and library media programs the instructional task is to prepare students who can function effectively in this information-based economy. Individuals who have the requisite skills to handle jobs in this economy will succeed, but those who lack such skills may be completely left out.

Summary

Major paradigm shifts in the emerging information economy mean that all librarians will need to rethink: (1) possible sources of information and the reliability of those sources; (2) appropriate ways to access those sources selected; and (3) formatting information and access for ease of use. *Information Power* (1998)[16] presents a view of library media services based on student information literacy needs. As the twenty-first century approaches, the school library media program and the local school must share a vision of the kind of world in which students will work and live and what information literacy means in that context. Instructional programs must help students develop the skills that make successful living in such a world possible. The rest of this book presents principles for the future school library media program.

Notes

1. Information Power–Vision Statement, 1998. URL source: http://www.ala.org/aasl/ip_goals.html.

2. Joel A. Barker, *Paradigms: The Business of Discovering the Future* (New York: Harper Business, 1993), 32.

3. American Association of School Librarians, *Information Power: Building Partnerships for Learning* (Chicago: American Library Association, 1988).

4. Philip M. Turner, "What Help Do Teachers Want, and What Will They Do to Get It?" *School Library Media Quarterly* 24, no. 4 (summer 1996), 208–12.

5. AASL/AECT, National Guidelines Vision Committee, *Information Literacy Standards*. URL source: http://www.ala/aasl/stndsdraft5.html.

6. American Association of School Librarians and Association for Educational Communications and Technology, *Information Power: Building Partnerships for Learning* (Chicago, Ill.: American Library Association, 1998), 38.

7. David V. Loertscher, *Reinvent Your School's Library in the Age of Technology: A Guide for Principals and Superintendents* (San Jose, Calif.: Hi Willow Research and Publishing, 1998), 3.

8. B. J. Fishman and R. D. Pea, *The Internetworked School: A Policy for the Future*. URL source: http://www.covis.nwu.edu/papers/fishman&pea1993.html# introduction.

9. American Library Association, *Access to Electronic Information, Services, and Networks: An Interpretation of the Library Bill of Rights, Adopted by the ALA Council, January 24, 1996*. URL source: http://www.ala.org/oitp/ebillrits.html.

10. These standards are spelled out with examples, content-area applications, and levels of proficiency in *Information Power* (1998), 8–43.

11. *Information Power* (1998), 122.

12. Jane A. Hannigan, "An Expanded Managerial Role in a Microcomputer Environment," in *The Library Microcomputer Environment: Management Issues*, ed. Sheila S. Intner and Jane A. Hannigan (Phoenix, Ariz.: Oryx Press, 1988), 207–8.

13. Benton Foundation, *The Learning Connection: Schools in the Information Age* (Washington, D.C.: Benton Foundation, 1997). URL source: http://www.benton.org/ library/schools/.

14. Future World International, *Rules-of-the-Game for a Changing World Economy* (Future World International, 1997). URL source: http://www.futureworld.co.za/.

15. Wolfgang E. Grulke, *The New Workplace: The Changing Nature of Work, Organizations and Business in the Information Economy*, 1997. URL source: http://www.afsmi. org/journal/sep97/sep-002.htm.

16. *Information Power* (1998).

5

People Principles

*But the real reason all librarians should become more skilled and knowl-
edgeable in affective and humanistic approaches to library/media work is
precisely because they are whole human beings whose feelings, values, and
attitudes do count as a part of themselves and their work. Their humanity
in their work, not the media, is their most important message.*[1]

Introduction

The authors have known poor school library media programs with
excellent facilities, modem technology, and a more than adequate
staff and budgets. On the other hand, we have known programs with
limited library and technology resources, limited staff, and minimal
budgets that were excellent programs. What makes the difference?
The really important element is the people and the ways in which
they relate to one another, to the children, and to the parents and the
community. Many professional education programs are successful in
teaching technical library skills; not so many are successful in helping students develop their people skills—the human relations and
communication skills that make the library skills effective. This
chapter presents people principles for future school library media
programs.

People Relations Are the Heart of
Child Development and Learning

Even at the beginning, we are all social beings. Breakthroughs in
methodology for assessing infants' perceptual abilities show that

even newborns are quite perceptive, active, and responsive during physical and social interaction. The newborn infant will imitate people, stick out its tongue, flutter its eyelashes, and open and close its mouth in response to similar actions from an adult or older child. Through crying and other distress sounds, the infant signals physical needs for food, warmth, safety, touch, and comfort. Infants' physical requirements are best met when delivered along with social contact and interaction. Babies who lack human interaction may fail to thrive. Such infants will fail to gain sufficient weight and will become indifferent, listless, withdrawn and/or depressed, and in some cases will not survive.[2]

Piaget pointed to peer interaction as one major source of cognitive as well as social development, particularly for the development of role-taking and empathy.[3] In the contexts of school, neighborhood, and home, children learn to discriminate among different types of peer relationships—best friends, social friends, activity partners, acquaintances, and strangers.[4] If the structuring of social experiences in a school allows children to have a variety of age, peer, and adult relationships in a wide variety of environments, we thereby promote social development. Rigid and formal scheduling may hinder this process. Hallinan states that formally structured educational situations, built around teacher-group interaction, tend to result in fewer peer interactions than less formal settings. Fewer socially isolated children are found in informal classrooms where activities are built around projects in which peers can establish skills for collaboration and activity partnership.[5] Readers of educational history will recognize that John Dewey had many of the same insights.

In terms of people principles, the future focus of the library media center program needs to shift toward enhancing the variety of informal social experiences for the students in the school. Visits from authors, peer tutoring, library helper programs, community volunteers, and programs from community agencies, adults presenting their families' stories, musical and dramatic programs, and other appropriate activities can be integrated into the curricular activities of the library media program so that students have the opportunity to interact with these adults and other children. Because of massive problems in many community/home situations, the basic human interaction skills of children will be acquired in the school setting.

Relationships Have an
Impact on People

The things we do are far less important than the relationships we establish or destroy. Library media specialists work hard at establishing and maintaining good relationships because they are critical to successful instruction, children's learning, teacher collaboration, and a successful school library media program. The focus needs to be on the people rather than on facilities, books, or technologies.

Getting people the things they need when they need them requires that we know our colleagues very well, so that we can read, review, select, and acquire the resources that will work best for them. Implementing this strategy will often mean spending a large amount of time with individual teachers or students, small groups, and with the whole school faculty so that the library media specialist will be able to anticipate requests, find appropriate software, and assist in the implementation of instructional plans. All of which indicates that we will need to take time from other activities to work on people relations—either by not doing those other things, or by doing them more efficiently.

Media Programs Reflect the Diversity
of the School and Its Community

Let us state this principle bluntly: No two school library media centers should look the same. No two school library media collections should contain identical materials. No library media programs should be the same. Doing it like someone else does it may mean that the library media program does not meet the needs of this particular school and these students and teachers. The reason for this principle lies in the difference among students and teachers in different schools. The instructional program of any school has to reflect the learning styles of its students and the teaching styles of its teachers as well as the organized curriculum of the school system.

In the factory model of education, all units—administrators, teachers, students, aides—had the same functions. You learned your function and it continued in the same way over time so that one could easily predict outcomes. In the newer the models of education which are student-centered and adapted to the learning styles of students and the teaching styles of teachers, there is no such regularity.

James Gleick's *Chaos: The Making of a New Science* suggests that science suffered through a "factory-model" period commonly called the "clockwork" theory of the universe, which was ruled by a series of scientific laws giving scientists a very stable view of the nature of the universe. Chaos theory began when scientists noted a variety of unpredictable results from very similar beginnings. Gleick goes on to apply this chaos theory to many fields.[6] Applying the chaos idea to library media programs leads to the conclusion that the combination of teacher styles, student learning styles, neighborhood setting, larger community context, and other factors will vary greatly from school to school. Each school will have a unique combination of factors that will lead to a unique library media program.

Learning Connections sums up this uniqueness as follows: "Every program should be designed to support, complement, and enhance the educational philosophy, goals, and locally-generated objectives of the district and school of which it is a part. Thus, while they may encompass many of the same elements, *no two programs will be identical.* Each will reflect the unique flavor of its particular school, teachers, students, and curriculum."[7]

This uniqueness does not mean there will not be similarities among library media programs. Even in chaotic situations, a variety of recognizable patterns emerge over time. The unique context of a particular school does mean that each program needs to be built around the particular set of dynamics and needs of that school, however—not modeled after other successful programs or developed from some mandated model of library media programs.

People Relations Are Crucial to Developing Children's Resilience

Bonnie Benard summarizes the research on resilience in children and youth:

> Some longitudinal studies, several of which follow individuals over the course of a life span, have consistently documented that between half and two-thirds of children growing up in families with mentally ill, alcoholic, abusive, or criminally involved parents or in poverty-stricken or war-torn communities do overcome the odds and turn a life trajectory of risk into one that manifests "resilience," the term used to describe a set of qualities that foster a process of successful adaptation and transformation despite risk and adversity. . . . We are all born with

an innate capacity for resilience, by which we are able to develop social competence, problem-solving skills, a critical consciousness, autonomy, and a sense of purpose.[8]

She points out that a growing body of effective school research[9] and numerous ethnographic studies[10] present a picture of those characteristics of the family, school, and community environments that may alter or even reverse expected negative outcomes and enable individuals to circumvent life stressors and manifest resilience, despite risk.

These "protective factors" fall into three categories: caring and supportive relationships, positive and high expectations, and opportunities for meaningful participation. Primary among the forces for resilience are the people principles found in caring and supportive relationships within the school library media program. The presence of at least one caring person—someone who conveys an attitude of compassion, who understands that no matter how awful a child's behavior, the child is doing the best he or she can, given his or her experience—provides support for healthy development and learning. Werner and Smith's study, covering more than forty years, found that, among the most frequently encountered positive role models in the lives of resilient children, outside the family circle, was a *favorite teacher* who was not just an instructor for academic skills for the youngsters but also a confidant and positive model for personal identification.[11]

Furthermore, as the research of Noddings has articulated, a caring relationship with a teacher gives youth the motivation for wanting to succeed: "At a time when the traditional structures of caring have deteriorated, schools must become places where teachers and students live together, talk with each other, take delight in each other's company. . . . It is obvious that children will work harder and do things . . . for people they love and trust."[12] Even beyond the teacher-student relationship, creating a school-wide ethos of caring creates the opportunities for caring student-to-student, teacher-to-teacher, and teacher-to-parent relationships.

For many children the teacher, the assistant, or the library specialist may be the only caring adult in the child's life. The library media center and its collaborative instructional programs can provide a wonderful environment for resilience factors to grow. Creating opportunities for students and teachers to imagine and deliver programs that celebrate the delight we find in one another's company, highlighting the family and life experiences of authors, illustrators, and storytellers who celebrate together—all such activities contribute to resilience for children and the adults who work with them.

Caring for each other is not a program or a strategy, but rather a way of relating to youth, their families, and each other that conveys compassion, understanding, respect, and interest. That is to say, caring is an important people factor in the school library media program. Individuals who cannot care should not work in the school or the library media center. Caring for one another is also the well-spring from which flow the two other resilience factors—high expectations and opportunities for participation—which will be discussed in chapter 6 of this book.

Collaboration Is Essential in Media Programs

Much has been written about collaborative learning or team teaching. The term *collaborative learning* covers a broad array of approaches often recognized by their more particular names, such as cooperative learning, simulations, or writing groups. Some endorse collaborative learning simply as an effective teaching strategy. Others see collaborative learning as much broader work that involves a different way of thinking about knowledge, learning, and being together in the world. Here are some typical strategies that have been used:

Group Investigations are structured to emphasize higher-order thinking skills such as analysis and evaluation. Students work to produce a group project, which they may have a hand in selecting.

STAD (Student Teams Achievement Divisions) is used in grades 2 to 12. Students with varying academic abilities are assigned to four- or five-member teams in order to study what has been initially taught by the teacher and to help each pupil reach his or her highest level of achievement. Students are then tested individually. Teams earn recognition based on the degree to which all team members have progressed over their past records.

Jigsaw is used with narrative material in grades 3 to 12. Each team member is responsible for learning a specific part of a topic. After meeting with members of other groups, who are "expert" in the same part, the "experts" return to their own groups and present their findings. Team members then are quizzed on all topics.[13]

In all collaborative learning settings, each member of a team is responsible not only for learning what is taught but also for helping teammates learn, thus creating an atmosphere of achievement. Cooperative or collaborative learning requires a number of people skills. A basic component in any attempt to introduce collaborative or cooperative learning for students is the modeling of collaborative behavior on the part of the instructional staff. One of the reasons for stressing the instructional consultant role of the library media specialist has to do with this modeling aspect. If the school staff wants students to learn how to work cooperatively, to deal with differentiated roles in learning, and to understand the particular strengths of individuals in a group process, the library media specialist needs to initiate activities with teachers that show the media specialist and teachers working cooperatively on planning and delivering instruction.

Another form of collaborative work is team teaching. Fogarty and Stoehr describe collaborative team teaching in terms of Gardner's multiple intelligences (verbal, logical, musical, bodily, interpersonal, and intrapersonal) and Fogarty's ten curriculum integration models (fragmented, connected, nested, sequenced, shared, webbed, threaded, integrated, immersed, and networked). Their book includes activities for building teams, exploring how to put power into themes, and ways to thread life skills through the subject-matter content. It includes cooperative structures for interactive lessons, strategies for developing relevant integrated units, and ideas for webbing themes to the intelligences and methods that infuse rigor into thematic units.[14]

Information Literacy: Final Report by the American Library Association Presidential Committee on Information Literacy paints a picture of a highly people-centered, collaborative school:

> The school would be more interactive, because students, pursuing questions of personal interest, would be interacting with other students, with teachers, with a vast array of information resources, and the community at large to a far greater extent than they do today. . . . Students' quests would involve not only searching print, electronic, and video data, but also interviewing people inside and outside of school. As a result learning would be more self-initiated. . . . Both students and teachers would be familiar with the intellectual and emotional demands of asking productive questions, gathering data of all kinds, reducing and synthesizing information, and analyzing, interpreting, and evaluating information in all its forms.[15]

There is no work situation that does not demand collaborative work with other people. Beginning in the earliest grades, the school staff can model collaboration as the mode of work that adults prefer. If the staff can collaborate in planning, instruction, and extracurricular activities, students will come to accept such a model as the normative thing. Collaboration can be extended beyond the school. Many of the educational reformers cited in this book consider the parents or primary caregivers of the child to be a largely untapped resource in the education of all children—more especially in the education of at-risk children. In particular, the Comer school model[16] is built on research that strongly suggests that the more collaboration between parents or caregivers and the school program, the larger the chances of success.

There are major obstacles to parent and caregiver involvement in the school program—often because of the work schedules of most parents and caregivers. In more than 60 percent of American families both parents work. Often parents and caregivers do not live in the neighborhood of the school because the children ride school buses to their assigned school. Many communities lack public transportation, or the transportation route plan does not include easy access to school facilities. An increasing number of families are single-parent families, adding to the pressure on that parent or caregiver and reducing the chance that the parent can be included in the school program. Parents and caregivers may also have a history of unsatisfactory relationships with public agencies. Some parents are never contacted by any public agency unless there is trouble. If the only time a parent or caregiver hears from the school is when the child is having difficulty or making trouble, the image of the school program becomes identified as "another one of those bothersome agencies always giving us trouble."

The library media specialist alone cannot create a parent-friendly school. Nonetheless, the library media specialist has many opportunities to ask parents and caregivers to participate in the school's library media program. Some parent-friendly suggestions:

1. *Include the parent-student-teacher association of the school.*
   The library media specialist needs to be a part of the PSTA association of the school so that programs of that organization can include information on the library media program, promote the use of materials in the library media center, and give parents and caregivers an opportunity to be involved in the instructional work that their children are doing in the library media center. Such participation may lead to PSTA programs in the library media center, displays of student work done in the center, oppor-

tunities for students to teach parents and caregivers in the use of various media resources (CD-ROM encyclopedias, online services, the World Wide Web, and so on), special programs about books and other resources to buy for their children (perhaps in connection with a book fair), and reading aloud programs that involve parents, students, teachers, grandparents, and community leaders.

2. *Review every program and activity of the library media center for parent potential.*
Library media programs have an incredible number of instructional activities and events. Every event in the library media center has the potential for parent or caregiver involvement. Include parents and caregivers on the media advisory committee and have that group participate in the planning and evaluation of library media program activities. Have programs at times when working parents can come. Never have an author or illustrator visit without including at least one night-time program. Ask parents and caregivers to take part in book talking, storytelling, giving (or receiving) instruction in the use of information resources, working with small groups or with individual children needing special help. On a periodic basis every library media specialist should review all activities from this perspective. Those activities that seem to have no potential for parent or caregiver involvement need to be carefully examined—it may be that those activities have very limited instructional value. The library media specialist will always look for ways to actively include many people in the library media program of instruction.

3. *Evaluate the library media collection from the perspective of parent or caregiver needs and interests.*
Chapter 6 of this book goes into more detail about expanding the library media collection to include resources of interest to parents and the larger community. At this point the authors want to stress the need for the library media center to be seen by parents and caregivers as a place where they can get the information resources they need to assist their children in being successful in their school experience, where they can learn how to do better home instruction for their children, and where they can find resources to deal with family needs and concerns that impact their children's lives. Such a collection assessment will demand that the library media specialist undertake a collaborative review of information

resources and programs available to parents and caregivers in public libraries, community colleges, local religious institutions, and community agencies.

The authors are not suggesting that the library media center should replace all of these other agencies and their resources and programs. Rather, the library media center and its catalog should have appropriate resources related to the educational needs of parents, caregivers and children. Among the finding tools of the library media center, parents and caregivers should also find information about the location of other resources in the larger community, and how to access them. The library media specialist should work collaboratively with other library agencies on joint or sequential programming of interest to parents and caregivers. In meetings with parents and teachers other suggestions for the collaborative involvement of parents and caregivers will be forthcoming.

Library media specialists should be warned that there is a long tradition in K–12 education that suggests that collaboration or cooperation are *not* normal. The factory model of education that suggested viewing all students as identical, also suggested that the activities of education could be set up as isolated units. Elementary education has often been done in isolated classrooms where one teacher was expected to be an expert in all areas of instruction. Library media programs have often been separated from any connection with what was happening in the classrooms. In high schools, what was done in one department was often related only to requirements for graduation and/or entry into higher education. Cross-departmental cooperative teaching was the rare exception. Current reform movements in middle-grade education stress the teaching of teachers with groups of students; such reforms seem to be spreading to other grade levels.

Almost all the literature about cooperative planning, team teaching, and other collaborative activities stress a curriculum that is holistic, focused on higher-order thinking skills, integrated across subject areas, and deliberately interdisciplinary. Working in this mode requires people skills because the professional staff is actually planning and implementing a curriculum based on the needs of their individual students. Such processes require hard work—learning tolerance of different attitudes and affects, listening actively to what other people say, fitting one's own work and schedule into the pattern of the whole group, and focusing on the final group project outcome rather than one's own contribution.

Such modeling may take the form of the individual staff members teaching the parts of the lessons in which they have the most expertise; or of their using a particular software package with which they are comfortable to demonstrate something in another format. Modeling can mean breaking a whole class down into smaller groups with each group working with a different adult on a particular part of a project. In this case, successful modeling also means bringing all of the parts together in an integrated whole. Involvement of outside experts as well as parents and caregivers in the instructional program moves the school toward making the whole village take part in the education of the child.

Cross-Cultural Communication
Is Essential to the Media Program

We have borrowed from cultural anthropology and communication studies the idea of cross-cultural communication.[17] People observing various tribal groups have noted that communication between groups is essential but often quite difficult because even those who use the same language may mean quite different things by the words they use. In many primitive cultures a wise elder of the tribe serves as the one who communicates between different tribal cultures and makes communication and commerce possible. When such communicators are missing, the breakdown of communication can result in warfare or at least major misunderstandings. Such breakdowns are not limited to primitive tribes, as we have seen in our modern world of Bosnia, Africa south of the Sahara, the Middle East, and with the militia groups in this country. Our world seems to have a hard time understanding what others are saying, what they mean, and what is important to them.

Education and the workplace are facing an increasingly diverse cultural situation. Current demographic predictions indicate that by the end of this century only 15 percent of new entrants to the workforce will be white males, compared to 47 percent in 1985. Most significantly, across the country people are facing the challenge of living in a multicultural society. Immigration, migration, and fertility patterns indicate that by the year 2010 about 38 percent of people under the age of eighteen in the United States will be African, Asian, or Hispanic American.

By that time, in seven states and the District of Columbia, more than one-half of the children will be minorities: Hawaii (80 percent), New Mexico (77 percent), California (57 percent), Texas (57 percent), New York (53 percent), Florida (53 percent), Louisiana (50 percent), District of Columbia (93 percent). Joe Schwartz and Thomas Exeter reported in the late 1980s that in nineteen states at least one-fourth of the population would be either African, Hispanic, or Native or Asian American.[18] In the 1990s, as experts predicted, most immigrants arrived from Asia and Latin America.

According to James P. Allen and Eugene T. Turner, 90 percent of these immigrants will settle in metropolitan areas, with the largest numbers coming to New York, Los Angeles, and Chicago. Each area in the United States, however, hosts its own unique cultural blend. Hispanic Americans, for instance, tend to concentrate in California and Texas, while significant numbers of Asian Americans can be found living in western coastal cities; African-American communities are more strongly represented in the east and southeast.[19] In studying such statistics, however, school officials should take into consideration the tremendous diversity in cultures, economic and family situations, and educational levels that exists within each ethnic group.[20]

The demography of school populations is changing as the diversity of America's population increases. Not only are the ethnic characteristics changing, but the increasing mobility of our population means that children bring different cultural perspectives into schools all over the country. Starting in the 1980s, the number of children of K–12 school age declined, forcing school systems to close facilities and make staff reductions. These demographic changes have a number of educational and workplace implications:

1. The workforce will grow more slowly than at any time since the 1930s.

2. The average age of the American worker will rise.

3. The number of entry-level young workers will decrease.

4. Immigrants and minorities will comprise a larger portion of the entering workforce.

5. Women will continue their strong influence on organizations.

6. The United States will see an increased mismatch between workplace needs and workplace capabilities, which is already placing demands on the educational system in terms of vocational/technology training.

7. Employers will have to consider potential workers from groups they once ignored.

8. Small businesses will bear a disproportionate share of the effort.

9. Kinds of work will continue to change.

10. The nature of the worker's family will continue to change.[21]

Executives and other administrators will be forced to learn how to manage a diverse employee population by cultivating, strengthening, and utilizing diverse talents and skills, rather than merely providing access to new groups. The existing cultural barriers to integrating new team members can be overcome by understanding differences of race, gender, disabilities, sexual orientation, and social class, and by recognizing that different groups may approach their work differently. The ability to deal with diverse cultural backgrounds and expectations will become a highly prized skill. Business leaders are already requesting that more understanding of cultural and ethnic diversity should form part of the educational programs of schools.

Even in the best of situations, communication breakdowns occur. The cultures of administrators, school systems, communities, and teachers are not identical. Although these cultures often use the same words, they do not always mean the same thing. A simple illustration of this cultural difference is found when a college teacher says, "Please read the assigned passage critically." The teacher is asking for a very careful reading and rereading of the passage to discover its meaning plus a careful analysis of the passage in relation to other passages previously read. The students hear, "This is an assigned reading; be sure to read it at least once before the next class." Site-based management may mean to the principal, "Now *I* have some control over how the money is spent." To teachers it may mean, "Now *we* have some control over where the money is spent." To the central administration it probably means, "Your school gets a little bit of money to spend as you see fit, but most of it must go to *system* priorities."

Often what is said by one group is misunderstood by other groups. As the school reform movement grows, that movement adds to the confusion by introducing new words for old ideas, and old words with new content. When you add to these cultures, the cultures of the national government, the state department of education, and of political action groups—the situation is ripe for disaster. Just being able to understand what others mean by what they say becomes a major task, which is made even more difficult if a person is responsible not only for understanding, but also for reinterpreting that understanding so that others can understand.

Library media specialists have often complained about being "caught in the middle" between administration, faculty, and students. It is true that cross-cultural communicators lead an interesting life! Still, the unique position of the library media specialist offers a chance for that person to become an informal interpreter to the "other side." The library media specialist is not a traditional teacher who gives grades to students; the library media specialist is an administrator, often with a budget allocation to administer. The library media specialist is also often supervised by someone in the local school and by someone in the school system. Often the library media specialist is one of the few professionals who works with all of the children and teachers in the school all of the time.

This position of being in the middle, working with administrators and teachers, taking a holistic view, and being careful not to be seen as joining the other guys, allows the library media specialist to attempt to interpret what is being said and done from another angle. Again, this role may not be a comfortable one for every specialist. Some simply "join" the teachers in opposition to those other cultures—especially the principal and the school system. Others "join" the administration and lose their contacts with the culture of the teachers. In ideal circumstances the library media specialist is not a joiner, but a bridge.

Chapter 7 of this book makes a strong case for flexible scheduling in the library media program, not only because such scheduling brings students to the library media center at the time of instructional need but also because such scheduling allows for time to consult with teachers. If everyone is always too busy to consult and help one another, what will happen to the instructional program? It will become a very poor instructional program. Teachers and all professional staff need time to plan, to teach, to evaluate, and to revise.

The library media specialist needs to have time to assist teachers at every step in this process. A library media center with excellent resources is not very useful unless people know what is there. Resources available in the larger community remain unavailable unless someone makes their availability known. The library media specialist has the responsibility to promote the use of relevant materials in the library media collection, to publicize the availability of resources beyond the library media center, and to create opportunities for the staff and students to explore the resources available. Much of this effort is public relations work. Creating signs, bulletin boards, announcements, and videotapes that promote resources and opportunities for learning is a large part of this effort. So is integrating the larger community into the finding tools of the library media center.

Suggestions for Community Involvement

1. *Use the online catalog to share information about the larger community.*
   If the library has an online catalog system, create entries that not only describe the books and other library material resources, but list community agencies, individuals, and places of interest. Such a catalog system would have entries for the local science center, museums, 4-H programs, the humane society, various volunteer agencies, local storytellers, community social service and health agencies, and so on. Each entry would give the name of a contact person, an address and phone number, as well as a brief description in the notes field.

2. *Make sure your vertical file includes information about the larger community.*
   Place materials about local and state agencies, interesting places, and people in the vertical file of the library media center under curriculum-related subject headings. Remember that a vertical file is only as valuable as the information in it; the library media specialist or aide will have to keep the file up to date.

3. *Encourage classes to produce materials related to what they are learning.*
   Select the best teacher and student productions to place in topical "learning boxes." Such boxes might include information on local history, ecosystems of the area, tornadoes, oceans, and so on.

4. *Alert people to opportunities for refreshment, renewal, and growth.*
   Because stress and burnout are such common aspects of the modem world, a wide array of techniques, classes, and other opportunities are available in most communities. Carter lists the following individual strategies for dealing with stress and burnout: biofeedback, buddy system, childhood energy, conflict management, desensitization, dreams, exercise, humor, ideology, imaging, leaving stress behind, looking forward, making lists, meditation, mental diversions, mental health days, morning routine, nutrition, peer coaching, personal inventory for fun, refueling your tank, relaxation, responding to student concerns, self-praise,

self-hypnosis, self-talk, sense of purpose, shunning the superman/ superwoman image, sleep, social support, teacher mind sets, time alone, and time management.[22]

The library media specialist can develop a bulletin board or e-mail listing of the opportunities within the school system's wellness program and in the community at large where people can find programs designed to deal with stress and burnout.

Summary

People relationships are critical to successful future media programs. The authors have stressed that relations do not only apply in the school environment, but must be extended out into the whole school system and the wider community. We believe that no media program is successful without applying these people principles which are the hardest to apply in real life. If it takes a whole village to raise a child, then the library media specialist had better have good working relationships throughout that whole village. A "whole village" library media program becomes an exciting center filled with diverse groups of people, all of whom view themselves as being learners, and as being instructors by example—of children in all areas of the village.

Notes

1. J. W. Powell and R. B. LeLieuvre, *Peoplework: Communication Dynamics for Librarians* (Chicago: American Library Association, 1979), 24.

2. A. Clarke-Stewart and J. B. Koch, *Children: Development Through Adolescence* (New York: Wiley & Sons, 1983), chap. 1.

3. Jean Piaget, *Moral Judgment of the Child* (London: Kegan Paul, 1932).

4. Sherri Oden, *Peer Relationship Development in Childhood* (Urbana, Ill.: ERIC Clearinghouse on Elementary and Early Childhood Education, 1981, ERIC Document Reproduction Service No. ED 207 668).

5. Maureen T. Hallinan, "Recent Advances in Sociometry," in *The Development of Children's Friendships*, ed. S. R. Asher and J. M. Gottman (New York: Cambridge University Press, 1981), 39–51.

6. James Gleick , *Chaos: The Making of a New Science* (New York: Penguin Books, 1987).

7. North Carolina Department of Public Instruction, Division of Media and Technology Services, *Learning Connections: Guidelines for Media and Technology Programs* (Raleigh, N.C.: North Carolina Department of Public Instruction, 1992), 1.

8. Bonnie Benard, *Fostering Resilience in Children*, ERIC Digest (Urbana, Ill.: ERIC

Clearinghouse on Elementary and Early Childhood Education, August 1995, ERIC Document Reproduction Service No. ED 386 327).

9. James Comer, "Home-School Relationships as They Affect the Academic Success of Children," *Education and Urban Schools* 16 (1984), 323–37. R. Edmonds, "Characteristics of Effective Schools," in *The School Achievement of Minority Children: New Perspectives*, ed. U. Neisser (Hillsdale, N.J.: Lawrence Erlbaum, 1986, ERIC Document Reproduction Service No. ED 269 500), 93–104.

10. S. B. Heath and M. W. McLaughlin, eds., *Identity and Inner-City Youth: Beyond Ethnicity and Gender* (New York: Teachers College Press, 1993). L. Weis and M. Fine, eds., *Beyond Silenced Voices: Class, Race, and Gender in United States Schools* (New York: State University of New York Press, 1993).

11. E. Werner and R. Smith, *Overcoming the Odds: High-Risk Children from Birth to Adulthood* (New York: Cornell University Press, 1992).

12. Nel Noddings, "An Ethic of Caring and Its Implications for Instructional Arrangements," *American Journal of Education* 96, no. 2 (February 1988), 215–30.

13. "Collaborative Leaning: Hearing Many Voices—Learning as One," *Washington Center News* 7 (spring 1993), 1–28.

14. R. Fogarty and J. Stoehr, *Integrating Curricula with Multiple Intelligence: Teams, Themes, and Threads. K–College* (Palatine, Ill.: Skylight Publishing, 1995).

15. The American Library Association, *Information Literacy: Final Report by the American Library Association Presidential Committee on Information Literacy* (Chicago: American Library Association, 1989), 74.

16. James P. Comer, "Child Development and Education," *Journal of Negro Education* 58, no. 2 (spring 1989), 125–39. N. M. Haynes and J. P. Comer, "The Yale School Development Program: Process, Outcomes, and Policy Implications," *Urban Education* 28, no. 2 (July 1993), 166–99. Note also chap. 4 of this book.

17. Ruth Burgos-Sasscer, *Why and How to Manage Diversity*. Paper presented at the annual international conference of the National Institute for Staff and Organizational Development on Teaching Excellence and Conference Administrators, Austin, Texas, May 22–25, 1994 (ERIC Document Reproduction Service No. ED 371 809). Heather Blenkinsopp, "Communicating Across Cultures for Reference Librarians Who Supervise," *Reference Librarian*, no. 45–46 (1994), 39–43. Russell M. Gersten, "The Language-Minority Student in Transition: Contemporary Instructional Research," *Elementary School Journal* 96, no. 3 (January 1996), 217–19.

18. Joe Schwartz and Thomas Exeter, "All Our Children," *American Demographics* 1, no. 5 (May 1989), 343–45.

19. James P. Allen and Eugene T. Turner, "Where to Find the New Immigrants," *American Demographics* 10, no. 9 (September 1988), 23–27, 59, 61.

20. Amy Klauke, *Coping with Changing Demographics. ERIC Digest Series Number EA45*, 1989 (ERIC Document Reproduction Service No. ED 315 865).

21. Rick Fischer, *Tomorrow's Workers: A Peek at What Demographers See. Workforce 2000*, 1990 (ERIC Document Reproduction Service No. ED 324 712).

22. Suzanne Carter, *Teacher Stress and Burnout. Organizing Systems to Support Competent Social Behavior in Children and Youth* (Eugene, Ore.: Western Regional Resource Center, 1994 (ERIC Document Reproduction Service No. ED 380 970).

6

Instruction and Collection Development Principles

Recent interest in libraries has focused on the contribution school libraries/ media centers might make to the current education reform movement. In particular, some reform advocates hope that library/media center staff will become key players in the effort to move teaching methods away from textbook-based instruction toward an emphasis on interactive and resource- based methods. What is needed is additional examination of the character- istics of schools that effectively use their library resources and of the sorts of barriers that present the greater availability and use of these resources.[1]

Introduction

Traditionally, instructional and collection development principles were discussed under the heading of library media programs. The authors have chosen not to discuss library media instructional pro- grams because such discussions often mislead people into thinking that there is a separate library media program. We take the posi- tion that there is no separate library media program and that everything that happens in the library media center must be related to the instructional program of the school. As people grow up they have a variety of experiences with libraries. Usually the earliest ex- periences make the most lasting impression.

Assemble a group of teachers, parents, and library media spe- cialists and ask, "What is the purpose of a school library media center program?" You will receive a variety of answers based on experience with libraries of all types. Responses will range from "I have no idea . . ." to "The program exists so that I can have a planning period free from supervising the children."

Administrators and teachers must understand that the basic focus of library media programs is collaborative instruction, not anything else. The whole program—from scheduling, physical arrangements, resources, pre- and post-school activities to book fairs—is designed to enhance the teaching/learning process in the school. The program does not exist to do its own thing and it can only be evaluated on the basis of its contribution to that instructional program. This chapter presents instructional and collection development principles for future library media programs as a part of the total instructional program.

The Media Center Exists to Support Instruction

If the library media center exists to support instruction, then the library media specialist exists to provide instruction cooperatively with other educators and the materials in the collection are there to be an integral part of that instruction. Media specialists have been viewed in a number of different roles—as bookkeepers, as storytellers, as people who keep things organized. However, in the context of education, the school library media specialist is an *instructor*. The library media specialist is trained to select appropriate materials for individual or group instruction and to support instruction by being a planner of instruction and a coinstructor with other teachers.

Information Power (1998) devotes an entire chapter to learning and teaching and presents cardinal learning and teaching premises that are basic to the school library media program. Specific goals for the library media specialist are outlined for each principle:

Learning and Teaching Principles

Principle 1: The library media program is essential to learning and teaching and must be fully integrated into the curriculum to promote students' achievement of learning goals.

Principle 2: The information literacy standards for student learning are integral to the content and objectives of the school's curriculum.

Principle 3: The library media program models and promotes collaborative planning and curriculum development.

Principle 4: The library media program models and promotes collaborative planning and curriculum development.

Principle 5: Access to the full range of information resources and services through the library media program is fundamental to learning.

Principle 6: The library media program encourages and engages students in reading, viewing, and listening for understanding and enjoyment.

Principle 7: The library media program supports the learning of all students and other members of the learning community who have diverse learning abilities, styles, and needs.

Principle 8: The library media program fosters individual and collaborative inquiry.

Principle 9: The library media program integrates the uses of technology for learning and teaching.

Principle 10: The library media program is an essential link to the larger learning community.[2]

To avoid misunderstanding, the authors (and *Information Power*) do not mean that instruction is the only thing the library media specialist needs to do. Naturally, the library media specialist will be engaged in a number of activities that make instruction possible: the acquisition and organization of resources for the library media center, the arrangement of the library media center itself, the provision of equipment and related software for classroom use, and various other management and accounting details. All of these administrative and maintenance activities make the instructional and collection development role of the library media specialist possible. However, it is very easy for such activities to become a priority, sometimes externally imposed by the administration, which squeezes out the instructional and consultative roles of the library media specialist.

As Drucker notes, "The first question in increasing productivity in knowledge and service work has to be: *What* is the task? What do we try to accomplish? Why do it at all? The easiest—but perhaps the greatest—productivity in such work comes from redefining the task, and especially from *eliminating what needs not to be done* [emphasis added]."[3] Often the library media specialist will have to promote these consultative and instructional roles because the administrative staff and teachers have only experienced the administrative or maintenance roles. True curriculum integration requires *time*—to plan with teachers, to select, acquire, and assemble materials and equipment, to teach cooperatively with teachers, to cooperatively evaluate what happened in instruction, to evaluate the library media collection, and to make changes on the basis of that evaluation. The complaint is often heard that "Principals and teachers only see us as clerks!" It may be that they got that impression from observing how the school library media specialist spends his/her time.

Every library media specialist needs to take a hard look at personal time allocation in the library media center and the time demands imposed by administrative staff and teachers. Often these colleagues do not know what managing the school library media center involves. Indeed, if the center is well managed, there is no reason for everyone to know how hard the media specialist must work to make it so. If the activities of the specialist are to be reprioritized to focus on curriculum integration, the specialist must find ways to limit the time impact of administrative and maintenance activities. When it becomes clear that the majority of time is spent on school library media center administration and maintenance, then a major shift in the understanding of the role of the school library media specialist is required. Numerous articles on time management in the school library media center would indicate that this is not an easy task.

Quality Instruction and Collection Development Recognize Various Learning Styles

Traditional models of instruction view the teacher as having a great deal of knowledge to impart to students who learn, more or less, in the same way. There is evidence to suggest that teachers tend to teach in ways in which they themselves have been taught.[4] A variety of techniques for presenting information and evaluating the retention of that information have been developed. Certain students have the ability to absorb and retain information presented by the teacher and to present that information back to the teacher at examination time. Other students do not possess that particular ability and must have other avenues for processing information.

As we have seen in the status quo model of education, the standard scheduling of instructional time is based on a factory model of instruction from the industrial revolution, which operates on a set of hard-to-change educational assumptions. Education became universal on a mass production model. The implications for school learning activities are information retention, rote memorization, standardized procedures, and testing. Those students who do not work well in this model are dropped out of the system or "tracked" into programs where they work with other students who also did not work well within the system. Barth calls this model the "transmission of knowledge" model of learning. He notes that the model has certain assumptions:

1. The ultimate purpose of education is the acquisition of knowledge.

2. Knowledge is what has been learned and recorded over the ages. It is categorized into the disciplines of mathematics, chemistry, history, and so on, each of which has a content and a structure that can be taught and learned.

3. There is a minimum body of knowledge in each subject (the curriculum) that everyone must know before leaving school.

4. Adults are best suited to make important choices about what children should learn.

5. If children are given much choice about how and what they learn, they will wander from the best path of knowledge.

6. Children are not naturally drawn to academic work and must therefore be externally motivated.

7. Children play on their own time, out of school. During school time they work.

8. The student who is having a lot of fun probably isn't learning very much. If learning involves some pain, it's likely to be good for a child.

9. Children learn most in settings where there are few distractions.

10. When children work together, cheating is more likely.

11. Some children are bright, some average, some slow.

12. There are individual differences among children, but if we group them by ability and vary the rate at which we present material to them, they will all have equal opportunity to learn.

13. The student who knows something is able to display that knowledge publicly, at the request of the teacher. The student who can't display knowledge does not have it.

14. Errors are mistakes. Mistakes are undesirable and must be eliminated.

15. Acquisition of knowledge can be accurately measured.

16. The best way of evaluating the effect of the school experience on a child is through a battery of standardized tests.[5]

Critics often recommend returning to the factory model and harshly criticize other models that are now claimed to be "not working." As noted before, Findley and Wyer identify the assumptions underlying much education in schools and industry: (1) all learners are alike; (2) learners are passive recipients of all messages; (3) learners are not themselves engaged in an active process of making sense of their lives; (4) learners need to be standardized; and (5) such an approach brings success.[6] In such a production model of education, it is little wonder that administrators, teachers, and library media specialists all work hard "just to get to 3 P.M. and end my shift on the assembly line."

Schools have been described previously as organizations with loosely coupled systems.[7] Such systems maintain consistency and resistance to change.[8] As institutions, schools have been able to ignore, absorb, and modify many revolutionary factors without much change in the factory model which is actually happening in classrooms and the library media center. The rigid scheduling of student, teachers and media specialists as production units continues.

In recent years an educational change model has stressed the needs of the individual student in the educational process, and to focus on different ways of learning. Braun, in the final report on *Vision: TEST*, sees the information-age model of the school as follows:

> We recognize that students learn in different ways, and we celebrate the diversity they bring to the learning process. In this model, teachers have many roles—facilitators, resource allocators, collaborators, researchers, etc.—as they help students not only acquire facts but also gather data, form and test hypotheses, do research, develop problem solving skills, and learn to work together. In this model, students—individually and in cooperative groups—are actively engaged in the learning process.[9]

To the constructionist, the process of education operates with a learner who is active in the learning process. Learning is complemented through real-world applications or simulations, and hypotheses are tested by actual experience. The constructionist process uses dialogue and mutual conversation. Learning how to think, problem solving, and decision making are skills that can be learned and improved. Higher-level cognitive skills are the goals of teaching and learning activities. The learner's personal state of development is recognized and accommodated in the educational process, and what we teach must be interesting and be taught in an interesting way.[10]

In this model, the student can move from the role of passive vessel to that of active learner; the teacher can move from the role of lecturer to that of counselor, mentor and adviser; the library media specialist can move from the role of resource provider to that of team teacher, cooperative planner, and instructional developer. The curriculum becomes increasingly interdisciplinary and the subject specialties of the staff begin to blur. Standard scheduling of classes becomes a barrier to learning and is replaced with block or flexible scheduling. The wider community (locally and at a distance) becomes a site for educational experience and a source of valued information for research and evaluation. Administratively, the staff and students of the school become involved in decision making, assessment of outcomes, and "site-based management."

This model of education is not confined to public education. In the March 1995, *Byte* magazine presented as a summary of the changing educational paradigms:[11]

Changing Instructional Paradigms

Old Paradigm	New Paradigm
Classroom Lecture	Individual Exploration
Passive Absorption	Apprenticeship
Individual	Group
Omniscient Teacher	Guide
Stable Content	Fast-changing Content
Homogeneity	Diversity

Much of current "constructionism" in education is an attempt to deal with multisensory ways of learning. The origins of constructionism lie in the realization that children learn from their interactions with the real world and that they have had, and continue to have, a great deal of experience in a real world outside the school world. Effective learning relates what is happening in school settings to the already developed framework of real-world experience that children bring to the classroom.

This active form of learning allows the student to bring already defined meanings to situations and perhaps to modify those meanings on the basis of new experience (sometimes called expanding the framework). The teacher does not say what the meaning or purpose of situations is; rather, children search out facts, analyze, and compare them to what they already know, developing their own conclusions along the way. There are many examples of this model in the educational reform movement. Here we present the whole language concept as one example.

Whole Language Instruction and the Media Program

The whole language movement attempts to integrate children's learning experience around real literature as it is published, not on condensed, watered-down versions of published works. Here the real world of the child is linked to the real world of literature and literary genre. In a traditional approach to education learning is broken down into small pieces. Children are asked to learn these pieces and are rewarded for their behavior. Teachers diagnose what children know and then remediate by teaching them what they do not know. Often the various small pieces are not assembled into any whole.

The whole language approach is very close to the opposite of this idea. Learning occurs through use of language and literature, not as a separate part of it. Texts are kept whole, not broken down into parts. Teachers observe and assess what children know and build upon their knowledge, designing a classroom environment and learning activities cooperatively with children so that they become internally motivated to team with others. The goals of instruction are broader and address affective considerations. Whereas in a basic skills program the goal is to teach children how to read and write, the goal of a whole language curriculum is to help children become avid readers and writers, to develop a love of learning.

The change from a basic skills to a whole language approach precipitates vast changes in the school library media center. Lamme and Beckett give three illustrations of these changes in terms of instructional programs: Theme Studies, Process Writing, and Literature-based Reading.[12]

Theme Studies

The main difference between theme studies and traditional units of study is that theme studies rely upon children's literature instead of textbooks. Children explore a topic in far more detail and spend much longer on each theme than in a textbook-driven program.

Children engaged in a theme study use the school media center to seek information about specific topics. They also use works of various genres to supplement their research. For example, fiction can be used to demonstrate attitudes and behaviors. Poetry can provide an aesthetic dimension to the theme study topic.

Theme studies require large numbers of trade books, which the children and teachers use to build the content of their instructional program. Library media specialists must work cooperatively with teachers to ensure that resources are available in the media center when needed. At certain times of the year, pulling books can be a full-time job for the media specialist. Flexible scheduling is also important to the success of theme studies. When the media center is available to individuals and small groups of children virtually all day, children are free to seek information whenever questions arise.

Process Writing

A process writing program provides another opportunity for children to turn to books.[13] When they encounter problems in their own writing, children look to published authors for solutions. For example, children might examine "real" books to see how authors introduce different characters without listing them. The concepts of authorship and illustratorship are vital to an interactive view of reading and writing.[14] Indeed, as children become authors themselves, they become interested in other authors as people and writers. When a class becomes "hooked," the library media center must be prepared with a good supply of books by the favorite author or illustrator. Children also want information about authors and illustrators, and the library media center will need a large collection of file materials to satisfy this interest.

Literature-Based Reading

These reading programs focus upon helping children become avid and reflective readers, rather than merely skilled readers.[15] Instead of being tested after reading, children share opinions about books, both orally and in writing. This change of focus draws readers to genre studies and studies of literary elements, again making demands upon the media specialist and the collection. For example, children who notice a pattern in a book are likely to request more books with that pattern. Media specialists can help teachers use children's comments to lead them to other good books, encouraging children to read and to respond at higher levels and in more complex ways to what they are reading. The discovery of patterns, differences, and repetitions with modifications is a part of the higher-order thinking skills process.

There are numerous other activities in a literature-based reading program that call for media specialist participation. They include reading workshops in which children select books based on their personal interests and keep reading logs or journals; Book Buddies programs in which more experienced readers read aloud to beginning readers in lower grade levels (as in the Reading Together programs), often holding the child in their lap in a rocking chair; and various sustained silent reading programs like D.E.A.R. (Drop Everything and Read), in which children use a specified time every day to read books for pleasure.

The role of the media specialist changes radically in a whole language setting. Obviously, the library media specialist in this model will need a vast knowledge of his/her own collection as well as the collections of other school and public libraries. Additionally, the library media specialist serves as a consultant during the planning and implementing of theme studies, as a teacher of information skills in the context of the use of literature and other language-based technology tools, and, it is hoped, as an instructional leader. Collection development moves toward the collection of quality materials that will help teachers and students become consumers and creators of literature.

Cullinan reported that many schools have been slow to recognize the potential of the media specialist in a whole language program.[16] Yet such leadership is critical. Teachers who have relied primarily upon basal readers, kit reading series, or textbooks for a number of years need models for selecting books, reading aloud, giving book talks, conducting book discussions, storytelling, and involving children with puppetry, flannel boards, and story enactment. Not only should the library media specialist share his/her expertise in these areas, but he/she can learn from teachers and read books that in previous times would have been the exclusive domain of classroom teachers.

Because whole language instruction requires a very large collection of books, a debate often arises over ownership and control of the books purchased to support whole language programs. Should new books be in classrooms where children have immediate access to them for their reading, writing, and theme studies programs, or should they be in the library media center and borrowed on a temporary basis by classroom teachers? Library media specialists will be familiar with the problem of classroom collections that become permanent collections to which other teachers and students have no access. This problem can be further complicated by the variety of funding sources for such programs. Often teachers have access to grant or special funding for the ordering of new books and literature-based technologies. Should classroom teachers be able to order books they want for their instructional program, or should all orders go through the media specialist? The authors take the position that all materials should be ordered and processed *through* the library media center and that all materials in every location should be available to *all students*. Having all materials listed in the library media center online catalog will go a long way to creating such a situation.

Instruction and Collection Development Must Deal with Multiple Intelligences

The authors borrow the concept of multiple intelligence from Howard Gardner.[17] Dr Gardner first proposed the idea of multiple intelligences in 1983 and has expanded on that idea ever since.[18] When the question is asked, "What makes a person intelligent?" the most common responses will often note a person's ability to solve problems, utilize logic, and think critically. These typical traits of intelligence are sometimes lumped together under the label of "raw intelligence." A person's intelligence, traditionally speaking, is contained in his or her general intellect—in other words, how each and every one of us comprehends, examines, and responds to outside stimuli, whether it be to solve a math problem correctly or to anticipate an opponent's next move in a game of tennis. Our intelligence, therefore, is our singular, collective ability to act and react in an ever-changing world.

In contrast, Gardner suggests that there are at least seven intelligences: linguistic, logical-mathematical, spatial, bodily-kinesthetic, musical, interpersonal, and intrapersonal. These varied intelligences arise out of individual and cultural factors, and will vary from person to person. The difference between this view and more traditional views of intelligence may be summed up by two questions. The traditional view of intelligence asks, "How intelligent is this person?" The multiple intelligence view asks, "How is this person intelligent?" It assumes that all children have ways of learning and mastering skills. If multiple intelligences are taken seriously in instruction, then there will need to be a variety of instructional approaches so that students with strengths in different areas can reach the same educational goals. Multiple intelligence theory also stresses that the child as learner is central to how classroom materials are selected and utilized both in the classroom and the library media center.

If every child may have different intelligence strengths, then the library media specialist will take into account the individual strengths of children as he/she builds a library media collection and provides instruction. Multiple intelligences require a varied format library media collection so that students and teachers have multiple channels to the same goal. While the backbone of the collection will continue to be print materials, other formats of information become critical. As an example, studying the work a particular author may require copies of the author's work, a video of the author at work, a cassette or CD recording of the author reading aloud from his/her work, and a multimedia presentation of at least one of the author's titles. Comparing these different formats of the same source and noting the differences, omissions, and additions would, of course, develop those higher-order thinking skills which are now part of every educational system.

Students and teachers will also want to become part of the creative process, so the library media center will need to have the essential tools required for students and teachers to create and illustrate their own literary efforts (perhaps in the style of the author or illustrator being studied). Such tools may be simple ones such as paints, brushes, paper, scissors. They can also be computer-based software that allows students and teachers to write, illustrate, and print in color their efforts. In some library media centers, literature-based learning is taken to its logical conclusion and the creations of students, teachers, and parents are put on display in the library media center, videotaped, and even added to the library's collection so that students can look up their own works in the online catalog.

Instruction and Collection
Development Involve the Whole School

Providing students and teachers with multiple opportunities for meaningful involvement and responsibility within the school is a natural outcome in schools that have high expectations. Meaningful participation is a fundamental human need. We believe that when schools ignore these basic needs of both students and teachers, schools become alienating places.[19] On the other hand, certain practices provide students and teachers with opportunities to give their gifts back to the school community and do indeed foster all the traits of resilience. Such practices include designing lessons that ask questions that encourage critical thinking and dialogue, and also encourage a more hands-on approach. Collaborative strategies with students include involving students in curriculum planning; in creating the governing rules of the classroom; in being responsible for their own conduct and the conduct of others; in real-life work situations; in cross-age peer tutoring, and child care; and in community service.

The library media specialist needs to work with teachers on curriculum planning so that appropriate resources and their implications can be acquired ahead of time (collection development), suggested at planning time, and utilized in instruction. Note that the suggested activities are not added on when students have some time to spend in the library media center. If the library media specialist is involved in curriculum planning and curriculum review with the teachers, then the collection development process for resources is strengthened because what is acquired will actually be used by the school community. The library media specialist can involve students in the evaluation of the media center's resources by asking them, "What did you think of that ?" or "Did you find what you needed for your project?" or "What would you suggest for this project?" More detailed evaluation ideas are presented in chapter 8 on planning and evaluation principles.

Students can also be involved in responsibility for the program and functioning of the library media center. Many library media centers have student assistants. Sometimes these "jobs" are based on who is available or are used as a reward for students who are successful in the instructional setting. Moving the student assistant idea into active participation will require thinking of the student assistant position as a real job. In one library media setting, students who want to be library assistants are asked to fill out a simplified job application and asked for three references, including a teacher, a parent or relative, and a peer.

Students who apply must be in good standing at school and are selected on the basis of their applications and references. Thus the real work world is modeled in the library media center setting, where the idea is that one applies for real work through a formal process. References based on good performance have the importance they have in real-life job seeking.

Cooperative Planning, Instruction, and Collection Development Are the Norm

In chapter 5 concerning people principles, we highlighted the need for collaborative activities on the part of professional school staff as a model for cooperation and collaboration among students. We also began a discussion of factors that promote resilience among children who are at risk. Here we stress the instructional roles including the communicating of high teacher expectations, which promote resilience.

One key to successful students is high expectations for students and teachers. Research has indicated that schools that establish high expectations for all youth—and give them the support necessary to achieve them—have high rates of academic success. They also have lower rates of problem behaviors such as dropping out, drug abuse, teen pregnancy, and delinquency than other schools.[20] The most obvious and powerful means for conveying positive and high expectations is the collaborative relationship level in which the teacher and other school staff communicate the *same message*: that the student has everything he or she needs to be successful.

The library media specialist must supply a wide variety of instructional resources and varied formats for materials, which are targeted to student needs. One teacher or one library media specialist alone cannot do this job! It must be a cooperative agreement among the whole staff. Through relationships that convey high expectations, students learn to believe in themselves and in their futures, developing the critical resilience traits of self-esteem, self-efficacy, autonomy, and optimism. As Tracy Kidder writes: "For children who are used to thinking of themselves as stupid or not worth talking to . . . a good teacher can provide an astonishing revelation. A good teacher can give a child at least a chance to feel, She thinks I'm worth something; maybe I am."[21]

Schools also communicate high expectations when the curriculum is structured and organized to support resilience by respecting the ways in which humans learn and acknowledging that individuals learn in a variety of ways. Such a curriculum and the resources that support it are thematic, experiential, challenging, comprehensive, and inclusive of multiple perspectives—especially those of emerging minority groups.

Collection development can support high expectations. The library media specialist does *not* select watered-down versions of literature or abridged guides to that literature. He/she collects materials at a variety of reading levels in the high expectation that students will be able to move from the simplest materials to the most complex over time. If students select a book beyond their reading level, the library media specialist does not refuse to let them take that book out!

In the computer-related resource area, selection of software is based on ease of use, but software that challenges the students and stretches their problem-solving ability is also selected. At all costs, software that requires drill and practice is avoided—instead, software is found that is structured in ways that present increasing challenges to the students as they become more skilled. Perhaps the most useful instructional software is that which keeps track of the student's progress and adjusts programs to provide new challenges.

Collection management includes the process of eliminating resources and related equipment from the collection. Students and individual needs change, so the process of instructional collection development must include weeding. In ideal circumstances, we would always have the most up-to-date and accurate information available to students and teachers. Weeding is the process that allows the library media specialist to remove outdated items and items that are in need of correction because of emerging facts. This process also allows for modification of the collection based on student needs. Weeding should include all formats and related equipment in the library media center. Far too many library media centers have closets and shelves full of equipment with no related software, software that will not work on any equipment, and machines that no one understands.

Instruction and collection development that support resilience build from perceptions of student strengths, interests, and experience. They are participatory and facilitative, creating ongoing opportunities for self-reflection, critical inquiry, problem solving, and dialogue. Grouping practices that support resilience promote cooperation among differing students and teachers, shared responsibility for teaching and learning, and a sense of belonging.

The Media Specialist as Instructional Consultant and Participant

Finding time to be an instructional consultant with teachers and to do cooperative teaching of students is difficult. As Turner notes:

> The development of the role of the library media specialist as instructional consultant, formalized in *Information Power*, has been neither

easy nor smooth. Studies have repeatedly revealed that the role of instructional design consultant has not been implemented to any significant degree. . . . Lack of time, training, and administrative support are a few of the barriers that prevent implementation of this role.[22]

But the media specialist must find that time by prioritizing functions and seeking administrative support to make schedules more flexible. Self-confidence is essential and the library media specialist must seek out the training which will equip him/her for that consultative role. The classroom is where change takes place and the library media specialist must gain collaborative access to what happens in that space. Planning with teachers prior to instruction, enriching the instructional process with appropriate resources and information utilization techniques, and team teaching make the most sense. Van Deusen studied flexible scheduling in the primary grades and found that flexible scheduling *combined with team planning* was the best-case scenario [emphasis added].[23]

There Are Many Paths to Media Instruction and Collection Development

Students and teachers learn in a variety of ways—which is another way of saying we are each intelligent in different ways. The library media center program must be structured so that this variety of learning styles or intelligence can be accommodated. Viewing the library media center as just another large classroom substitute is to invite the perception that it is irrelevant to learning. The library media instructional program and collection will increasingly encompass a variety of work areas for teachers, students, and staff who may work on a project for only a few minutes or who may be working in small groups over several grading periods. Chapter 10 on facilities principles discusses the design of such a multipurpose, technologically oriented media center and offers some suggestions for dealing with traffic problems and the noise created by multiple use and scheduling.

As more and more hardware and software allow for integration of graphics, pictures, and scanning of printed materials, some very effective instructional modules can be created that encourage students to explore resources from computers located in classrooms or laboratories remote from the school library media center. When we finally get to the point where we can transmit information and television over the same cables to the desktop computers in classrooms, school library media specialists will be able to present information through television, demonstrate the use of resources, and allow students to use those same resources at one desktop computer located in a classroom. The World Wide Web already demonstrates how many different kinds of resources and sources of information can be accessed from a desktop computer and a Web browser program. Combinations of voice, television, graphics, and software are already available in many multimedia configurations. *Information Power* (1998) highlights the possibilities: "By linking students with the unlimited learning opportunities available throughout the learning community, the school library media program provides a bridge between formal, school-based learning and independent lifelong learning."[24] The complexities of the emerging learning community illustrates the that the major task which the library media specialist must undertake in the collection development program of the library media center.

School library media programs are not as far away from that future as we may think. In one school system, computer laboratories have been abandoned in favor of having several computers in each classroom and all computers networked together with a large desktop computer acting as a file server. This computer-based communication system makes available to teachers and students many instructional programs, graphics production, and word processing tools. Students simply go to a computer, type in their names and are presented with a menu of options.

In several of the schools, the library media center online catalog is also accessible from the same computer and is listed as a option on the menu. When a computer-based local area network is used to interconnect the classrooms, any library media specialist can develop ways in which to connect the library's finding tools—the online catalog and the circulation files—to that network so that teachers and students have access to these resources without leaving the classroom. In some schools, CD-ROM databases are also networked out of the school library media center so that students can utilize these bibliographic tools from computer laboratories or classrooms.

Because of this local area network, teachers and students have access to high-quality printing on several laser printers attached to the network. A student produces a project, and then selects either the ink-jet printer in the classroom or the high-quality printer in the production laboratory of the library media center. In several classrooms the teachers have removed the dot matrix printers because of noise, and replaced them with ink-jet printers. Additionally, students can go the library media production area and use hand scanning devices that allow graphics to be scanned from print copy into a computer file for use with various graphics programs. There is now a large file of student-produced computer graphics available on the file server. Students can use the classroom or library media center computer to call up a graphics program and use their graphic stored on the student's own disk.

Everyone Is an Instructor and Collection Developer

The formal distinctions created by professional certification and differential hiring lead us to think that some people administer, some people teach, some people clean up or serve food, and others have specialized tasks. Some library media specialists seem to feel that they are the only qualified selectors of library materials. Viewed from an adult and salary perspective, such distinctions make sense. Viewed from the perspective of the child, and often the parent, such distinctions are very abstract and often make no sense at all. Appropriate behavior, learning styles, what is important, high expectations of everyone, and how one survives are learned from the full circle of persons the child contacts. Anyone working as staff or volunteer in the school is instructing all of the time.

If the library media collection is to reflect and support the instructional program and the larger community supporting the school, collection development must not be exclusively a professional task. Rather, ways need to be developed so that students, parents, and community members can be involved in suggesting materials, contributing materials, and evaluating materials that make up the library media collection. Media advisory committees become one place where this collaborative collection development process can begin. Creating multiple ways for students, PSTA groups, parents, volunteers, and members of the community to make suggestions will also help. Does your media center have a suggestion box where people can place suggestions for new materials? At PSTA meetings, is there time for making suggestions, informal conversations, a table display of new materials? Does your school invite community leaders to visit the library media center and help with suggestions for the selection and evaluation of materials?

When all people involved in the school see themselves as instructors who model appropriate attitudes, instruction, and behavior, and when this fact is openly acknowledged by the whole staff and supported by the principal, the conduct of the adults in the school changes radically. They realize that what they say to each other, how they treat each other, and their attitudes in general are all being noticed, and often copied, by the children. All adult conduct in a school needs to be professional in the sense that everyone is on duty full time when in the school. In terms of attitudes and behavior, there is no time at school when anyone is off duty. Sloppy habits, emotional outbursts, conduct unbecoming to adults should all be noticed, evaluated, and terminated. For the child, "big people" have a consistent style of conduct, operate under the same rules, and model appropriate behaviors at all times.

When the Menninger Clinic in Topeka, Kansas, tried this approach at the Kansas State Hospital, the recovery rate for poor-risk patients increased dramatically. What degree or certification a *person* has makes no difference in these areas. We already know that children can sense, and make use of, inconsistencies in adult attitudes and behavior. Children learn very early when to wait for daddy, or talk to mom, and how to exploit differences between authority figures in the home. By the time children come to school, they have a full range of skills in adult manipulation.

As they enter the system, they are quick to test out all of the adults in the environment to see what inconsistencies exist and how they can be exploited. Successful school environments are those in which the staff has come to common agreements on what behaviors are appropriate for a learning environment, and what kind of adults we want the children to become. Once these decisions are made, we can start acting out our decisions by modeling appropriate teaming behavior and appropriate adult conduct with one another and with children. Be warned, such team planning for individual students takes time. Many schools have had difficulty with this approach because of the large commitment of time it requires *before* results can be demonstrated.

We can take this concept beyond the school building. More than twenty-five years ago, child psychiatrist James Comer and his colleagues at Yale Child Study Center experimented with a two-year school intervention program in two inner-city elementary schools in New Haven, Connecticut. Based on his observations, Comer concluded that children's experiences at home and in school deeply affect their psychosocial development, which in turn shapes their academic achievement. Conversely, poor academic performance is in large part a function of the failure to bridge the social and cultural gaps between home and school.[25]

In Comer's School Development Program improvement is based on building supportive bonds among children, parents, and school staff to promote a positive school climate.[26] The Comer program is designed to create a school environment where children feel comfortable, valued, and secure so that children will form positive emotional bonds with school staff and parents and develop a positive attitude toward the school program, which promotes the children's overall development and, in turn, facilitates academic learning. This program relies on staff collaboration and parent involvement to promote consistent expectations of high student achievement and excellent student conduct.

Future Roles for the Media Specialist

As discussed in the next chapter on scheduling, flexible scheduling of the library media program is essential. Unless the program is based on the varied instructional needs of students and the curriculum it will fail. Because instruction never ends, the media center program never stops! What was begun in one instructional time period can easily continue over a much longer period of time. Skills acquired during one session can be built upon in the following session with little loss of skill levels. The library media program can be regarded as the continuous acquisition of information skills necessary for students to be successful in their work as students. The teaching of those skills will be dependent on the curriculum of the particular school and the process of instructional consultation. In terms of collection development, the library media specialist must create ways for the total library media collection to be under continual, collaborative evaluation. If instruction is continuous, collection building and weeding must also be on that schedule. We can not afford to have unused or useless materials in the collection; there is simply not enough space.

Acting as a instructional consultant to teachers requires thinking cooperatively about the whole instructional program as a multiyear enterprise. It will be difficult to break out of the nine week instructional mode into a mode that suggests that instruction continues across several years. In part, this difficulty results from the fact that school systems still insist on standardized evaluations and scores at specified times. In the school reform movement these efforts are justified on the grounds of accountability and supported by the many political forces who want to know "what they are getting for their investment."

Yet instruction is not a nine-week, semester-long, or yearly activity; rather, it is an activity that continues through many years—even a lifetime. Teachers and library media specialists need to step back from the yearly perspective and think about the overall process of educating these children in this school over several years. Fortunately, the library media specialist is one of the few staff members who will have contact with all of the students throughout their years in the school. Chapter 8, on planning and evaluation principles, details a process for gaining this multiyear perspective.

Most of the suggestions in this chapter require additional time and staffing. Library media specialists know that even with careful planning there is never enough time. It should be obvious, but the authors will again point out that excellent library media programs deeply involved in the instructional process require additional staffing. To be truly effective, every library media specialist needs a capable full-time media assistant who does not have other responsibilities in the school. In larger schools, there will need to be more than one professional library media specialist and several assistants. The authors realize that in times of budget cutting, demands for additional staff may fall on deaf ears; however, it should be clear that true educational reform demands specific services from the library media program that cannot be provided with current staffing patterns.

Summary

The authors have suggested that the staff of the school need to review everything that is happening from a multiyear perspective and seek ways to make instruction collaborative, student-centered, and relevant to what the students are learning in school and in life. We view the library media specialist as a teacher among teachers; we view the library media center as a major support and resource for the instructional program of the school; we see the information-finding tools of that center as resources that point teachers and students to resources in the school, in the neighborhood, in the community, and in the world.

The library media specialist works cooperatively with others to create a teaching/learning environment and collection that brings out all the most positive capabilities that students have. The goal of instruction is to tap the learning styles and intelligence of students and teachers in ways that communicate high expectations of everyone. The goal of collection development is to provide a wide array of resources arranged to stir imagination, motivate, and enhance the learning styles of students and teachers. Continually evaluated, the library media collection should become increasingly relevant to the actual as well as the potential needs and interests of the students and teachers of a particular school.

Notes

1. National Center for Education Statistics, *Libraries/Media Centers in Schools: Are There Sufficient Resources?* (Washington, D.C.: Office of Educational Research and Improvement, July 1995).

2. American Association of School Librarians and Association for Educational Communications and Technology, *Information Power: Building Partnerships for Learning* (Chicago: American Library Association, 1998), 58.

3. Peter F. Drucker, *Managing for the Future: The 1990s and Beyond* (New York: Truman Talley Books, Dutton, 1992), 98.

4. Daniel D. Barron, " Constructionism: New Ways to Love Them to Learn," *School Library Activities Monthly* 12, no. 6 (February 1996), 48–50.

5. R. S. Barth, *Run School Run* (Cambridge, Mass.: Harvard University Press, 1980), 8–9.

6. Charles A. Findley and Jo-Anne Wyer, "Learning in the Information Age," in *Proceedings of the International Conference on Computer Assisted Learning in Post-Secondary Education, May 5–7 1987* (Calgary: School of Education, University of Calgary), 9–16, 19.

7. Karl E. Weick, "Technology as Equivoque: Sense Making in New Technologies," in *Technology and Organization*, ed. P. S. Goodman, L. E. Sproull, and Associates (San Francisco: Jossey-Bass Publishers, 1990), 1–44. Quote is from p. 31.

8. Karl E. Weick, "Educational Organizations as Loosely-Coupled Systems," *Administrative Science Quarterly* 21 no. 1 (March 1976), 1–19.

9. Ludwig Braun, *Vision: TEST (Technologically Enriched Schools of Tomorrow). Final Report: Recommendations for American Educational Decision Makers* (Eugene, Ore.: International Society for Technology in Education, 1990, ERIC Document Reproduction Service No. ED 327 173), 1.

10. Findley and Wyer, "Learning," 12, paraphrased.

11. Arthur Reinhardt, "New Ways to Learn," *Byte* 20, no. 3 (March 1995), 52–72. Quote is from p. 52.

12. Linda L. Lamme and Cecilia Beckett, *Whole Language in an Elementary School Library Media Center* (Syracuse, N.Y.: ERIC Digest, 1992, ERIC Document Reproduction No. ED 346 874).

13. Lucy M. Calkins and Shelley Heroin, *Living Between the Lines* (Portsmouth, N.H.: Heileman, 1990).

14. Linda L. Lamme, "Authorship: A Key Facet of Whole Language Instruction," *Childhood Education* 66, no. 4 (winter 1989), 83–86. Linda L. Lamme, "Authorship: A Key Facet of Whole Language," *Reading Teacher* 42, no. 9 (May 1990), 704–10. Linda L. Lamme and Linda Ledbetter, "Libraries: The Heart of Whole Language," *Language Arts* 67, no. 7 (November 1990), 735–41.

15. June C. McConaghy, *Children Learning Through Literature* (Portsmouth, N.H.: Heileman, 1990). Ralph Peterson and Maryann Eeds, *Grand Conversations: Literature Groups in Action* (New York: Scholastic Press, 1990). Kathy G. Short and Kathryn M. Pierce, *Talking About Books* (Portsmouth, N.H.: Heileman, 1990).

16. Bernice E. Cullinan, "Latching on to Literature: Reading Initiatives Take Hold," *School Library Journal* 35, no. 8 (April 1989), 27–31.

17. Howard Gardner, *Frames of Mind: The Theory of Multiple Intelligences* (New York: Basic Books, 1983).

18. Howard Gardner, "Multiple Intelligences Go to School: Educational Implications of the Theory of Multiple Intelligences," *Educational Researcher* 18, no. 8 (November 1989), 4–9. Howard Gardner, "Teaching for Understanding—Within and Across the Disciplines," *Educational Leadership* 51, no. 5 (February 1994), 14–18.

19. Seymour B. Sarason, *The Predictable Failure of Educational Reform* (San Francisco: Jossey-Bass, 1990).

20. Michael Rutter et al., *Fifteen Thousand Hours* (Cambridge, Mass.: Harvard University Press, 1979).

21. Tracy Kidder, *Among School Children* (New York: Avon, 1990), 14.

22. Phil M. Turner, *Helping Teachers Teach: A School Library Media Specialist's Role* (Englewood, Colo.: Libraries Unlimited, 1990), 34. Kathy G. Short and Kathryn Pierce, *Talking About Books* (Portsmouth, N.H.: Heileman, 1990)

23. Jean D. van Deusen, "The Effects of Fixed versus Flexible Scheduling on Curriculum Involvement and Skills Integration in Elementary School Library Media Programs," *School Library Media Quarterly* 21, no. 3 (spring 1993), 173–82. Quote is from p. 173.

24. *Information Power* (1998), 122.

25. Norris M. Haynes and James P. Comer, "The Yale School Development Program: Process, Outcomes, and Policy Implications," *Urban Education* 28, no. 2 (July 1993), 166–99.

26. Daniel D. Drake, "Student Success and the Family: Using the Comer Model for Home-School Connections," *ClearingHouse* 68, no. 5 (May–June 1995), 313–16. Daniel D. Drake and Bernard Hinsdale, "A Village Comes Together: The Comer Model," *School Community Journal* 4, no. 2 (fall–winter, 1995), 79–89. James A. Block, *School Improvement Programs: A Handbook for Educational Leaders* (New York: Scholastic Inc., 1995).

7

Scheduling Principles

How much time do we have?
525,600 minutes in 1996
Everyone has the same amount of time!
O.K., then why don't I have enough?
(Overheard in a library)

Introduction

This chapter looks at scheduling principles as they affect the library media program and services. A number of studies over the past two decades demonstrate that increasing instructional time is beneficial to students' achievement. Increasing instructional time means making adjustments in scheduling, including cutting down on the interruptions in instructional time, making instructional time more flexible to allow for the completion of projects, and eliminating extrainstructional activities from instructional time. Karweit reviewed the research on school time and learning. She distinguishes between *allocated time* which is the time scheduled by legislatures (length of the school year) or local administrators (when classes begin and end, what interruptions will be allowed), and *engaged time*, which is the time students are actually engaged in learning—sometimes called "time on task." She says, "The actual use of scheduled time depends on many other factors, including the students' school attendance and the erosion of instructional time by noninstructional activities and events. Finally, given that instruction is taking place, the instruction may or may not be needed and the student may or may not be paying attention."[1]

She suggests that better use of time available and rescheduling of activities may increase engaged time on task. Gilman and Knoll also reviewed the factors diminishing instructional time and conclude that less than 30 percent of the average school day is devoted to instruction. Rather than extending the school day or year, they urge more efficient time management and reevaluation of the urgency of noninstructional activities.[2] Strange summarized the studies of increasing instructional time and suggested that the actual amount of time allotted for instruction may be the single most important factor associated with student performance.[3]

Administrative policies create the largest loss of instructional time. Such policies may be imposed by the school system administration, the state legislature, or the state department of public instruction. Gilman and Knoll list the following time-loss activities: "pep sessions, convocations, activity periods, school musical and dramatic practices, fire and tornado drills, programs sponsored by various community groups, fund-raising activities, study halls, home rooms, announcement times, collection of funds for lunch, milk breaks, recesses, bathroom breaks, discipline problems, and time for passing from one class to another."[4]

Enough Time and Staff Are Essential to Media Programs

Before discussing other scheduling principles, it is important to understand the different meanings of time in the school setting. Cambone notes that while administrators typically organize time in a linear way (by the clock), teachers (and library media specialists) experience time in multiple ways:

> They are, in no particular order, student time, teaching time, learning time, innovation time, managed time, administrative time, cyclical time, political time, and experienced time. These are simultaneously experienced time constructs through which life is lived in schools—in fact, it is the nature of time for teachers that different aspects overlap and interact with each other constantly.[5]

Scheduling implies arranging time to get things done. The problem is that everyone has multiple things to do! Library media specialists and teachers do not simply live at school; they also must maintain their personal, family, and social lives beyond the school.

So, frequently, they find themselves overloaded with demands for their time as the needs of students increase, the marking period ends, or the winter holidays approach. Sometimes people become so overloaded that they experience "timelock,"[6] where the different gears of their living clock grind to a stop, the ability to attend to tasks is diminished, and almost nothing gets done.

School reformers have suggested that reforms take time—time to discuss issues, time to meet with parents and community, time to participate in planning, time to revise curriculum and schedules. The central problem is that time is not a commodity that can simply be added to the school day. Lengthening instructional periods into block schedules, providing planning periods, lengthening the school day, going to year-around schools, by themselves, do not provide much of the time expected. In part the problem lies with the multiple kinds of time demands placed on teachers and library media specialists. Even if they had all the time in the world, they could not readjust their work and schedules to get everything done.

Scheduling and time only make sense if we realize that everyone has multiple professional and personal demands on their time and that time demands from students, peers, administrators, and parents will vary from school to school as well as from grade level to grade level. Within this context, the only way more time can be found is to prioritize time on the basis of planning and goal setting. For this reason, chapter 8 of this book presents principles of planning and evaluation for library media programs. Once the library media specialist knows what the goal priorities are and develops objectives to move toward those goals, some time decisions can be made. Without planning, the library media program can go into timelock and very little is accomplished.

Having suggested that the time available needs to be spent on the priorities of the library media program, the authors do not want to imply that if library media specialists would just get organized, all problems would be solved. For flexible scheduling to work, or for the instructional consultant role to be effective, there *must be* additional staffing in library media centers. Offering instruction at the time and point of student need requires time to plan with teachers, scheduling of blocks of time with students, and time for evaluation afterward so that the next instructional process will be more effective. If the library media specialist is to perform all of his/her professional roles, there must be additional staff even in the smallest schools.

Additional staffing can mean additional professional media personnel, library media assistants, student media helpers, and volunteers. Much of the materials preparation, budget accounting, and media center maintenance can be handled by other staff. In the ideal situation the library media specialist would have enough support staff to allow full-time players in professional roles. However, any librarian in any type of library can tell you that a lot of routine maintenance functions must be handled at the moment, and one cannot wait until someone is available to help out. Some library media programs will be fortunate enough to have full-time or half-time support staff as library media assistants; other programs will have to depend on volunteers and student assistants. In any case, getting the varied jobs done in the time available will require extra hands to share in part of the work.

In any discussion of the staffing of library media centers, there is always the question of staff training. Often this discussion starts with, "But it is so much easier to do this complex task myself, in the way I want it done, than to train someone else to do it!" True, doing it ourselves is always easier. It may not accomplish what we want to accomplish in the long run, but it is always easier. People do not understand instructions; they do not intuitively understand just exactly how we want the job done; and they often make assumptions or do things beyond what we specifically wanted. Often we have to retrain and redo work that has been done.

In view of all of these problems, it is no wonder that even when library media specialists have additional staffing, it is often underutilized. Library media specialists are faced with an extremely hard choice: Either do the job yourself the way you want it done, or take the time to train your staff and volunteers so that they do the job the way it should be done. Because we have so much to do, the authors suggest taking the second option—spend some time doing good training so that you will have time to do the instructional and consultative things you need to do. One major problem with this suggestion is that few preservice library education programs give their students any training in instructional development or their staff development roles.

The authors would like to add a few notes on volunteers (parents, community members, or student assistants). Volunteers are *not* free! Carefully selecting, training, nurturing, and rewarding volunteers takes a great deal of time and energy. If you have not used volunteers before, talk with other agencies or librarians in your area who have used them. Programs that are run by volunteers may be a significant part of the library program, especially in these days of limited budgets and even more limited staffing. However, you should watch out for:

1. Promoting an attitude that says, "If volunteers can do it, it must not be worth much." A variation on this theme is, "Since you are doing so well with free help, why do we need to fund that program?"

2. Accepting individuals who want to volunteer but are clearly unsuited for the activity in question. Such individuals might be the overprotective parents of children wanting to be near their children, individuals with morbid curiosity about children, individuals with psychological problems, those who are out to "save" the library patrons with a specific religious faith or philosophy, or those who would physically or psychologically abuse your patrons.

3. Creating jobs for volunteers that are really only the routine clerical jobs of the library—the jobs that no one likes. There is a lot of routine, boring, and heavy work in a library media center; be sure that everyone (including you) has an opportunity to participate in that kind of labor, but also in important work—reading aloud to students, attending special staff development workshops, hearing a children's author, helping in the selection of materials, building a library display or diorama.

4. Developing volunteer use and program "on the fly," so that things are never done the same way twice. If individuals are responsible for your library programs or services, they need policies and procedures manuals as they work with your patrons. *Everyone* meeting the public should present the same policy to the patrons. A comprehensive introduction to these policies and procedures (for the library media center and the school) should be built into the training program for these individuals.

5. Excluding certain types of persons from your volunteer programs. Be sure that the design of your program (hours, location, activities, promotion) does not unintentionally exclude certain people. Be sure that no one is excluded because of ethnic background, disability, age, sex, sexual preference, or other factor. Roy has summarized the various concerns about the use and abuse of volunteers in his "Volunteers in Public Libraries: Issues and Viewpoints."[7]

Collaboration Means
Dealing with Schedules

Throughout this book the authors insist that collaborative activities—in planning, in teaching, in evaluation and assessment, and in community relations—are essential to the successful school. Most collaboration fails for lack of time. Most time problems are caused by poor or inappropriate scheduling. Just as all of the resources in the library media center are there to support instruction, so all of the time available in the school should support instruction. There is no time or place in the school where instruction does not take place. Anything that happens in the school—good or bad—is part of the instructional process. When staff members who have assigned tasks arrange to meet and do other things, they are instructing students. When staff members gossip in the hallways, they are instructing students. The ways in which staff members treat each other face-to-face and when they refer to one another in front of students is instructional. Sometimes the instruction we are giving children is unintentional and we would not actually *want* to teach the children what we *are* teaching them in those situations. If all time is viewed as instructional, then we need to carefully analyze what we are doing with time and what that activity says to students. If the members of school staff are spending more than half of their time in noninstructional activities, we must find ways to cut down those noninstructional activities.

Noninstructional activities can be very demanding. Here are some suggestions for cutting down on them:

1. *Keep a time log.*
   In traditional work analysis one of the most successful tools is the time log or time journal. Most people who have work experience do not know how they are spending their time because they become habituated to the ways in which they do their jobs. A time log is a simple way of recording, on a regular basis, what we are doing. Some studies of work suggest that the day be broken down into fifteen-minute or thirty-minute slots and each staff member asked to fill in what happened in each slot. In the authors' experience, most people find a summary worksheet at the end of the week to be as useful. Some people will find that keeping a daily journal helps them to remember what actually happened. A sample worksheet is shown on the following page.

Sample Weekly Worksheet Summary

Program Task	Time	Group	Count
Supervising Circulation	5 hours	all school	378
Storytelling	2 hours	Pre K, K	45
Information Skills			
Almanacs	2½ hours	3rd grade	25
CD-ROM	3 hours	4th grade	45
Literary Elements	2 hours	1st grade	56
Reading Guidance	3½ hours	varied	15
Teacher Consultation	4 hours	3rd grade	3
		1st grade	4
		5th grade	2
Videotaping School Assembly	2 hours	all school	325
Catalog Maintenance	2 hours	all school	
Circulation System Maintenance	2 hours	all school	
Materials Selection & Preparation	5 hours	all school	
Technology Troubleshooting	1 hour	2nd grade	23
	1½ hours	4th grade	26
	½ hours	5th grade	20

This table is only an example. Individual library media specialists will have other functions and programs to list. If the library media specialist summarizes weekly worksheets into semester or yearly totals, he/she can create a fairly accurate picture of how time is actually spent.

2. *Fill out a school library media time priority chart.*
   Wright and Kulleseid have both suggested that one way for library media specialists to deal with the time problem is to analyze in detail: (1) time spent on various library functions, (2) priorities of various functions, and (3) skills levels for each function.[8] A sample library media time priority chart with instructions will be found at the end of this chapter. This is a more detailed and time consuming exercise, but the effort spent may be rewarded when we can actually see how our time is spent and compare that time with our instructional priorities.

Flexible Scheduling Is
Essential for Media Programs

As noted in chapter 1, flexibility in instruction recognizes differences in the ways students learn and teachers teach. Rather than having identically scheduled times for all classes in the school library media center, scheduling is based on consultation with each classroom teacher so that library media activities are correlated with classroom instruction and time is allowed for different rates and styles of student learning. Such flexible scheduling allows the school library media specialist and teachers to plan extended periods during the day for specific instructional uses; it can also include the daily scheduling of a particular class or group of students for up to a week.

Substantial benefits result from flexible scheduling in the library media center. Van Deusen studied fifth graders and found convincing evidence that media specialists were more closely involved with the curriculum and that there was an increase in the information skills integration into the curriculum in circumstances of flexible scheduling.[9] Toor states that with flexible scheduling there are improvements in access to resources, information analysis skills, and critical thinking skills.[10] Lankford cites the report of the National Education Commission on Time and Learning, *Prisoners of Time*, which begins by stressing that American education has held the amount of time allotted for education constant for the past one hundred fifty years. The theme has been "learn what you can in the time we give you." She criticizes fixed schedules because they limit the access of students, teachers, and media specialists to the "teachable moment" and points out that fixed schedules also severely limit the amount of time teachers and media specialists have for cooperative planning.[11]

Lankford describes a project to provide elementary schoolchildren with flexible library access including such elements as factors leading to project succes; people's attitudes as the greatest obstacle to change; how the project was sold to librarians and principals; project problem solving; and lessons learned during the project's first year. For media specialists the overriding concern seemed to be, "What happens if I give up *my* control in the library?"

Here is her summary of what the school system learned about flexible access:

1. It is beneficial to the learner in terms of enhancing information-gathering skills, increasing an appreciation of literature, and conducting activities which foster lifelong learning and library use.

2. What is taught and learned in the library media center cannot be separated from what is taught and learned in the classrooms.

3. Multiple activities and multiple grade levels can function in the library media center at the same time.

4. Flexible access results in no loss of control by the library media specialist, but enhances her/his role in the teaching/learning process.

5. Flexible access helps create students who are excited about learning and who become self-motivated learners eager to conduct and complete research projects.

6. Kindergartners and first graders can find their own way to the library for checkout of materials and can acquire basic skills necessary to later success in information research.

7. Flexible access and multiple usage increase noise levels and produce some disorder.

8. Flexible access gives visibility to the creative skills of the library media specialist. All of the roles—teacher, organizer, leader, resource specialist, reading consultant, and curriculum wizard—become obvious in planning sessions with teachers and students.

In 1991 the American Association of School Librarians issued a position statement on flexible scheduling which encouraged planning between library media specialists and classroom teachers as well as both scheduled and unscheduled visits by students. The statement went on the affirm that "an open schedule must be maintained. Classes cannot be scheduled in the library media center to provide teacher release or preparation time."[12]

All Schedules Affect the Media Program

Library media scheduling can flounder if other school schedules are not also flexible. If everyone must do something at a specified time—in any area of the school—eventually, that rigid schedule will create conflict with flexible scheduling. Often union contracts or system-wide policies demand that teachers have a planning period each day. It is very easy for a principal to confuse the role of the media specialist with those of other subject or activity specialists who visit the schools to provide specific instruction such as art, music, or physical education. By placing all specialists in one classification, the principal is able to decide that scheduled time in the library media center can be utilized to allow teachers a planning period. If instructional activities are interrupted by a series of scheduled noninstructional events, even flexible instructional periods suffer. Flexibility in instructional use of the library media center can be severely hampered by external factors and administrative policies.

External factors include weather emergencies, time taken by in-service training, parent conferences, telephone calls, athletic celebrations, elections, or staff development days. All these factors may actually cancel school days. The activities and responsibilities of the school library media specialist outside the local school are also external factors affecting the amount of time available to plan with teachers and cooperatively provide instruction.

Library media specialists need to remember that even flexible scheduling will have structure. Ohlrich stresses that there is a structure in even the most flexible scheduling of the library media center.[13] First, there is the schedule or time frame of the curriculum itself. What is taught in a particular grade and at what time of the year? For the "teaching moment" to occur in the learning of information skills, such skills must be keyed to what is being taught in the curriculum.

Second, there is the school and school system schedule which determines nine-week or session schedules, when grades are due, when tests are given, and what holiday and staff development days are mandated. Nothing can be taught by teachers or media specialists when the students are not available. Third, there is the schedule of each individual grade level and how instruction is done. Teachers may vary the time when certain subjects are taught; they may teach so that particular subjects are shared among classes, and across grade levels. Fourth, there is the schedule created for the media specialist's own job—time to plan, time to eat, time to do administrative work. Although these elements cannot take over the schedule, they do need to be thought about and built into the schedule.

Schedules Are Based on Children's Instructional Needs

The factory model of education assumed that everyone would learn the same things at the same time. Rigid scheduling within a classroom or in a whole school makes a couple of false assumptions about the teaching/learning process:

1. *All units of time are identical.*

   This assumption leads to thinking that anything can be scheduled at any time without regard to prior activities or subsequent activities. Instinctively we know that this assumption is wrong. When children have been engaged in a very exciting physical activity, they are not immediately ready for sitting down at a table and doing quiet work. Mother even used to warn us not to go swimming for at least a hour after eating! There needs to be a rhythm to activities in the school that allows for a variety of learning activities in a variety of styles. The rhythm of the school schedule should be based on the needs of children, not the needs of staff or the school system.

2. *Time of day does not influence teaming.*

   This assumption flies in the face of the fact that individuals have different biorhythms which influence some people to be "morning people" and other people to be "night people." Scheduling difficult, abstract learning projects early in the morning for night people is a mistake. Obviously, we cannot totally ignore the schedule of the rest of the world. Deliveries must be made; food must be prepared; maintenance must be done.

   Still, school leadership teams can do a much better job of arranging the schedule than they currently do. They can begin by finding out about the learning styles of their students, and making as much adaptation to those learning styles as possible. Because each student has a life outside school it is also essential to know about personal health and home life particulars that impact the students' ability to learn. Throughout K–12 education there has been rethinking about schedules, which have moved away from the "time-block" concept in which all subjects are taught on the same time schedule. Time-block scheduling was once even a part of elementary education with school system level orders mandating when particular subjects were to be taught during the day, and when students were to be moved from one place to another.

   In one large urban school system during the 1980s, the system actually required that students be "rostered" into the school library once a week for forty-five minutes. The North Carolina legislature in appropriating funds for school technology included in the law a statement that, "students will spend at least 30 scheduled minutes with a computer each week." Most educators now realize that different subject areas, different instructional styles, and different student learning styles require different amounts of time. Some specific considerations:

1. *Review any "pull-out" activities that require that some students be removed from their classrooms.*

    In most school systems pull-out activities mean that some students are not in instructional settings with their peers because they are participating in tutoring, testing and evaluation, or other specialized activities. Each pull-out activity needs to be evaluated in terms of the value of that activity compared with the value of in-class instruction.

The authors are not arguing that pull-out activities are necessarily bad, but only that they need continual monitoring and evaluation. In one school setting, the number of pull-out activity hours per week exceeded the total number of classroom instructional hours! Pull-out activities also have the drawback of identifying students who have special needs to their peers. It would be much better if we could arrange to have time, and staff, so that special needs could be met in the context of classroom instruction. Probably any rethinking of pull-outs needs to include ways to include special activities and specialists in the life of the classroom. In this context, specialists can work with part of the class in a small group while the teacher works with another small group. With luck, there may be a teaching assistant who can also be working with a small group. Amazing things happen when students work with an adult in groups of fewer than ten!

2. *Review all noninstructional activities in the school.*

    As previously pointed out in this chapter there are numerous activities in the school that fall outside the regular instructional program. But, as we pointed out in the chapter on instruction, every activity in the school instructs. Most school staffs will find that they have too many noninstructional activities in which what is actually being taught during those activities has not been carefully examined. For example, what are we teaching when we have assemblies and programs for the whole school? Such activities can have very valuable instructional components *if* they are planned as a part of the instructional program. Anyone proposing a whole school activity (including the principal) should be able to justify that activity on instructional grounds.

Such instructional planning would include preparing students for the event scheduled for the whole school, arranging the event so that teachers and students are not simply passive receivers of information, and following up after the event. Having an author visit a school or a theatrical group present a play requires that teachers and students have some background knowledge of what has been written, what techniques were used, what it means, and exposure to other examples of similar works. It is most effective when teachers and students actually have hands-on experiences with the work of the guests. Such hands-on experience could include reading aloud the works of the visiting author, having actors in the theatrical group visit classrooms prior to the event, writing stories using the words of the author, or creating displays or artifacts that illustrate the event.

The event itself needs to be evaluated. Does its scheduling allow time for questions from the audience? Does the event schedule allow for small group or individual class meetings with the presenters? Is the content of the event clearly related to the goals and objectives of the instructional program? Is the event a one-time activity or will there be other clearly related events following? (One-time guest speakers or events with a passive audience are not worth having even if they are free!)

All events need to have follow-up. When human beings experience an exciting or meaningful event they should be encouraged to talk about it afterwards. They create poems, stories, artifacts to help them remember the event; they show pictures or videos of the event; they relate the event to the rest of their lives. If such events do have meaning, then teachers and students need opportunities to talk about what the event meant, to celebrate how good it was, to create something by which to remember it. An author visit or theatrical performance in a school is not over until such a follow-up is a planned, integrated part of the instructional program.

Notice how this integrated event process differs from the typical management of such events in your own experience. How often were school assemblies, dramatic productions, visits from school district or community leaders, tornado and fire drills actually thought through as instructional experiences? The authors hold to the view that all activities in the school are instructional and therefore these activities must be *intentionally* instructional, not just instruction by accident. We realize that the local school cannot control all of the event intrusions into the instructional program of the local school, but the staff can certainly limit the number of intrusions that are clearly for no instructional purpose, or are public relations for the school system such as photo opportunities, or simply time fillers.

3. *Review all out-of-school events.*

We all remember excellent field trips. We also remember when field trips were simply excuses to be out of the school and not in an instructional setting. There is nothing inherently wrong with field trips, or other out-of-school activities; however, all such activities need to be reviewed in light of their instructional content and relationship to the goals and objectives of the instructional program. Again, such activities need pretrip preparation, clear instructional goals and objectives, and follow-up.

Summary

The library media specialist needs to be included in the schedule review process. Often he/she will be able to suggest information materials, community resources, or activities that strengthen the instructional, participatory content of events. Also, the library media specialist can plan displays, activities, and instructional programs in the library media center which reinforce the instructional content of the events. Preparing students for such occasions through storytelling, book talks, learning centers, or video visits with authors can make events even more meaningful. Arranging cooperative follow-up activities with teachers can strengthen the instructional impact, even sometimes the life-changing impact of such experiences.

It seems obvious that the library media specialist should also evaluate all events in the library media program itself in the ways suggested above. There is so much instruction needed in schools at all levels that we can ill afford to have activities or programs in the library media center that are not carefully integrated into the instructional program, cooperatively taught, and followed up in ways that strengthen the instructional components. In the future, the library media specialist needs to be an instructional leader who takes a long view of the whole instructional, coinstructional program and repeatedly asks, "How does this event (program, activity, unit) relate to what we have done before and what we have said we plan to do in the future?"

Remember that scheduling is not a nine-week, semester, or annual event; rather, it is a multiyear process. Since somebody needs to take the long view of things, the authors suggest the library media specialist for that role. Vision and the ability to do long-range planning are priceless assets and can raise appreciation of the value of the library media specialist to new heights.

School Library Media Time Priority Chart

Column one lists various instructional and maintenance functions typical of a school library media program. There is space for additional functions. Estimate the amount of time you spend each day and place in column 2. Multiply the daily amount by the number of days in the school year and place that time in the column 3. (It may help to have someone else estimate with you—an assistant, a volunteer, a teacher.) In column 4 rank the importance of each activity in terms of your program objectives: 1 (essential); 2 (very important); 3 (important); 4 (optional); 5 (unnecessary). In column 5 rank your preference for carrying out each activity: 1 (enjoy greatly); 2 (enjoy); 3 (sometimes enjoy); 4 (neutral); 5 (do not enjoy). In column 6 rank your performance of each activity: 1 (excellent); 2 (very good); 3 (good); 4 (adequate); 5 (need more training/practice). Column 6 allows you to assess your own need for staff development; if there are high priority activities in which you do not feel comfortably competent, you have identified an area where you can seek out additional training or education.[14]

Activity Type	Time Each Day	Annual Time	Ranked* Priority of Activity	Ranked** Preference for Activity	Ranked*** Expertise Performance
Instructional					
Providing student instruction					
• individual-class meetings with teachers, students or staff (one-to-one, or group)					
Planning activities					
• for LMC					
• for the school					
• for other groups					
Program evaluation					
Collection evaluation					
Administrative					
Training of others (volunteers, students or support staff)					
Supervision of others					
Scheduling use of LMC materials, equipment, or space					
Record keeping and maintenance					
Inventory					
Financial accounting					
Budget building and justification					
Grant proposals, etc.					
Selection					
• professional reading					
• examination and evaluation					
• consultation with others					
Acquisition (ordering)					

Activity Type	Time Each Day	Annual Time	Ranked* Priority of Activity	Ranked** Preference for Activity	Ranked*** Expertise Performance
Processing/preparation					
Cataloging/classifying					
Filing cards, vertical file, etc.					
Circulation duties (checking out and in and statistics)					
Overdue notices and retrieval					
Materials shelving and storage					
Materials and equipment weeding					
Materials repair					
Hardware repair					
Equipment and materials delivery					
Off-air taping of TV					
Materials production (print and nonprint)					
Housekeeping (room arrangement, etc.)					

*Ranked priority: 1 (essential); 2 (very important); 3 (important); 4 (optional); 5 (unnecessary).

**Ranked preference 1 (enjoy greatly); 2 (enjoy); 3 (sometimes enjoy); 4 (neutral); 5 (do not enjoy).

***Ranked performance 1 (excellent); 2 (very good); 3 (good); 4 (adequate); 5 (need more training/practice).

Notes

1. Nancy L. Karweit, "Should We Lengthen the School Term?" *Educational Researcher* 14, no. 6 (June–July 1985), 9–15. Quote is from p. 10.

2. David A. Gilman and Sharon Knoll, "Increasing Instructional Time: What Are the Priorities and How Do They Affect the Alternatives?" *NASSP Bulletin* 68, no. 470 (1984), 41–44.

3. L. W. Strange, *School Achievement Related to Time of Instruction and Other Factors* (Indianapolis, Ind.: Indiana Department of Public Instruction, February 1984).

4. Gilman and Knoll, "Increasing Instructional Time," 43.

5. Joseph Carmbone, "Time for Teachers in School Restructuring," *Teachers College Record* 96, no. 3 (spring 1995), 512–43.

6. Robert Keyes, *Timelock: How Life Got So Hectic and What You Can Do About It* (New York: HarperCollins, 1991).

7. Loriene Roy, "Volunteers in Public Libraries: Issues and Viewpoints," *Public Library Quarterly* 5 (Winter 1984), 29–40. Loriene Roy, "Volunteers in Public Libraries: A Pilot Study," *Public Library Quarterly* 8, no. 1–2 (1987–88), 127–45.

8. Kieth C. Wright, *The Challenge of Technology: Action Strategies for the School Library Media Specialist* (Chicago: American Library Association, 1993). Eleanor R. Kulleseid, *Beyond Survival to Power for School Library Media Professionals* (North Haven, Conn.: Shoe String, 1985), 85–86, 166–67.

9. Jean D. van Deusen, "The Effects of Fixed versus Flexible Scheduling on Curriculum Involvement and Skills Integration in Elementary School Library Media Programs," *School Library Media Quarterly* 21, no. 3 (spring 1993), 175–77.

10. Ruth Toor, "Focus on Flexible Scheduling," *School Library Media Quarterly* 19, (fall 1990), 36–37.

11. Mary D. Lankford, "Flexible Access: Foundation for Student Achievement," *School Library Journal* 40, no. 8 (August 1994), 21–23. Lankford cites: The National Commission on Time and Learning, *Prisoners of Time: Report of the National Education Commission on Time and Learning* (ERIC Document Reproduction Service No. ED 378 686).

12. American Association of School Librarians, "Position Statement on Flexible Scheduling." URL source: http://www.ala.org/aasl/positions/PS_flexible.html.

13. Karen B. Ohlrich, "Flexible Scheduling: The Dream vs. Reality," *School Library Journal* 38, no. 5 (May 1992), 35–38.

14. Eleanor R. Kulleseid, *Beyond Survival to Power for School Library Media Professionals* (Hamden, Conn.: Library Professional Publications, 1985), 85–86, 166–167.

8

Planning and Evaluation Principles

Above all, assessment focuses on how well the program fosters students' learning and their development into active, independent members of the learning community who use information effectively, creatively, and responsibly.[1]

A plan is a course of action for the future. Prior to taking action, a competent administrator will sit down, determine what is to be achieved and why, decide what activities indeed need to be carried out, and develop steps to carry out the planned activities. . . . Unless there is a plan you are attempting to follow, you can never be really sure that you have accomplished what is desired. The competent administrator wants no surprises.[2]

Introduction

Once a library media program develops, it tends to go on without any review or change. What we have done in the past tends to be what we continue to do. This inertia can only be overcome by a continuing planning and evaluation process. The authors grant that it is more comfortable simply to continue in our old program patterns and not subject our program to criticism and the need for change. But planning and evaluation are critical tasks because every public institution is in a zero-sum budget situation. That is, if we want to do something new, we will have to abandon something we are now doing because there is not enough money to do both. This situation is not likely to change. Administrators, teachers, and library media specialists must repeatedly evaluate everything they are doing to see what is pushing the school toward its goals, what is irrelevant, and what is hindering progress toward achieving those goals.

Some factors hindering movement toward goals are not under the control of the local school. Sometimes we just have to live with policies, rules, and position statements that are antithetical to children and the teaching/learning process. That such things exist is not the question; the question is, Are we doing all that we can, given what we can control, to move our school toward the goals we have defined? This chapter considers what comes prior to planning, some basic principles of planning, and how the library media specialist plans in the midst of his/her busy schedule.

Planning and Evaluation Are Not the First Steps

The first step is not planning, evaluation, a formal review of mission and goals, or a needs assessment. The first step is an *awareness of need* for change in current procedures and programs so that your library media center can help the school move toward its goals. If everyone on the school staff is satisfied with the way things are going, do not start to plan! Indeed, you cannot plan anything! If you try, you are probably asking for trouble. Many planning guides and brochures for libraries stress formal needs assessment before making decisions. Here, we stress that even before such a formal assessment process, there needs to be a widespread awareness of some need for change.

Major studies[3] of the infusion of innovations into organizations stress at least one step before planning: the *recognition of a need for change*. So long as everyone is satisfied with the way things are going, little will be accomplished. Once a need for change is recognized, the library media specialist can raise questions about school library center needs as they relate to the mission and goals of the school. But unless that awareness is there, any discussion of needs is irrelevant. Planning and evaluation can only take place in a school setting that is hospitable to these processes. Any planning or evaluation process implies change.

The library media center staff have to be willing to step back and take a hard look at what they are doing, what the future directions are, and what changes need to be made. None of these actions is easy or comfortable because we are redefining the role of the library media program in the instructional life of the school. The whole process is a political one. The library media staff need to involve all of the important players—teachers, administration, students, parents, and community—in the process. Successful planning and evaluation require commitment from a host of participants.

Planning and Evaluation Are Goal-Driven

Planning and evaluation have direction. Planning asks the question, "What will move us toward our school's goals?" Evaluation asks, "How well have we done in moving toward our school's goals?" We do not just plan in order to be planning, or evaluate so that we can be evaluating. Goals are created when we understand the mission of the school and the school system. As the National Education Association Special Committee on Educational Technology notes:

> Understanding our mission is very important. One educator stated our central purpose very clearly. He said, "Will technology transform education? No. That transformation must take place first in education's true workplace—the minds of its decision makers. It requires a shift in focus from what technology is or does to what it enables educators to do." *The planning focus should be on the individual educational needs of students and how educators meet those needs rather than on technology* [NEA emphasis].[4]

Under the section on program administration the new national standards for school library media service note: "Principle 6: Ongoing assessment for improvement is essential to the vitality of an effective library media program."[5] This principle does not mean that every school library media specialist will make the same plans. Rather, goal-driven planning and evaluation are always unique to a particular school setting because the goals of each school are unique—based on the particular needs of teachers and students in a particular place at a particular time. The media specialist must understand the uniqueness of the particular school setting.

The chaotic nature of schools has already been mentioned. This chaotic nature makes what works in one school hard to implement in another school. At the same time, the authors realize that there are major forces pushing toward common or standard goals for all schooling. The factory or cookie-cutter model of education is still with us. In at least one state a move to return more control and power to local school districts has been contradicted by the state's assertion that how schools and teachers will be judged is going to be based on test results covering areas defined by the state, not the local school board. Good planning asks, "What are we going to do *in this school* to meet the unique learning and life needs of our students?"

Library media specialists are always planning! We plan when we work as instructional consultants with individual teachers; we plan when we do collection development; we plan when we work with the school leadership team; we plan when we work with other library media specialists or system-level personnel. The purpose of planning is so that we can make good decisions that have results consistent with the mission of the school. The purpose of evaluation is to inform ourselves about how well we planned and what impact our programs had. Planning without evaluation is useless. The ways in which people plan vary, and there are numerous techniques for the planning process. Even so, every planning process has certain common elements:

1. *Mission and goals*
   All planning is an attempt to move an institution, or some part of that institution, toward some defined goal. We plan so that our activities are not random or traditional, but goal-driven. If we do not plan, then the library media program has a very great chance of not contributing to the goals of the school.

2. *Current program assessment*
   We cannot plan if we do not know the current state of our programs. Creating a baseline of data about our program and how the administration, teachers, and students feel about that program is an essential beginning step.

3. *Measurable objectives*
   Once we know our goal(s) and the current state of affairs, we need to develop specific program and instructional objectives that can be measured. Some people react very negatively to quantitative measures of programs: "We are doing a lot of really fine things with children that are very hard to measure!" Yes, but what are you doing that moves the school toward its goals? All planning depends on being able to define in measurable terms how we are going to assess our progress toward the goals of the particular school in which the library media program operates.

4. *Resource evaluation*

   After defining some specific program objectives it becomes necessary that the library media specialist and his/her media advisory committee must ask, "What resources—human and informational—do we have to meet these objectives?" This question is best answered by seeking evaluation of the library media center's resources from teachers and students in an ongoing way. We not only want resources that are related to the objective; we want resources that teachers and students can use effectively to meet the instructional objectives.

5. *Implementation strategies*

   With specific objectives, we can seek ways to use teachers', students', and media specialists' skills and the resources of the library media center to meet these objectives. Strategies ask the question, "What are we going to do to meet this objective?"

6. *Evaluation processes*

   Evaluation is the other side of planning. We can never know how well we are doing our jobs, or meeting our objectives, if we do not have some form of evaluation of what we are doing and how well the library media program is meeting the instructional objectives of the school.

This cycle of planning, implementing, and evaluation is ongoing. We do not plan just once; we are always planning, implementing our plans, evaluating our work, and starting all over again. We can represent the process graphically:

Planning and Evaluation Cycle

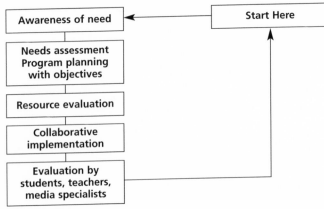

Note: Because needs, user populations, and resources change, this process must be continually repeated.

Planning and Evaluation Are Messy Processes

Because the school library media center exists in the midst of an operating school, which in turn is part of a larger operating system, planning efforts are going to be rather messy. Our local plans will have to fit into the larger context of a top-down bureaucracy where everyone is busy.

Lankford points out that "Everyone has ideas, but if we used all the ideas the library might exceed the square footage of the school. A word about costs is therefore in order."[6] In the planning process we need to have big program dreams; the messy part comes when we try to fit those dreams into the available space, or we hear from the associate superintendent for finance about the cost of adding additional doors or changing electrical wiring in the school to accommodate those dreams.

Planning and Evaluation Are Collaborative Efforts

There is no more important collaboration than the collaborative work of planning and evaluation of library media programs. Planning and evaluating alone is always a disaster; there are simply too many variables for anyone in a school to plan or evaluate alone. If we do not plan and evaluate collaboratively, we can not work collaboratively. In almost all of the school reform movements the stress is on cooperative involvement of all of the stakeholders in the education process. For example, in the Comer School Development Program, three principles underlie the whole cooperative effort:

1. Schools must review problems in open discussion in a *no-fault* atmosphere.

2. Each school must develop *collaborative working relationships* among principals, parents, teachers, community leaders, superintendents, and health care workers.

3. All decisions must be reached by *consensus* rather than by decree.[7]

Each Comer school designs cooperative planning and work on the basis of three teams:

The School Planning and Management Team

This building-level governing and management body is headed by the principal and comprises teachers, administrators, parents, support staff, and a child development specialist. As a team they are responsible for identifying targets for social and academic improvement, establishing policy guidelines, developing systematic school plans, responding to problems, and monitoring program activities.

The Mental Health Team

This team is headed by the principal and includes teachers, administrators, psychologists, social workers, and nurses. Together they analyze social and behavioral patterns within the school and determine how to solve recurring problems, applying child development principles in their decision making.

The Parents' Group

The goal of this group is to involve parents in all levels of school activity, from volunteering in the classroom to school governance.

Planning and Evaluation Have Setbacks, Failures, and Major Disasters

Failure and problems are the real tests of cultural participation. If we can stick together when things are not working, we have developed a real living culture in the school. It is fairly easy, if time-consuming, to plan when we can agree and when every plan works out. But life is not like that. Real-life planning always includes evaluation. We need to know how our plans are working out in the real world of schooling. Without the feedback from honest evaluation, we can never know if our plans are working or not.

The evaluation process is never an easy one. If a number of people have been involved in the planning process, all those people have a stake in the success of the planning process. Naturally, they want things to work out as planned. Almost always, evaluation tells us that we are not doing quite as well as we might. Often evaluation tells us that we are missing the mark by a very wide margin. Typical reactions to this planning evaluation cycle include:

1. *The desire to "fudge" the data*
   There may be pressure within the school and from above to interpret data in the best light. Or, as a recent case in Connecticut illustrates, to actually change test results *after* children have taken tests in order to get higher evaluation results. Statistically, such fudging gets easier and easier as we use desktop computers and statistical software packages to analyze our data.

2. *The refusal to wait for results*
   This reaction is most often seen in "fad" schools where every new trend, teaching technique, or technology is immediately adopted, only to be abandoned when the next fad comes along. The reaction is strengthened because those who fund schools (county commissioners, state legislators, Congress) always want immediate results on their investments. In the teaching/learning situation we are dealing with a multitude of variables within the school and in the larger community. Often meaningful results can only be measured over several years. When we keep making changes, adding new activities, refocusing the efforts of teachers and administrators, we ensure that no true evaluation will ever take place. Because we do not know how we are doing, we can assume we must be doing well.

3. *The rejection of the planning–evaluation model*
   Given all of the problems, it is tempting simply to decide that the school is too busy to engage in planning or that the school has too little control over what happens to make any difference. In many school groups the very mention of planning and evaluation causes a negative reaction based on past experience.

4. *The insistence that important activities cannot be measured*
   Some individuals and institutions are rightly concerned about logical reductionism, which states, "If you cannot count it and put it on the computer, it does not have meaning or importance." These folks fear that we are measuring the wrong things with standardized testing and other "bubble-fill-in" procedures. Some of these fears are justified because many important factors in the teaching/learning process are in the affective domain where counting is extremely difficult and the data that can be collected

through interviews, journal writing, or filming require careful qualitative interpretation. One institution of higher education known to the authors even boldly states, "Some very important aspects of the educational processing are difficult to measure; our school excels in these areas."

The library media specialist must deal with the objections to planning and evaluation. There is no alternative to an effective and efficient planning and evaluation process. But a major problem with planning and evaluation is the amount of time these processes take. Involving a lot of people in a planning process is time-consuming. For people to participate in a meaningful way, they must come to understand what is actually happening in the school, they must agree about possible options to deal with problems, and they must develop a common vision of what the school is to become. Put in cultural terms, they must build a common culture with a common vocabulary of meaning—they must leave their separate cultures because they have so much investment in the success of the school culture.

The ways in which a school staff organizes time will either allow for planning or cause planning to become impossible. Chapter 7 on scheduling principles discussed some of the ways the school staff can schedule their time more efficiently. The central idea of scheduling principles is that all scheduling of time in the school is based on instructional needs, not other factors. If we need time to plan and evaluate our work, we will have to take that time out of the day. When we clutter up our day with many activities and meetings, we effectively destroy any possibility of planning collaboratively.

Good Planning and Evaluation
Is a Multiyear Process

Future planning and evaluation require breaking out of the academic year mode of thinking. Most school systems and other institutions have longer planning and evaluation cycles. Almost everyone has participated in some kind of five-year-plan process. Yet most people in schools tend to limit their vision of planning, implementation, and evaluation to the traditional academic year. Part of the problem has to be with testing. School systems and state departments tend to arrange testing at the end of nine-week sessions and at the end of the year. The concept of "finals" in higher education has leaked down into even the elementary school. A legislative proposal in North

Carolina (Summer 1998) would even extend standardized tests down to the second grade! A lot of planning, implementation, and evaluation is based on the previously mentioned factory model of education applied to time. "We have x amount of time, and everyone will be able to learn what is necessary in that amount of time; then we will evaluate (test) their learning." Such thinking does not acknowledge that children and adults learn at different rates and in different ways.

The authors illustrate the possibility of breaking out of the annual cycle as follows:

1. *The goals of a school can be stated in a multiyear fashion.*
   For example:

   - Between kindergarten and the fifth grade all students at _____ school will apply all of their abilities to the task of becoming a knowledgeable and useful citizen of our community and the world.

   - The educational programs, staff, parents, and community of this school will be organized to provide all students with multiple opportunities for learning and personal and social development to meet these goals.

   - Through the instructional program and other services, all students will have multiple opportunities for learning how to access, retrieve, enjoy, critically review, and modify, produce, and communicate information useful to their work as students and citizens.

2. *The measurable objectives of the library media program must also be stated in a multiyear fashion.*
   The multiyear concept is one attempt to break out of the problem of "not having enough time to do the job right." Planning and evaluation of library media programs in this context demand that we think in terms of the total career of the child in the instructional program of the library media center. For example, in an elementary school we can begin by asking a series of constructionist questions:

   - *What experiences in reading, listening, viewing and evaluating of information resources does the child bring to kindergarten?*
     Subquestions might include: Is this child familiar with the preschool programs at the public library? What television programs does the family watch together? Do the parents of

this child read aloud to him/her on a regular basis? Does the family subscribe to newspapers and magazines? What attitudes do the parents have about reading and related activities?

- *What strategies does the child entering kindergarten use to identify, access, evaluate, use, and communicate information?*
  Subquestions might include: Does this child know his/her alphabet letters and their order? Can this child name different sources of information? Can this child tell you where he/she found a particular piece of information? Can this child tell a story about a recent event? Can this child share a family story? Can this child participate in a story-building activity with other students?

Such questions focus on the learning constructions (or emergent literacy) the child brings to the library media situation. Naturally, the answers to these questions will vary from child to child depending on their previous experience in the home and in the community.

We can continue by asking several *outcome* questions:

1. *What experiences should the child have during these six years in reading, listening, viewing, and evaluating information resources to be prepared for success in later schooling and in society?*
   Subquestions might include: What reading and creative writing experiences do we want to create for children throughout the curriculum of the school? How does the library media program contribute to that process? In what contexts do we want information skills to be taught? Is there an appropriate sequence for information-skills instruction? What production and evaluation experiences do we want children to have with varied media during their time in this school? What do computer-related technologies contribute to this process? Who in the community can serve as role models for the children in these areas? How do we create information-skills experiences in the extracurricular activities of the school and the community?

2. *What information skills should the child have during these six years that will allow him or her to identify, locate, evaluate, enjoy, use, and communicate knowledge to peers, teachers, family, and the larger community?*
   Subquestions might include: How do children become critical consumers of mass media? What information-production skills are appropriate to different grade levels and curriculum areas?

How can we incorporate the chosen information skills into the instructional program of each classroom? What different information resources does the library media program need so that teachers and students can compare information sources? What types of communication outlets does the program need so that students are encouraged to communicate their ideas with peers, teachers, parents, students in other places, and adult leaders in the local community?

These questions assist the library media specialist in overcoming the yearly kind of thinking. We are instructing all the time and we need to plan and evaluate on that basis.

Media Programs Must
Have Continuous Feedback

It is tempting to think of planning and evaluation as once-in-a-while activities. The cycle of educational accreditation reviews by state departments of education or regional accrediting agencies tends to support this view: "Well, they're coming again so let's do some data gathering, evaluate our programs, and plan for the future." Almost all accrediting agencies have now moved toward a continual review process to try to overcome this "occasional" type of thinking.

Library media program planning and evaluation need to be thought of as a continual process. We need to create mechanisms that will allow us to get continual feedback and data about the library media program so that we can fine-tune programs and services to meet changing needs. Classical evaluation theory divides evaluation into two types: formative evaluation, which is used to make corrections while a program is ongoing, and summative evaluation, which takes a snapshot of how well the program is meeting its instructional objectives at a particular point in time. Such summative evaluation is often done on an annual basis for personnel and programs.

In the context of multiyear planning and evaluation, the authors would argue strongly for *lots* of formative evaluation procedures and a very limited number of summative evaluations. The library media program needs to be self-correcting as the currents of the instructional program change. The library media program is like a ship in a constantly changing current, where regular course corrections are essential. In the past, we have too often insisted that a separate information-skills program would continue no matter what happened in other areas of instruction and no matter what the needs of teachers and students were. That must change.

Formative evaluation of the library media program takes two forms: informal data gathering and formal data instruments. Examples of informal data gathering can include:

1. Feedback about a particular library media program or service from the media advisory committee during one of their regular meetings, obtained by asking, "What did you all think of _____?"

2. Feedback from a teacher through the same type of question posed at the end of a cooperatively planned and executed unit of study: "How did this unit work for you and your students?" or "What suggestions would you have for doing this unit next time?" or "Should we try this unit with Mr/Ms _____'s class?"

3. Feedback at the end of a particular activity or instructional unit by asking students questions such as, "What did you think about that?" or "How should we do this next time?" or "What was the hardest part of this activity?"

4. Feedback from a teacher, parent, public librarian, or administrator who observes an activity or instructional unit and offers informal comments immediately afterwards.

5. Feedback from a journal of your own impressions of the instructional unit. Such an informal journal might ask such questions as, "What was the most effective part of this unit?" "What needs to be changed?" "How did the students and cooperating teacher react to this unit?"

Such informal feedback is extremely valuable in assessing how other people see the library media program. It provides the type of qualitative data that are hard to collect in formal evaluation procedures. One problem with such informal approaches lies in the fact that the evaluator often has an ongoing relationship with the library media specialist and may want to avoid saying anything that would harm that relationship. A variety of anonymous techniques can be used to overcome this problem:

1. *Create an Instructional Unit Suggestion Box*
   At the conclusion of the unit, ask students and teachers to write brief comments on a slip of paper and put them in the box.

2. *Create an Instruction Unit Learning Center*
   Put a tape recorder in a study carrel on which teachers and students can record their comments. Place a list of possible questions on the carrel wall:

WHAT DID YOU LIKE BEST ABOUT THIS UNIT?

IF YOU HAD ONLY ONE RESOURCE (LIST THEM HERE) WHICH WOULD YOU CHOOSE?

WHAT DID YOU EXPECT TO LEARN THAT YOU DID NOT?

WHAT OTHER BOOKS WOULD YOU LIKE TO SEE ADDED TO THE LIBRARY MEDIA CENTER ON THIS TOPIC?

3. *Create an Anonymous Correspondent*
   If the school has an e-mail system, create a "virtual person" so that teachers and students can sign on to the system as that person and send you their reactions to library media center programs and instructional units and offer suggestions to the library media specialist. It is true that some individuals will misuse such anonymous methods and the library media specialist may get some responses that are offensive and some that are useless; however, student and teacher feedback on an anonymous basis may prove to be a very effective evaluation tool.

Sometimes it is helpful to gather data on a more formal basis for purposes of collection evaluation, program evaluation, and personnel evaluation. Such formal evaluation does not replace the informal communication and feedback process; often it simply confirms what the library media specialist already knows from informal feedback. The nice thing about carefully designed formal evaluations is that we can aggregate the data so that we can observe trends in the evaluation of the library media program's specific instructional units and different parts of the library media center collection. Examples of formal evaluation can include the following.

Teacher and Student Instructional Unit Evaluation Forms
Immediately following an instructional unit or program in the library media center, the media specialist distributes a simple form and asks students to complete it. The content of the form will vary depending on grade level and instructional unit. Here are examples:

1. Student Instructional Unit Evaluation Form

Library Media Center—Evaluation

Instructional Unit _____ Class _____

(fill in before class)   *(fill in before class)*

1. What I liked best about this unit was:

2. We used the following resources in this unit (check the one you used most):
    □ CD-ROM   □ Encyclopedia   □ Almanac   □ Magazines
    □ Atlases   □ Books   □ Online Resources
    (vary list depending on unit)

3. One thing I wanted to know that I could not find was:

4. I understood what was presented by *(fill in name of media specialist)*:

    □ very well   □ O.K.   □ not very well   □ not at all

5. The materials for this unit are:
    □ very useful   □ useful   □ not useful   □ worthless

6. For this assignment, we need more materials about:

7. Next time we have a class, would you please:

Evaluation forms for students will vary from unit to unit and from school to school. This form is only a suggestion and may need to be simplified for specific situations. Other questions of concern in a particular library media center can be substituted for the questions here.

2. Teacher Instructional Unit Evaluation Form

Teacher Instructional Unit Evaluation Form

Class _____ Unit _____

1. The Instructional Unit Planning was:
   ☐ very helpful   ☐ helpful   ☐ not very helpful   ☐ no help

2. We can improve the planning of instructional units by:

3. The Instructional Unit used the following resources (please circle the appropriate response for each one):

CD-ROM	very useful	useful	not very useful	useless
Almanac	very useful	useful	not very useful	useless
Magazines	very useful	useful	not very useful	useless
Atlases	very useful	useful	not very useful	useless
Books	very useful	useful	not very useful	useless
Online	very useful	useful	not very useful	useless
Software	very useful	useful	not very useful	useless

(vary list depending on unit)

4. For this unit, we need to add the following materials to the library media center:

5. The time allowed for this instructional unit was:
   ☐ long enough   ☐ not long enough   ☐ too long   ☐ really too short

6. Next time we do this unit, let's

This form can be more complex than the student form and can seek responses to a wider range of issues. Take this one example: Completing forms is not much use until we can aggregate the information into some more useful format. The authors would make the following suggestion:

Student Preference Lists

The student form seeks information on various formats of information materials. Following several instructional units, the student preferences can be summarized in the graphic format below. As more data on student preferences are gathered, it is possible to focus on format preferences in different instructional areas and create a graph covering a longer time span. Note several cautions about this chart: (1) Student preferences should be carefully compared with teacher and library media specialist preferences. (2) The availability of a format may affect the preference rating. For example, if students must wait to use an online service or a CD-ROM, they may prefer other formats because of ease of access.

Such charts are helpful over a multiyear time period because they can show changes in both student and teacher preferences of formats in specific areas. This chart clearly shows the library media specialist that if any funds have been invested in CD-ROM products for reading, work must be done with teachers and students to increase the use of that format. The preference for online services in all subject areas is low. Is this fact due to lack of experience, lack of equipment, or lack of staff development? Students studying geography are making almost no use of magazines. Do we need to change our subscriptions?

We can also utilize the student evaluation forms and the teacher evaluation forms to evaluate the library media center collection. Because the form lists the various Dewey classification numbers used in instructional units, over time we can collect data on the effec-

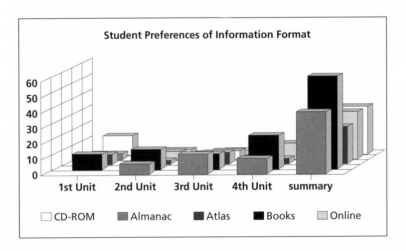

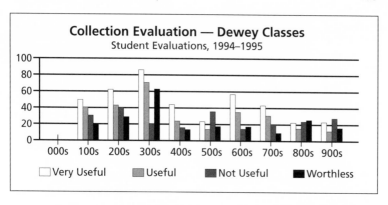

Collection Evaluation — Dewey Classes
Student Evaluations, 1994–1995

□ Very Useful   ■ Useful   ■ Not Useful   ■ Worthless

tiveness of the collection in instruction. Creating such graphs over a multiyear period allows the library media specialist to conduct continuous evaluation and development of the collection. Because funds for collections development are always limited, we need to identify those areas of the collection that are most in need of that development. The chart above displays Dewey class student evaluations in increments of 100.

Note several things about this graph: (1) Not all classes are evaluated because the 000s were not used in instruction. (2) We have used the total number of students who ranked materials in each classification. (3) The graph clearly shows that several classes (500s, 800s, and 900s) need development. (4) The graph could be made more useful by using more specific Dewey classes instead of the larger100 units.

Other charts could be created from the two data formats included in this chapter. We can compare teachers' evaluations of the instructional planning process in different subject areas or grade levels. We can assemble lists of suggestions for improvement from both students and teachers. We can chart the usefulness of various formats from the student and teacher perspectives.

Summary

The authors do not intend that library media specialists should use these specific evaluation techniques or chart presentation ideas. They are only illustrative. The point is that the data that are collected need to be put to some use in ways that are easy to understand. The library media specialist needs to collect data continually so that he/she can notice what impact planning and program are having on the instructional program. Most of this process is political in the sense that we are not just collecting data but are striving to present those data in graphic formats illustrative of what impact the library media program is having on progress toward the school's goals and objectives.

Notes

1. American Association of School Librarians and the Association for Educational Communications and Technology, *Information Power: Building Partnerships for Learning* (Chicago: American Library Association, 1998), 108.

2. Inez L. Ramsey and Jackson E. Ramsey, *Library Planning and Budgeting* (New York: Franklin Watts, 1986), 3.

3. Arthur Levine, *Why Innovation Fails* (Albany, N.Y.: State University of New York Press, 1980). E. M. Rogers, *Diffusion of Innovations*, 3rd ed. (New York: Free Press, 1983). M. Sokol, "Innovation Utilization: The Implementation of Personal Computers in an Organization" (Ph.D. dissertation, University of Maryland, 1986).

4. National Education Association Special Committee on Educational Technology Report (Washington, D.C.: National Education Association. Special Committee on Educational Technology, 1989), 11. They are quoting Rhodes, L. A., "We Have Met the System—and It Is Us!" *Phi Delta Kappan* 70, no. 1 (September 1988), 28–30.

5. *Information Power*, 108.

6. Mary D. Lankford, "Design for Change: How to Plan the School Library You Really Need," *School Library Journal* 40, no. 2 (February 1994), 20.

7. Jacquelyn Zimmermann, ed., *The Comer School Development Program, Education Research Consumer Guide, Number 6*, 1993, ERIC Document Reproduction Service No. ED 363 679.

9

Budgeting Principles

Economics is defined as the study of scarce resources. . . . Allocating these scarce resources means determining how to use, spend, or divide the resources, in other words, how to spend the library's budget, how to allocate hard disk space to store computer files, how to schedule employees' time . . . or how to manage personal time. In each case, choices have to be made to make the best use of limited resources.[1]

Introduction

Because so many library media centers have very limited budgets, it is tempting to avoid a discussion of budget on the basis that there is so little money to talk about! There may be very little to talk about, but how that money is spent says a great deal about the real goals and objectives of the library media program. Budgeting is where planning actually becomes real. Just as with time, we spend money, no matter how little we have, on what we think is important. Because budgeting is the financial component of planning, the budgeting process should reflect the goals and specific objectives of the school's program. When a library media program and a school do not base their budgeting on goals and specific objectives, it is easy to be taken in by every fad that comes along. The long-term Miller and Shontz studies of school library media expenditures show that library media programs that do not plan can easily spend all of their resources on technology and end up with no funds for other resources.[2]

Such problems are not unique to school library programs. Most academic libraries are constantly facing the spiraling costs of serial publications. If an academic library staff is not very careful, the total acquisitions budget can easily be taken over by serials, leaving nothing for acquisition of books, microforms, recordings, and so forth. As costs continue to rise, the library media specialist must continually do budget planning in the context of changing goals and objectives of the school. There are constant demands from a variety of sources for the few dollar resources of the library media program.

Budget Planning Is Objective-Based

As the authors have stressed repeatedly in this book, there is no independent library media program. That program and its resources are based on the instructional program of the school. Library media specialists cannot buy materials based on their own personal or professional interests; they cannot build a collection on what worked at another school; they cannot base their selections on what the most aggressive, outspoken teachers want. Budgeting for resources and the technologies to support those resources must be based on a clear understanding of the goals and objectives of the school as these are worked out in instruction. Budget decisions are not always based on such rational understandings. As Polley notes, "The history of modem education is littered with the trash of technology left behind by unrealistic purchases, naive users, and vendors working on a quota system."[3]

One of the major reasons for the failure of many programs and technologies in library media center programs and in the overall instructional program of schools arises from the lack of careful budget planning. We should spend no funds without being able to justify how and to what extent these funds will move the school's instructional program toward its goals and objectives.

The authors know that neither the school library media specialist nor the administration of the school has absolute control over how funds are spent. Special allocations from school districts, from federal categorical funds, or from state legislatures may require that certain types of expenditures be made. Once in a while the brand name of a particular resource or technology is specified in the funding agencies' guidelines! It is a hard saying, but we need to beware of any funding that requires that the school and/or the library media program violate the local school's goals and objectives. If a funding source demands that we initiate a new program outside those specified in the school's goals and objectives, we are probably better off without that funding.

Enhancing the library media program budget with grant proposals poses the same type of problem. The library media specialist cannot simply seek any grant that is available. All grant ideas must be filtered through the lens of the school's goals and objectives. The question to ask is, "Does this grant request push our library media program in the direction of the school's goals and objectives?" If the request requires new programs, additional work, or different resources from those in the school's stated goals and objectives, then we had better not submit it.

Again, the authors know that school systems and state departments do not always follow their own goals and objectives and that state legislative bodies often have goals and objectives that do not agree with those of other agencies. However, the library media specialist needs to have a firm grasp on the local school's goals and objectives and the ways in which these are being implemented in the school. Whatever funds the library media specialist controls need to be allocated toward those goals and objectives.

Budgeting Is Subject to the Laws of Economics

While this book is not the place for specific discussions of the laws of economics, it is still important to understand that everything the library media specialist plans and implements is still subject to the same rules of the game that affect every business in the world. To be more specific, every service and program of the library media center is subject to the laws of economic utility. Some economic definitions will help:

Utility—Represents the sense of well-being or satisfaction a consumer derives from a particular market bundle. When the library media specialist asks students and teachers to evaluate a specific program or resource in the library media program, he/she is asking about the utility of that specific resource or program. No program that has low utility can survive.

Marginal Utility—The additional satisfaction received from an additional unit of a commodity or service, all other factors being constant. We see this concept operating in a library media center when students or teachers ask for some information resource "just like the one we had last year!" Or "Tell us another one of those strange, funny stories!" Or "Do you have any more books about little dogs?" Marginal utility has limitations caused by diminishing utility, which we define below.

Diminishing Utility—Recognizes the fact that as we consume more and more of a service or commodity, we get less and less satisfaction. In popular culture this idea is sometimes called "the law of diminishing returns." In library media terms, this concept means that a good idea will wear out with the students and teachers. Sometimes the good idea wears out very, very fast. The library media specialist needs to know through planning and evaluation when the law of diminishing utility is beginning to operate in the library media program.

These economic concepts explain why we cannot plan to budget more funds for last year's services and programs. Naturally, there will be some carryover from one year to another and we will have new students to introduce to our good resources and programs; however, we cannot just keep doing more of the same because the economic concepts tell us that the consumers' feeling about those resources and programs will change. We could continue to do the same old things, but over time those things will lose their appeal to larger and larger groups of users. If users have alternative sources of resources and programs, they will turn to using those sources instead of the library.

At first, as more programs or services of the same type are added, we will get the effect of marginal utility. Most students and teachers (our consumers) will receive additional satisfaction from having additional access to these programs and services. But soon the rules of diminishing utility will come into play, and no matter how hard we work, there will be less and less satisfaction. Faced with these economic concepts, it is difficult to see why anyone would want to plan a budget on the basis of simply adding a percentage to last year's budget. Yet that is what is often requested. Adding a percentage to a line-item budget is simply a way of saying, We are going to do all of the things we did last year, but we will have additional funds to do more of the same.

This is a recipe for disaster in retail business and in libraries! Budget planning is a process of constantly realigning the funds that we have to meet new consumer demands that change all the time. For this reason, the previous chapter on planning and evaluation stressed that we need to have continual feedback from students and teachers about the library media program and resources. Realistic budget planning depends on such feedback so that we can allocate funds to areas of critical need.

Budget Planning Requires Examination and Promotion of Sources of Income

There are a number of potential sources of funds for school library media programs:

1. Federal funds, including Title I and Title XI funds, Eisenhower math and science grants, Vocational Education funds, Exceptional Children allocations. Many federal funds are in categorical accounts, which means that the funds can only be allocated for specific purposes or to serve specific populations of students.

2. State funds including state department of education per capita funding for instructional materials, local education authority funding for salaries, resources, and equipment, and special allocations (usually at the state level) for one-time funding of new thrusts in education. Many times these special allocations will be technology-related and no funding is supplied for continued support or maintenance.

3. Local funds, including fines, local board funds, partnerships with business and industry, memorials, PSTA support, or book fair receipts.

4. Capital outlay funds, including allocations for new facilities, renovations, and other facility-related improvements.

5. Special funds and grants, including local, state, and federal grant sources.

In all budget planning, the basic question remains, "How does the library media program get its fair share of those funds that come to the school?" The answer to that question is, "Through library media program *involvement* in the total instructional program of the school. In schools where the library media program is seen as essential to the success of the school's program, and, more especially, the success of the instructional program of individual teachers, there will be active support for the library media program receiving an adequate share of the budget allocated. No funds come automatically to the library media program, even if funds are allocated to the library media center by state law. The library media specialist must argue for a share of these funds on the basis of the utility of the library media program to the total instructional program of the school.

Cost/Benefit Analysis of the Program Must Be Done

There is never enough funding for library media programs. How does the library media specialist select what will be funded next year? The authors have already stressed that the priorities of the school's goals and objectives will play a major role in such decisions. Another major factor is cost/benefit analysis. Cost analysis asks, "For each student (or class) served, what is the cost of a particular program?" Benefit analysis asks, "What benefit did each student (or class) receive from this particular program?" Both questions are worth asking on a continuing basis. The more powerful question is, "What is the relationship between the costs of a particular program and its benefits to students (or classes)?"

Traditional budgeting focused on *inputs* to the library media center: how much money was available for materials, for equipment, for maintenance, for contracted services, or for travel? In the past accrediting agencies often asked for input type data: number of books per student, number of seats in the library, total floor space, periodical subscriptions, number and type of audiovisual materials and equipment. The typical line-item budget for expenditures in libraries reflects this input type of thinking. Cost/benefit analysis moves our thinking toward *outputs* of the library media program. Such thinking continually asks, What is the benefit of this particular activity? Who does it benefit? and, What does it cost per student (or class)?

Libraries have not usually collected cost data about the various aspects of their programs. In fact, it has only been in the last decade that cost finding has become a part of library literature.[4] If we do not identify the specific programs and services offered in the library media center, then we cannot ever know what each service costs. It follows that the library media specialist has no way to justify a particular library media program to those who fund it! Knowing what specific programs and services cost is the first step in cost/benefit analysis. This process begins when the library media specialist begins to estimate the amount of *time* he/she spends on planning and delivering specific programs and services.

Detailed cost center analysis includes not only the time spent, but also direct costs such as equipment, materials used, supplies, and indirect costs such as utilities, telephone, maintenance, and so on. While such detail is useful and could be pursued, it is important to remember that the largest cost in any library media center is for personnel and their benefits. If we can estimate the time spent on various activities, we can determine where our cost centers are.

Notice that the authors are not suggesting a detailed, minute-by-minute analysis. Ideally, what is needed is a fair estimate of the time spent over a semester or year in various programs with various groups of teachers and students. If the library media specialist follows one of the procedures suggested in the chapter on planning and evaluation for monitoring time use we have the basis for some cost analysis. Once we know how much time we are spending on various activities and how many students and teachers we are serving with each activity, we can create some time/people/cost ratios. The hourly cost of the time of the library media specialist can be calculated by determining the cost of annual salary and benefits and then dividing that figure by the total number of work hours in the year. For example:

Calculating the hourly cost of media services
Annual Salary = $28,500
Benefits = $4,845 (17% of salary)
Total = $33,345
Total hours = 1,440

Every hour the library media specialist spends on an activity can be said to cost $23.16. Note again that this cost figure is only for the time of the library media specialist, not for materials used, equipment related to those materials, or other costs of keeping the library media center open. If there is an assistant or volunteers, their salary figures would need to be included in costing out activities. An analysis of time spent may reveal cost centers shown in the chart in the following page.

This example is oversimplified because we are only counting the costs of the library media specialist's time. Still, the example shows that different activities have different costs per unit of service. Library media specialists cannot assume that all activities are equal. On the other hand, the authors have deliberately built the model to

Sample Cost Center Analysis
School with 450 students
Hourly cost = $23.16

	Time	No. Served	Cost	Cost/ Pupil	Yearly Average	Yearly No. Served	Yearly Cost
Activity: Information Skills	6 hrs.	125	$139	$1.11	216 hrs.	4,500	$5,003
Yearly cost per student = $.90							
Activity: Storytelling	2 hrs.	45	$46	$1.02	72 hrs.	1,620	$1,668
Yearly cost per pupil: $1.03							

show great differences in costs per student. This does not mean that the library media specialist should concentrate all efforts on the low-cost-per-student item! For example, all school activities such as videotaping school assemblies are very low cost per student. If we follow the low-cost rule, the library media specialist would try to increase the number of all school activities requiring videotaping. How would such an effort match with the school's instructional goals and objectives?

Many activities of the library media specialist involve one-to-one activities—that is, the activities are very labor-intensive and very expensive. We need to understand those costs, but the library media specialist may find that the school's instructional goals and objectives stress individualized instruction and team planning of instruction, so the costly activities must be supported. Once the library media specialist knows where he/she is spending time, he/she can ask the other important question, "What resources were used for this program and service?"

If the library media specialist cooperatively plans a social studies unit involving the study of a Latin American country (or countries), what information resources of the library were used? Remember that in chapter 5, we suggested collecting evaluation data on the basis of types of resources used. We can utilize a similar process here. The cost/benefit type of thinking allows the library media specialist to ask some hard questions about resources and programs:

1. *What do the activities and programs in the media center actually cost in terms of time spent on their preparation, implementation, and evaluation?*

Once we know what different things cost, we can ask the even harder question, "Are we spending our time on things that really make an instructional difference?" When the library media specialist finds high-cost items that are not clearly related to the instructional program goals and objectives, those activities should be evaluated for termination. We cannot afford to spend time on things that cannot be instructionally justified.

2. *What resources of the library media center are most utilized by the instructional program and what resources are least utilized?*
   At all levels of public education, instructional activities tend to repeat over time. If the library media specialist takes the time to analyze collection and equipment utilization, he/she can make informed decisions about which areas of resources need to be weeded and which areas need to be enhanced by additional acquisitions. Resources utilization becomes a key part of the collection development process. In flexible library media programs we do not have space for materials or equipment that cannot be clearly related to the instructional program of the school. As one media specialist said, "We have access to funds when we can't use them, and we have budget needs when there are no funds!"

Long-Range Budget Planning Strategies

1. The library media specialist should: Develop and prioritize a two-to three-year major purchase plan that includes expensive materials (such as encyclopedias), needed media equipment, upgrading for the catalog and the circulation system network where appropriate, and software. This purchase plan should be based on the long range instructional planning of the school so that planned purchases support the instructional program. Be sure that the media advisory committee is involved in this process. Get cost estimates on each part of this plan and keep the cost estimates current. If special funds become available, the library media specialist has a purchase order ready to go. Many library media specialists have maintained a resource "want list" for years so that when monies were available, they could quickly create a requisition. This idea merely extends that notion to all of the major purchases in the media center.

2. Know what programs and resources of the media center are getting the most wear and tear. Working with the instructional staff and the data gathered by the planning and evaluation process suggested in this book, the library media specialist should be able to identify collection areas and related equipment that will require replacement, upgrading, or additions. Because the opportunity to spend funds comes so rarely, we want to spend the money where it will do the greatest good.

3. Resist the temptation to accept special funding for anything that is not in your priority listing and do not accept gifts-in-kind that are outside your priority purchase areas. It is often tempting to accept gifts from the PSTA, a local business, or some other well-meaning group because they are free. That is simply not the case. Nothing in the library media center is free and if it takes up space, requires effort to maintain, and is outside instructional priorities, it is very costly!

4. Keep a multiyear perspective on budget and spending. The media center is in operation for the long haul. The coordinated instructional program will not end during this calendar year. Often library media specialists get discouraged about the lack of funding and abandon the budget planning process. Remember: Everything is multiyear, including the library media program. What we can not get this year, we can break down into its components and purchase over time.

5. Seek out other sources of funding for the media program. No media program will ever have enough funding to do the job that is demanded by good cooperative instructional use of the library media center and its resources. However, the media specialist is not alone in having this problem. Universities and colleges never receive funding from regular sources that would pay for more than one-fourth of the costs of having students. Those agencies have increasingly turned to seeking out sources of grant funding to help them. Library media specialists need to become informed about the public and private sources of grant funding and become skilled in the process of making grant applications.

Note that the authors are not suggesting that the school or the library media specialist seek out "just any old grant." Grant activity, like instruction, is goal-driven. If the school has clearly defined goals and objectives, grants should target areas that strengthen those goals and objectives, not cause additional work for the staff.

Summary

The school library media program and the total school never have enough funds to do their jobs adequately. This situation demands that library media specialists take great care about how their limited funds are allocated. If all the resources in the library media collection are for the purposes of instruction, then all the funds spent should also directly support instruction. The library media specialist should be able to justify the spending of any money on that basis. If the library media specialist and the media advisory committee have planned goals and objectives, all budget expenditure and time expenditures should be clearly related to those goals and objectives.

Notes

1. Bruce R. Kingma, *The Economics of Information: A Guide to Economic and Cost-benefit Analysis for Information Professionals* (Englewood, Colo.: Libraries Unlimited, 1996), 3.

2. Marilyn L. Miller and Marilyn L. Shontz, "Expenditures for Resources in School Library Media Centers, FY 1989–1990," *School Library Journal* 37 (August 1991), 32–42. Marilyn L. Miller and Marilyn L. Shontz, "Expenditures for Resources in School Library Media Centers, FY 1991–1992," *School Library Journal* 39 (October 1993), 26–36. Marilyn L. Miller and Marilyn L. Shontz, "The Race for the School Library Dollar (Expenditures for Resources in School Library Media Centers, FY 1993–1994)," *School Library Journal* 41 (October 1995), 22–33.

3. E. Polley, "The Effects of ATS-6," paper presented at the National Institute of Education Conference on Educational Applications of Satellites, February 1997 (Washington, D.C.: National Institute of Education).

4. Philip Rosenberg, *Cost Finding for Public Libraries: A Manager's Handbook* (Chicago: American Library Association, 1985).

10

Facilities Principles

We do not have a space problem. We have a space allocation *problem! Too much space is being used for activities that have nothing to do with instruction; too little space is allocated to the essentials of instruction. How much space in your media center is really used for instructional purposes instead of being used to house equipment, unused books, and an informal teacher lounge?* (Overheard in a media coordinators' meeting)

Introduction

The planning and design of library media facilities is not a new concern for library media specialists. The 1975 national standards, *Media Programs: District and School,* provided a detailed list of recommendations about media facilities, which included square footage recommendations for specific activity areas. The current standards for school library media services, *Information Power* (1988), includes recommendations in similar areas. *Information Power* under Program Administration includes "Principle 7—Sufficient funding is fundamental to the success of the library media program."[1] The statement includes funding "adequate to underwrite necessary facilities expansion and maintenance."[2]

Truett found that what library media specialists most wanted was a larger or expanded facility.[3] Many school library media centers have operated in the same space for years. Often the lighting, wiring, and arrangements of the library were adequate for library functions when lots of equipment was not required and most resources were in print form.

Many facility planners viewed the library media center as another classroom that simply had a lot of books around the walls. Some library media centers may still be suffering from the open school era, which put the library in the center of the school as a large open hallway. Many library media centers will have been modified to deal with electrical outlets and power for a variety of media equipment and clerical support equipment. As computers grew smaller, some major facility renovations of an earlier day—raised floors, special electrical circuits, current requirements of at least 220 volts—will have been reduced. Some designers seem to feel that having information available in computer-based systems eliminates the need for any facilities space for books and magazines, and the library media specialist will need to be on guard. There are electrical, storage, environmental, security, and physical arrangement concerns that every library media specialist must face. This chapter presents facilities principles for library media centers, which we hope can be useful well into the twenty-first century.

Media Centers Must Be
Inviting and Attractive

An excellent floor plan, flexible programming arrangements, and well-selected resources can all be wasted if the library media center facility is not a warm, inviting place. As Jussim noted:

> The effect of a media center upon its occupants is the result of a complex set of factors which range from the morale of the staff, the often unconscious influence of its decor and layout, the flexibility of its arrangement, the variety of surfaces, volumes, spaces, textures, colors, and traffic patterns.[4]

Walling refers to the "ambiance" of the media center as "the feeling one has in a place, including its physical aspects."[5] Ideally, students and teachers feel welcome and comfortable in library media centers—safe and encouraged to explore.

Every library media specialist needs to evaluate what the media center says by its layout, its signs, its displays, and its colors. Colors are especially important. A small, crowded facility can still be painted with bright colors and illuminated with colorful posters and signs. The authors know of a perfectly awful example that illustrates this principle. One media specialist decided that books in the collection and periodicals should all be bound in the same color—the best price was a dark gray with white lettering. Over a period of years the collection became gray and undistinguished looking, and so did the library media center. Certain factors influence the "feel" of a library media center.

Ceiling Height

The larger the media center, the higher the ceiling should be. No one should feel as if they need to stoop to get into or work in the library media center. One problem with very high ceilings is their impact on small children—a very large open space may be frightening. But it is not necessary for the ceiling of the library media center to be at only one level. Lowered ceilings can create a sense of intimacy in parts of the area. Stores forced to use large warehouse-like buildings with high ceilings often paint the high ceilings, pipes, ducts, and part of the upper walls with a flat black paint and use lowered light fixtures so that the upper area tends to disappear. This effect is heightened if the lower areas of the facility are painted in bright, attractive colors.

Colors

The colors used on walls, bulletin boards, carpets, tile, and ceiling areas should complement and blend with other areas of the school. We need to use bold colors for accent points. Many library media centers will depend almost completely on artificial light. In these circumstances, the colors selected should be checked in that light. Artificial light sources can dramatically change the colors. Remember to consider the colors of equipment, carts, and shelving when thinking about how colors will blend.

Textures

The feeling of a library media center can be dramatically changed by the textures of wall covering, carpet, chairs, tables, and other furnishings. It is important to avoid a "hard" look, created by selecting equipment and paneling covered with shiny, reflective paint or vinyl. We need to soften these hard areas with varied textures on furniture and wall hangings, and varied materials on the ends of shelf units.

Signs

Library media specialists also need to be aware of what their posted signs say about the media center. How many negative signs (DON'T, STOP, NO) does your media center have? How often does a sign say, "PLEASE" and "THANK YOU"? A sign in a New York City Park illustrates this problem:

> NO PETS
> NO SKATE BOARDING OR SKATING
> NO RUNNING
> NO BICYCLES OR MOTOR BIKES
> NO BASKETBALL OR STICKBALL
> NO LITTERING
> NO DRINKING
> THIS IS YOUR PARK . . . ENJOY IT!!

Furnishings

How we furnish a media center also has an impact on how the library is viewed. Throw away broken chairs, tables, and other furnishings. Fix what can be fixed and give it an attractive color and/or texture. Make sure that everything in the center is clean and usable. Often a media center is made less inviting and attractive because of the lack of storage and workroom space. Again, Truett found that media specialists ranked the need for more storage space and work room areas fairly high on their list of changes.[6]

An inviting media center is also uncluttered. The facility may looked as if it is being used, but it should not look like the random area for equipment, stuff for the next (or the last) party, or a place to store as yet unopened boxes. Clutter is a potential danger for everyone—especially those with some physical disability.[7] Keeping traffic areas clear, major furniture items in place, and tabletops clean is essential.

Facilities Design Must Be Flexible

Truett surveyed library media specialists and children's librarians in public libraries concerning their reactions to library facilities. She found that they most valued spacious open facilities with windows that provided good lighting. The biggest complaint was lack of space in which to do media center programming. She goes on to point out that technology has added new dimensions to the need for flexible space.[8] Areas for recording, duplicating, and editing are going to become increasingly important.

A library media center can be organized to create a number of learning and production centers simply by rearranging the center's shelving, partitions, and display cases. In other situations, actual construction of walls or purchase of partitions will be necessary. The key to such redesign of the facility is flexible space. If sufficient electrical outlets exist, and if computer-related technologies can be made movable so that "instant" study/production areas can be created, then the possibilities for multiple, flexible use of the facility increase.

Where the school has a local area network, some library instruction/production activities can take place away from the library media center. Just as television has been distributed throughout schools through cable systems, it is possible to distribute the use of the online catalog, CD-ROM devices, and utility programs throughout the school. Some computer-based instructional programs now allow the media specialist to design instruction sequences that can be utilized by teachers and students over the local area network.

Newer technologies mean that more and more instruction must be done in small groups either because of lack of equipment, or the desire to move away from whole class instruction into more appropriate learning groups in several places within the library media center. The concept has changed from a large classroom with lots of books to an area that can be rearranged to contain a variety of learning activities all happening at the same time. Movable, lightweight partitions, study carrels, and shelving on wheels can be used to create temporary learning activity areas.

The library media specialist will usually have to do most of the rearranging without help, so it is very important that the objects to be moved be lightweight. With space-age plastics and lighter metals now available, chairs, tables, partitions and carrels can be sturdy yet easily movable. Avoid heavy metal tables, attractive but immovable wooden tables, and partitions that require disassembly to be moved. The facility should be designed so everything can be moved around easily. This design idea translates into not having ceiling support columns in the library, avoiding changes in floor level like those caused by storytime pits, or steps without ramps. Later in this chapter, design considerations for persons with disabilities will be presented. Many of those design considerations will also be useful when trying to rearrange the library media center.

Facilities Design Must Be Future-Oriented

Facility design is conceived on the basis of (1) the mission of the school and its library media program; (2) the curriculum, teaching techniques, and learning styles of students and teachers; (3) the quantity and format of resources and related equipment; and (4) the number and age of the students. These are all important factors; however, we need to remember that for any one of these factors the present situation is already in the process of change. One illustration of these rapid changes is found in the types of audiovisual equipment used in schools. As the curriculum and teaching techniques have made more and more use of VCR equipment and computer-related technologies, the use of 16mm film and related equipment has declined. As computer software programs allow for the creation, duplication, and distribution of graphics, sound, and video throughout a classroom or a whole school, the necessity of moving equipment on carts from place to place is reduced.

Because we do not get to plan and build library media centers very often, the library media specialist and the media advisory committee must plan carefully when the opportunity occurs for a new library media center or a renovation. When in doubt, plans should include generous square footage allowances for all functions and construction that allows maximum flexibility. Space is not only important for resources, programs, and equipment; it is also critical to the people—students and teachers—who use the library media center. The research on the effects of overcrowding points out that how people function is strongly influenced by the amount of personal space available.

Children learn better if they perceive that they have space in which to learn and some control of access to that space. Teachers are more productive in planning and administration if they can create (even temporarily) a comfortable space where they are not distracted by noise, traffic, or other interruptions.[9]

As more and more computer-related technologies are introduced into the instructional program of the school, the library media center will need to be redesigned again and again to accommodate new formats, equipment, and new connections. Later in this chapter we will discuss principles specifically related to the use of computer-related technologies. Suffice it here to say that space adequacy, flexibility, and adequate electrical power are crucial to the successful use of these technologies.

Facilities Design Must Make Media Centers Accessible to All

In accordance with Public Law 101-476, Education of the Handicapped Act Amendments (1990) revised from P. L. 94-142, library media centers must be barrier-free and able to accommodate wheelchairs and other devices used by persons with disabilities. Section 504 of the Rehabilitation Act of 1973 includes access rights for persons with disabilities. The Americans with Disabilities Act has generalized these requirements to the whole community's environment.

Walling as well as Wright and Davie[10] have provided some basic considerations in making the library media center accessible to all teachers and students. Walling stresses that students with disabilities have information needs just like their nondisabled peers, but goes on to state:

> There are important differences, however, that cannot be ignored. These differences can become barriers to information access. Some create barriers to communication, others interfere with the students' ability to use their bodies to retrieve materials from the shelves or to use the material once it is retrieved.[11]

Although attitudes about persons with disabilities remain the major barriers to information access for them, the library media center facility design impacts almost all teachers and students with disabilities.[12]

Many people with disabilities need extra space to use the library media center effectively. Just getting around in a wheelchair means taking up eight square feet of space or four times that of a person who walks. Many people will appreciate a library media center where the floor covering does not present an additional barrier to access. Unfortunately, the needs of different disability groups conflict at this point. Carpets make moving a wheelchair more difficult but smooth or waxed floors may cause mobility-impaired persons to fall. A solid, unwaxed wood floor, or a low pile carpet with a hard finish is a good compromise. A number of disabilities limit the reach of disabled people so that they need adjustable tables, lowered shelves, and the ability to move computer-based technologies into range. People not only need extra space, they may also need modifications in traffic patterns such as wider aisles, space around tables, activity areas, or doorways, and sign systems.

All sign systems need to be thought of as visual, tactile, and auditory systems. Important signs, such as fire alarms, should not only make noise but also make a visual signal. Visually impaired teachers and students will have to feel the signs because they have raised letters or braille impressions. Some students with cognitive or perceptual disabilities may also need areas in which they can have private space to utilize information resources. Such spaces can also be utilized with equipment that tends to make noise (speech synthesis devices, computer-based voice output, recorded books, and so on).

Many times information resources for persons with disabilities must be converted into a format that the individual can utilize. This format change often means additional equipment and technology such as video readers, braille printers, special attachments for speech output or input, and other enlargement devices. The facility must have places to use and store this equipment. Format conversion can also mean large print, recorded, or braille materials, which require special shelving. Library media specialists will find additional information on the impact of the Americans with Disabilities Act on library facilities and programs in:

William Borucki, *Libraries and the Physically Disabled: An Updated Guide to Information and Their Sources* (Buffalo, N.Y.: Co-operative Colleague Communications, 1993, ERIC Document Reproduction Service No. ED 366 128).

Donald D. Foos and Nancy C. Pack, *How Libraries Must Comply with the Americans with Disabilities Act (ADA)* (Phoenix, Ariz.: Oryx Press, 1992).

Albert Scheimann, *ADA Compliance: What Are We Doing?* (Kent State University, Master's Research Paper, 1994, ERIC Document Reproduction Service No. ED 376 855).

T. R. Switzer, "The ADA: Creating Positive Awareness and Attitudes," *Library Administration and Management* 8, no. 4 (Fall 1994), 205–08.

Facilities Design Must Plan
for New Technologies

The rapid increase in the variety of computer-related technologies used as library media resources means that most library media centers and other types of libraries lack adequate electrical power to use these technologies. Many libraries were evidently designed in a time when one light bulb was all that a room needed. Electrical outlets with sufficient power are a chronic problem. Many readers will remember the wonderful *New Yorker* cartoons of the family living in a one-room apartment with an increasing number of appliances plugged into one light socket.

Even where local electrical codes require an outlet for every six feet of wall, many public institutions are built without that standard being applied. No matter where you decide to place your equipment, you can be sure that the electrical service will have to be moved to serve that location. Remember that adding strips of serial plugs along a wall or installing power columns floor to ceiling does not increase the amount of electric power available; it merely gives us more places to plug things in and blow the circuit breakers.

Most of these additions are wired in series, so that additional equipment simply puts more strain on the system. In an older facility, there may be no telling how many plug sockets have been wired together as a group. In one school library known to the authors the equipment cannot be used while lunch is being prepared in a nearby kitchen. Large computer network systems must have a power source separated from the rest of the circuits in the facility. Sometimes the requirements of the system will mean a major rewiring of the area of the facility. The electrical demands of any technology system should be clearly specified by the vendor of the system, even if that system is supplied by another group or manufacturer.

Even in the smaller library media center with limited technologies it is still a good idea to have the electrical systems of the media center checked for capacity. There is no point in turning on a series of desktop computers and finding that there is not sufficient power to operate them; or that you cannot operate a VCR in another area of the center once the computers are turned on. Where there is excessive demand for electrical power, desktop computer systems often give strange error messages, or simply refuse to work, no matter what we do.

Electrical concerns include: (1) running whatever computer-related technologies are required simultaneously without creating "brownouts" or throwing circuit breakers, (2) avoiding electrical systems changes that might damage equipment or software, and (3) ensuring a power supply for the systems when the power fails. Placing equipment on separate circuits from lights, air conditioners, and other operating equipment will help with the electrical power issues.

In areas liable to suffer radical changes in electrical power from the electric company some kind of backup power source will be needed. All electrical systems are subject to high-demand periods in which the amount of electrical power available cannot be maintained at a sufficiently high level. When full power returns, there is often a surge of electrical power through the system. Surge suppressors or protectors for individual desktop equipment will help in keeping damaging surges out of equipment and software. Since we cannot always have electrical power, the library needs some way to ensure that when "lights go out," valuable data is not lost from the system.

Many businesses and libraries purchase backup power supplies that are wired into the electrical circuits so that when power fails, the power backup system comes on. The simplest of these systems are mounted on a computer card inside the desktop computer and allow for a safe shutdown of the system and saving of files. More elaborate systems allow the system to keep operating on backup power. Such uninterruptible power sources are expensive, but well worth the price.[13]

Uninterruptible power supplies (UPS) provide backup battery power when the main source of power goes out. The basic, inexpensive models are stand-by units that allow electrical power to flow from the electric company to the computer until the power fails or drops below some threshold voltage (usually around 100 volts). When this happens the unit takes over and supplies power to the computer system.

Online UPS use the electric current from the electric company to charge batteries that feed the computer at all times. These units often function as surge suppressors and provide a more even flow of current. UPS for local area networks (LANs) usually involve a more expensive device to protect the file server when current is interrupted. Because LAN systems may cover several buildings or areas, UPS devices are also attached to the individual workstations throughout the system.

Cabling and Wiring Concerns

Any newer technologies in the library media center require thinking about what to do with wires and cables. The library planners face a problem familiar to the early "hi-fi" purchaser. The system comes in components that must be connected with cables, and each component requires an electrical outlet. Because of rapid developments, the future requirements of computer-related technologies cannot be predicted. Whatever the current wiring capabilities of the library are, we can be sure they will be inadequate later. Cables cannot be run just anywhere in the library media center. Loose cables on the floor can cause accidents, and most fire codes forbid the use of extension cords of any kind. Micaela and Micaela suggest several steps in anticipating future wiring/electrical needs:

1. Use high-quality carpet tile with a built-in antistatic feature so that flat wires can be run anywhere in a room.

2. Provide wall-mounted, dual-channel wiring raceways on all perimeter walls so that electrical outlets can be placed at any location on these walls.

3. Use underfloor wiring ducts that can be accessed at any point.

4. Install raised, accessible flooring systems in locations where there is a concentration of terminals and cables.

5. Modify outlets into combination electrical, data, and telephone units.

6. Provide six-outlet plug strips for each computer workstation.[14]

Often floors are concrete or tile without cable conduit in the floor. Sometimes ceilings are suspended ceiling systems and cables can be run above the office area, but how do they get from the desktop to the ceiling? A variety of wall-mount and power-strip columns are sold to help solve these problems. Even institutions that have cable conduits running through electrical tunnels may face problems. At least one large university library planned to run cables campuswide to provide remote access to its online catalog system. There were cable conduits described in the campus engineering plans. Such conduits did exist, but had already been filled with cables by student engineers. The institution was required to install new conduits for the library cables.

Cables come in a variety of forms, all of which must be run between various terminals and main computers. The slowest cables are twisted-pair cables and are often used in desktop computer-based circulation and catalog systems. As automated system demand grows, organizations turn to coaxial cable, which is faster, harder to work with, and more expensive. But fiber optic cable is very secure and operates at high speed, handling many different signals at the same time. But fiber optic cable is the newest cable technology and is also more expensive.

Bryce describes optic fiber as being made by "drawing a large glass, called a preform, out over a long distance until it is one long piece of pure glass whose diameter is measured in millionths of a meter: microns."[15] Fiber optic cables have two parts: a core and a cover called a cladding. Light signals pass through the core and the cladding refracts (bends) the light back into the core. The whole cable is covered by chemical coatings and a plastic covering. In such systems, light signals from LED devices travel at high speed down the cable to the receiving stations. When compared with the metal cables, fiber optics has several advantages: (1) the data rate of the cable (fiber optics can carry a signal at 1,000 megabits per second); (2) resistance to interference (many forms of static and electric signals cannot penetrate the optical fiber system); (3) lack of signal distortion (fiber optics maintain excellent signals over the cable with very low error rates); (4) security of the system (fiber optic cables are difficult to tap and do not radiate signals like metallic cables); (5) resistance to explosion (fiber cables do not have the spark potential of metal cables and, since they have no metal parts, lightning damage is less likely); (6) smaller, lighter cables (cables can be installed in places where coaxial cable cannot be placed).[16]

Not every library media center will need expensive cable. The choice of a particular cable will depend on the demands on the system, the number of computers and terminals to be connected, the speed of transmission required by the system, and what network connections are required by the school or school system. Coaxial cable is often recommended because of its resistance to noise interference and its capacity. However, coaxial cable is more difficult to string and must not be placed on the floor as it must not be abraded, severed, crushed, or shorted. Fiber optic cable is the most expensive to purchase and install, but can handle the largest amount of traffic. Until recently, making new connections in fiber optic cable required professional installers, but several companies have now offered devices to make this process easier.

The Impact of Technology on Facilities

The introduction of newer technologies in school library media centers means serious change in the way things are arranged in the library. While a great deal is written about computer equipment, upgrading systems, selecting new peripherals, and other technologies, very little has been written about the furniture librarians use to hold computer-related technologies and the people who will use them. First-time desktop computer users often assume that the space/electrical requirements for computers are the same as for electric typewriters. They are not. Desktop computers are not a single unit; rather, these machines have detached keyboards, monitors, printers, and often other peripheral devices like external modems, floppy disk drives, or CD-ROM drives.

Desktop computers have a variety of users, so that the layout for one location will not work for all locations. Small groups of students may need space around a computer terminal for cooperative research; other library users may use desktop computers or terminals for short periods, and may prefer to use them while standing. Laboratory computer areas may require additional work-table space to accomodate related instructional materials and a place to take notes. Whole class instruction may require an overhead projection device attached to the computer and the ability to dim the lighting in an area of the library media center. The library media specialist will need to study the particular instructional functions to decide the best environment for particular applications.[17]

If the monitor is placed on top of the computer with the keyboard in front of the computer a minimum of thirty inches of desktop is required. Often the computer is placed on a small table that serves as a computer stand and has a drawer where the keyboard unit can be stored when not in use. Some devices have a drawer mechanism that allows the keyboard to be suspended in front of the computer when in use. Several of these drawer mechanisms allow for adjustment of height and distance from the front edge of the table, making them useful to a wider range of individuals.

Another option is moving the monitor to a suspended-arm device that can be moved around above the tabletop. If the computer is placed on its side in a vertical computer stand on the floor, the small typewriter tabletop can hold the keyboard and the monitor. These adjustments assume that the connecting cables will be long enough to reach between devices, and that placing the computer in a stand on the floor is safe. Special desks are made to allow for more secure storage of the computer and keyboard because the desk folds up, or a roll-top desk type cover can be pulled down.

Standard desks are not a good location for computer-related technologies. Desks are typically two to four inches higher than typing tables. Use of the keyboard is more difficult if the individual must reach up to use it. This "reaching up" is a major cause of carpal tunnel syndrome.[18]

Placement on a side table or mobile unit is to be preferred. No matter what is done with the typical typing table or desk extension, another location will need to be found for the printer. Local area networks deal with this problem by placing printers and other output devices in a remote location away from the workstation. The human problem becomes, "How do I know that what I'm printing is being done without paper jams, or other problems?" A number of printers close to where people work may be cheaper than having people get up and go to visit the printer. Such visits usually turn into social occasions.

Several desktop systems are available with special extension surfaces for printers, computers, and keyboards. Sometimes these desk systems allow for the printer and keyboard to be hidden when not in use. Another type of desk system allows for the desk surface to be transparent so that the monitor can be placed in a sloped tray under that surface and the computer and keyboard can be placed in hidden drawers. Such desk systems allow for viewing by looking down (rather than straight ahead) and allow the desk to be used for other purposes when the workstation is not in use. These desk systems are expensive ($600–$1,000), and not everyone is comfortable with the viewing arrangement. There is also the problem of glare from overhead lights on the glass or plastic window above the monitor. Like glasses, the flat surface will need to be cleaned regularly so that hand smudges do not interfere with vision. Top-of-desk placement of computers has created a demand for small "footprint" machines that take up a minimum of desk space. Careful thought should be given to the footprint area of the workstation system being considered: How much tabletop or desk space is required? What is the most comfortable way to use the keyboard and view the screen? Where will the system on/off switch be located?

Security Concerns in Facilities Design

As library media centers increase their use of computer-related technology to provide information for teachers and students, the problems of security for these systems have increased. One of the most disheartening events in the life of a library media specialist happens when the school is broken into and very expensive equipment is stolen or vandalized. The concentration of small desktop computers, VCR players, and study carrel TVs in the library media center creates a security problem. As equipment becomes smaller and easier to use, it also becomes easier to steal. There is a good "on-the-street" market for such equipment or for components (memory cards, CPU cards, modems, drives, keyboards, monitors) of computer systems.

There are security "tie-down" systems that make the removal of equipment difficult. In the United States, companies like DARTEK (Dept. 976, 949 Larch Avenue, Elmhurst, IL 60126, 800-832-7835) and GLOBAL (1050 Northbrook Parkway, Dept. 52, Suwanee, GA 30174, 800-845-6225) offer a variety of tie-down options. Such companies also offer more expensive devices such as devices that ring an alarm when equipment is unplugged from the wall, and noise, heat, and motion detectors that turn on lights and send an alarm to a central location where the police are called.

A good part of the security problem (as well as the user assistance problem) can be solved by locating equipment in proximity to staff locations so that staff can observe, supervise and assist the users. Unattended equipment tends to attract security problems including abuse of equipment and software, theft, and illegal copying. A basic rule of location is, "Never place equipment in an area where it can be seen from outside the building."

Some abuse of public access systems results from "hacking," which is the introduction of software commands into the computer software operating system by individuals who know how to get into the management areas of disks, computers, and local area networks and create annoying messages, destroy file access, cause memory problems, and generally make trouble. Such software commands can be entered from the keyboard, placed on a floppy disk, or sent through e-mail. Many hackers' activities are harmless in the sense that no data are destroyed or modified; however, some hackers leave viruses on the computer hard disk or on floppy disks they have overwritten.

Computer viruses are small software programs that give the computer instructions usually involving how file access is managed, or modifying what appears on the screen. These programs may even modify the operating system of the computer so that basic internal software commands are no longer executed and the computer stops operating. These viruses often erase hard disks, or File Access Tables

(FAT), so that all existing information and programs are lost and the whole disk must be reformatted.

Library staff will need to monitor their systems for these possibilities. Several companies have produced antivirus programs that prevent viruses from being loaded by automatically scanning any disks that are inserted into the system. There are also programs which will check e-mail content and downloaded files *before* they are processed by the system. Whenever a particular terminal or network is turned on, a program is run to detect viruses, and a virus detector program is loaded, which stays resident (TSR) in the system. The user is warned if any disk contains viruses. Most of these systems will allow for files on the hard disk to be "locked" into a read-only status so that changes cannot be made in loaded programs and no programs can be loaded onto the computer without knowing the password to the locking system.

Library media programs can also avoid problems by establishing policies about the use of private floppy disks. No disk is to be used on the systems without going through the virus testing programs on a computer at the entrance to the public access area. If there is a such a policy in the library media center, it needs to be a part of the acceptable use policy that students and their parents sign prior to accessing the computers.

Besides the main file servers for library automated systems, the library media specialist and the media advisory committee will need to plan the environments for all of the various terminals connected to that system. Many libraries will opt for local area networks for connecting the various automated functions together. Such LAN systems will need to be placed in locations where cables can be run. Many buildings do not have conduit for cabling their systems and must arrange for installation of conduit in overhead areas with drop poles or around base boards.

Ergonomic and Health
Concerns in Facility Design

As work has been shifted from traditional manual library operations toward concentrating most work on computer-related technologies with video display terminals (VDT), many health concerns have emerged. Robertson has published a library media center guide that includes recommendations on the design and placement of computer-related technologies.[19] People often work at terminals in a very fast and continuous way. As they work, they use the same group of muscles repetitively—especially the arms and hands, as well as the eyes. At the same time, all of the large muscle groups in the body are held immobile for long periods. This combination of factors results in repetitive stress injuries (RSI).[20] The repetitive movements can cause muscle and bone damage to those who work continually at such machines.

The most frequently mentioned problem is carpal tunnel syndrome (CTS), which is a very painful and debilitating condition involving the nerve and tendons that run from the forearm into the hand through the tunnel created by the wrist bones. As we move our hands and fingers, the tendons run against the sides of the tunnel causing the tendons to swell and pinch the nerve. This pinching causes tingling, numbness, and excruciating pain. Typing at a badly placed keyboard (too high, too low, too awkward) can produce CTS.

In addition to CTS there are other painful conditions that can result from poorly designed work areas. Cervical Disk Syndrome involves pain, numbness, and muscular spasm caused by compressed spinal disks pinching off the cervical nerves in the neck. A poorly placed monitor that causes unnatural head positions is the cause of much CDS. People also report rotator cuff injuries, which involve pain and limited motion in the shoulder, caused by inflammation of one or more of the rotator-cuff tendons in the shoulder. Tendinitis is a swelling, tenderness, and weakness in the hand, elbow, or shoulder due to tendon swelling. It is also the result of repetitive actions that stretch these tendons unnaturally and too often.

Other concerns focus on difficulties in viewing the monitor display and the effects of low and very low frequency radiation and the electromagnetic fields created by computer monitors. McKimmie and Smith summarize the recent technical literature on extremely low frequency (ELF) electric and magnetic fields emitted by computer video display terminals. They point out that when library employees of one library were surveyed, more than 60 percent used a video display unit for more than one half of their workday. They urge that librarians use "prudent avoidance" (p. 18) whenever possible with these display devices. Specifically, they suggest: (1) rearranging work areas so that people are not working in close proximity to the sides and backs of video monitors; (2) sitting at least an arm's length away from display devices; (3) turning off

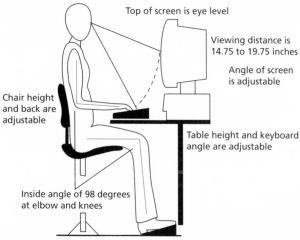

Top of screen is eye level

Viewing distance is
14.75 to 19.75 inches

Angle of screen
is adjustable

Chair height
and back are
adjustable

Table height and keyboard
angle are adjustable

Inside angle of 98 degrees
at elbow and knees

Foot rest for short operators

these devices when they are not in use rather than using a screen saving program; (4) avoiding leaning on, or sitting next to video display devices; (5) taking regular breaks from work at video display terminals by having rotating work assignments throughout the library; and (6) involving the library staff in decision making about workstation placement and work area arrangements.[21]

These ergonomic concerns can be summarized in a few words: those who work at desktop computers in the library media center should have a physical environment that is comfortable and that does not cause undue eye strain or muscle fatigue. Most problems can be avoided by having furniture that encourages good posture, refocusing the eyes regularly, allowing for frequent breaks or changes in work routines, and arranging the work area so that there is sufficient space for equipment and everything needed to do a job is within easy reach. Many present media center installations have not taken any of these ergonomic issues into account—especially for library staff. In the United States, the Occupational Safety and Health Administration (OSHA) was expected to issue a workstation ergonomics standard during 1994 although the regulations did not become law until 1996.[22]

Many businesses have modified their work areas because of more than 12,000 complaints filed under the Americans with Disabilities Act. Most of these complaints have been settled out of court when businesses agreed to make workstation changes. Costs have ranged from $150 to $1,000 per workstation.[23]

The figure on the previous page illustrates a workstation area that conforms to the ergonomic standards.[24]

Media specialists should be concerned about some specific design aspects:

Chairs

The chair should have an adjustable seat height that allows for a wide range of adjustments—between fifteen and twenty-one inches. If several people use the same workstation it is important that the chair be easily readjustable (probably with pneumatic height adjustment) so that each worker can be seated with thighs on a horizontal plane, lower legs vertical, and feet firmly on the floor. Because people vary in height, a footrest for shorter people may be necessary. If the seat is too high and the legs dangle, circulation to the upper legs is cut off. If the seat is too low, the arms will be at an uncomfortable angle when using the keyboard or mouse. The chair should also have a back that is adjustable for both tension (How hard do I push to move the back of the chair?) and height (Where does the back of the chair meet my back?). The figure below illustrates some of these design concerns:

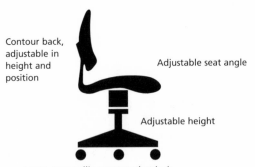

Contour back, adjustable in height and position

Adjustable seat angle

Adjustable height

Large, easy-rolling casters that lock

People come in all sizes, so work chairs must be very adjustable. Average size simply will not work for chair design where people are working over long periods. Andrea and David Micaela point out that chairs need to be carefully chosen because people's dimensions are not average but very diverse. They stress the importance of adjustability in all areas and suggest that the adjustable features include seat, arms, back height, and back of chair tilt.[25]

Keyboards

The traditional keyboard is designed so that smaller, weaker muscles must do all of the work. These QWERTY keyboards are a main factor in causing repetitive stress syndrome.[26] There are keyboard designs that allow the largest fingers to do most of the work, but very few offices have had any luck introducing them because people who can type do not want to learn a new system. Keyboards should be adjusted so that the upper arm and lower arm are at a right angle (90 degrees) when the hands are on the keyboard. Hands and arms should be in a straight line, Usually, chair height adjustment can take care of these matters.

Most keyboards can be adjusted for slope. The keyboard slope should allow for a flat wrist position. If people have difficulty with wrist fatigue, a wrist cushion at the base of the keyboard should be tried so that the wrists can be rested on that cushion between keystrokes. There are a number of specialized keyboards that allow the user to change not only the slope of the keyboard but also the arrangement of keys and the placement of various function keys. Examples of such keyboards include:

Mykey Keyboard–ErgonomiXX, Inc., 525-K E. Market Street, Box 295, Leesburg, VA 22075, fax 703-771-1137. Mykey provides a QWERTY keyboard divided and sloped for natural hand positions, built-in palm rests, function keys on a clock face, center-point trackball, and rear, adjustable elevators for the keyboard.

Select-Ease Keyboard–Lexmark International, Inc., 740 New Circle Road, NW, Lexington, KY 40511, 800-438-2468, fax 206-936-7329. Select-Ease Keyboard provides a keyboard in two halves, which can be twisted, turned, or even split apart.

Monitors

Unlike typewriters, VDT devices are a source of light. This fact means that the placement of lights (including light from windows) needs to be carefully studied. External lights can create glare on the screen of the monitor. For example, try reading an automatic teller machine at a bank when the sun is shining directly on the screen. Reduction of overhead lighting, use of window blinds, and the use of antiglare polarized screens can reduce glare. When lighting is reduced, the worker may require special lighting for printed text or notes that must be read and input onto the computer screen.

Flicker on VDT devices is caused by the fact that when a beam of electrons excites a place on the CRT, it glows, but as soon as the beam leaves that spot, the spot begins to fade. If an image is to remain on the screen, it must be constantly refreshed. When this "refreshing" does not occur frequently enough, the display seems to blink (fade, bright, fade, bright) or flicker. If the image of the screen is very bright, flicker is more apparent. If the office area around a VDT screen is dark, the images on the screen will appear to flicker more. If the display shows dark characters on a light background, there will be more flicker because of the large amounts of lighted area on the screen.

Flicker is more noticeable in areas of the screen outside the direct line of sight. These peripheral areas seem to stop flickering when the user looks directly at them. The ways in which people perceive (or do not perceive) flicker varies greatly. As people get older they tend to notice flicker less. Flicker can be controlled by increasing the refresh rate on the screen or by a higher-quality screen coating that holds its luminescence longer. Each library media specialist will have to devise his/her own strategies for facilities planning and maintenance in his/her specific school situation. The authors offer the following suggestions:

1. *Include facilities maintenance in instructional planning.*
   As the library media specialist plans with teachers, he/she needs to have in mind the current state of affairs in the library media facility and its resources. If there is going to be a maintenance activity involving the computers in the library media center, what alternatives do we have to suggest? If a part of the collection is checked out for binding or repairs, what are the alternatives we can suggest? When the technology does not work, what can we suggest as an alternative?

2. *Be creative in the use of facilities and resources.*
   There are many ways to study a particular topic in the school setting. It is tempting to continue doing what has worked very well. However, often repeated use of particular resources, facility areas, and equipment means breakdowns, and damaged instructional resources. We know that technology has its own appeal, and that can cause a problem. Sometimes wear and tear on the library media center can be cut back by involving other libraries and community agencies in instructional planning and implementation. Think about all of the alternative ways we study a topic

and be sure to include resources and people from outside the regular school program in your planning.

3. *Move things around to meet different instructional needs.*
The authors cannot overemphasize the need for flexible use of facilities in the library media center. The library media specialist will often have to rearrange the facility to deal with different programs on a weekly basis. While this rearrangement does not mean moving everything, it often means creating a variety of instructional areas within the library media center. The more flexible the tables, partitions, shelves, and equipment carts are, the easier job we will have rearranging the center for different instructional events.

4. *Budget for the upgrading of the electrical system in the library media center.*
Remember to include funds in the school or media budgets because the media specialist can be sure that the demand for more electrical outlets and more electrical power will increase every year. Often electrical wiring strictly limits the flexibility of the library media center because where we want to do something there is no power. The chapter on facilities in this book makes some suggestions concerning creating a flexible electrical power system.

5. *Consider the whole school as the library media center.*
Part of the emphasis on flexibility in facilities has to do with the possibilities for physically moving parts of the media collection around the school. Such thinking requires that the school staff stop thinking about the library media center as a location and begin thinking about the library media program as something that can happen anyplace and anytime in the school. Library media instruction can take place in the classrooms, in the cafeteria, in the halls—wherever people need the service.

As schools begin to use local areas networks (LANs), it is possible to move some library media services onto the network and into all areas of the school. For example, a networked school can have the online catalog, CD-ROM information sources, and various instructional programs available throughout the school. The authors have seen too many library media centers where all of the varied technology-based information resources were crowded together into an already overcrowded media center. As information sources move toward more and more technology-based resources, library media specialists need to think in terms of "distributed services." The advantages of a computer terminal and telephone in each classroom are hard to overestimate.

In public and academic libraries there is now a strong move toward offering services that the library patrons can use from their homes and offices. The authors would suggest that this trend is also needed in schools by having information resources and personal services available to students, teachers, and parents by means of a local area network or a dial-in service.

Summary

School facilities and library media facilities are changing very rapidly as information resources become available in a wider variety of formats. Library media specialists need to plan for future library media services in terms of distributed services, which will make the program of the library media center available throughout the school. The next chapter will look at the implications of technology developments on library media programs in the school.

Notes

1. American Association of School Librarians and Association for Educational Communications and Technology, *Information Power: Building Partnerships for Learning* (Chicago: American Library Association, 1998), 109.

2. *Information Power*, 110.

3. Carol Truett, "A Survey of School and Public Children's Library Facilities: What Librarians Like, Dislike and Most Want to Change about their Libraries," *School Library Media Quarterly* 22, no. 2 (winter 1994), 91–97.

4. E. Jussim, "Personal Space and the Media Center," in *Media Center Facilities Design*, ed. Jane A. Hannigan and G. E. Estes (Chicago: American Library Association, 1978), 9.

5. Linda Lucas Walling, "Granting Each Equal Access," *School Library Media Quarterly* 20 (summer 1992), 16–22. Quote is from p. 218.

6. Truett, "A Survey," 93.

7. Walling, "Granting Each Equal Access," 221.

8. Truett, "A Survey," 94.

9. Jussim, "Personal Space," 8–9. Kay E. Vandergrift, "Persons and Environments," in *School Media Quarterly* 4, no. 4 (summer 1976), 311–16.

10. Walling, "Granting Each Equal Access." Kieth C. Wright and Judith F. Davie, *Serving the Disabled* (New York: Neal-Schuman, 1991).

11. Walling, "Granting Each Equal Access," 216.

12. Wright and Davie, *Serving the Disabled*, 29–46.

13. P. F. H. Rose, "Keeping a Steady Current," *Computer Shopper* 14, no. 8 (August 1994), 290–314.

14. Andrea A. Micaela and David Leroy Micaela, "Designing for Technology in Today's Libraries," *Computers in Libraries* 12, no. 10 (November 1992), 8–15. Quote is from p. 13. Idem, "People, Assistive Devices, Adaptive Furnishings, and Their Environment in Your Library," in *Preconference Institute on Library Buildings, Equipment, and the ADA—Compliance Issues and Solutions, New Orleans, 1993* (Chicago: American Library Association, 1996).

15. J. Y. Bryce, "Fiber vs. Metal," *Byte* 14, no. 1 (1989), 253–58. Quote is from p. 253.

16. Bryce, "Fiber vs. Metal," 255–56.

17. Micaela and Micaela, "Designing for Technology," 10.

18. D. A. Harvey, "Health and Safety First—Ergonomic Issues Have Taken a Backseat to Performance, Resulting in a Growing Tide of Computer-Related Injuries. Change is Needed Now!" *Byte* 16, no. 10 (October 1991), 119–28.

19. Michelle M. Robertson, "Ergonomic Considerations for the Human Environment: Color Treatment, Lighting, and Furniture Selection," *School Library Media Quarterly* 20, no. 4 (summer 1992), 211–15.

20. Harvey, "Health and Safety First," 119–128.

21. Tim McKimmie and Janet Smith, "The ELF in Your Library," *Computers in Libraries* 14, no. 8 (September 1994), 16–20.

22. C. Rubin, "Workstation Comfort Boosts the Bottomline—Companies Should Prepare to Adapt Work Areas to Meet New Guidelines," *MacWEEK* 8, no. 10 (January 3, 1994), 101–03.

23. "Ergonomic Regulation," *PC World* 12, no. 1 (January 1, 1994), 72.

24. Kieth C. Wright, *Workstations and Local Area Networks for Libraries* (Chicago: American Library Association, 1993), based on a preliminary draft of the Library of Congress Collections Services VDT Ergonomics Committee report: Ergonomics and VDT Use, finally issued 1991 and reissued 1992. Printed in *Computers in Libraries* 13, no. 5 (May 1993), 52–53.

25. Micaela and Micaela, "Designing for Technology," 15.

26. K. Seidel, "As RSIs Skyrocket, Companies Are Finally Taking Ergonomics Seriously," *PC Week* 10, no. 25 (June 28, 1993), 126.

11

Technology Principles

People have always lived and worked in a "technological society," and the adoption of new technologies is a recurring issue. What is different about today?—the pace of technological change, the scope of its effects (global and beyond), the complexity and interdependence of advanced technological subsystems, and technology's value and place within the culture.[1]

Introduction—The Digital Revolution

There is a great deal of hype about the impact of computer-related technologies on our lives. But we have always lived with some technologies—we could not have developed civilization without them. As Kerka states: "Technology has existed throughout history as the processes and products by which humans have coped with and changed their environment. It can be considered the tools that extend human capabilities, the systems within which the tools are used, and an approach to the management of the environment."[2] Current computer-related technologies allow us to transform all forms of information into a digital format and to transmit that information at high rates of speed to any place in the world. Nicholas Negroponte, founder of the Massachusetts Institute of Technology's Media Laboratory, and Alvin Toffler, author and social critic, have called this digital information age the Third Wave. They contend that the world has experienced three major changes, or waves, in areas such as communications and employment. The third wave, on which we are riding, is characterized by higher levels of education and constant retraining, using telecommunication controlled and disseminated by individuals and organizations via computers.[3] In this information world, Ogden estimates that knowledge is doubling every 16 months.[4] Craver notes that rapid changes in technology and the skills needed to compete successfully in the workforce will force higher and different standards in education. She emphasizes that the information skills—the ability to acquire, organize, and use information—will be critical in such a society and that the library media program can provide education in these critical areas.[5]

The impact of rapidly changing technology on the workforce is highlighted by Marcusse, who points out that the future information-age technology will allow workers to telecommute, live anywhere, and work more efficiently. As this flexibility increases, lifestyle values are becoming more of a priority for both employees and companies. As employers expect more productivity, employees will want more flexibility about hours, places of work, and work groups. The changes brought about by new information technologies also present enormous social challenges that are only beginning to be addressed.[6]

The two chief challenges are: learning to cope with an increasing pace of change brought about by the changing technology, and coming to terms with a sudden, significant expansion of the definition of what it means to be literate in an information-based, high-tech society and economy. The Library Instruction Round Table of the American Library Association points out that bibliographic instruction, which focuses on the need to make library patrons become more proficient in locating and using information, is a major contributor to information literacy in this new information age.[7] This chapter presents a series of technology principles together with implications for future school programs and the related school library media implications.

Libraries Will Have Multiformat Collections

Some writers have argued that printed materials are now irrelevant and that all libraries should move to digital formats of information located on-site or at remote sites so that library patrons can access information from personal computers in their homes and offices. They go on to suggest that physical libraries may disappear and the role of librarians will change so that they become trainers of individuals seeking information. They urge that libraries of all types move aggressively into digitized information services and become "virtual libraries."[8] The Miller and Shontz studies of school library expenses suggest that as school libraries invest increasing funds in computer-related technologies, they spend less and less on print materials.[9] This pursuit of the digital or virtual library may be a major mistake.

Crawford suggests that the virtual or digital libraries are impossible, and the ideal of an all-encompassing solution is unrealistic because of costs and the state of technology. He stresses the continuing valuable roles of libraries as places for personal enrichment and places to learn more about things and suggests that these roles will merge with the new technologies to make the library a constantly evolving institution.[10] In a 1995 book, *Future Libraries: Dreams, Madness, and Reality*, Crawford and Gorman argue that policy makers and library administrators are being drawn uncritically to the idea of the virtual library and the "library without walls."[11] These webs of electronic resources are supposed to displace books, physical libraries, and most library staff.

Some librarians believe the virtual library to be imminent, adequate, and cost-effective. Crawford and Gorman offer a counter-argument to "technolust," which assumes that every new technological development is worthwhile. They offer ways in which librarians can embrace advanced technologies while retaining their libraries' role as service-oriented repositories of all formats of organized information and knowledge. They present evidence of the continuing value of books and print collections among diverse media.

Funded by the W. K. Kellogg Foundation, the Benton Foundation interviewed library leaders, conducted a public opinion survey, and held a conference of Kellogg's Human Resources for Information Systems Management grantees to assess the challenges libraries face in the digital age. The report summarizes the current situation in the following manner:

> With the role and impact of personal computers still fluid in this emerging digital world, now is the time for libraries to seize the opportunity and define their role with an aggressive public education campaign. . . . Do not shy away from the need to come up with new community-based alliances for libraries—strategic partnerships that can weave a network of community public service information providers to enhance each other's value . . . to the communities they service.[12]

While the authors use many of the new computer-based technologies on a daily basis for teaching, research, and writing, we would argue for a school library media center and a program that stresses the value of all formats of information and, in particular, the joys and values of reading as a part of lifelong enrichment and empowerment. We have noticed that at all library association meetings the longest lines and biggest crowds are found at the booths featuring children's book authors and illustrators who are autographing their latest efforts. We firmly believe that the joys of reading by yourself, reading aloud, and learning to put good ideas on paper so that others can enjoy them will continue to be significant forces in our lives.

The authors do not disparage other formats. Watching students access facts, graphics, or a series of sounds related to a particular topic, then convert these into presentations, clearly illustrates the usefulness of these formats. Much of the excitement about multimedia has to do with the fact that information available at a multimedia workstation can be retrieved, converted, transmitted, and "morphed" into new and interesting formats.

The library media program can provide many opportunities for students and teachers to experience new ways of learning and new ways of working together in flexible groups. As the emerging center of technologically based information services, the library media center has access to information in many formats: print, video, audio, digital, remote, local. Library media specialists not only have access to information and related equipment, but, more importantly, they have a long tradition of using various information formats for instructional purposes.

The library media program provides access to information, as well as access to many of the computer-based tools that allow students and teachers to transform those formats to meet their own instructional needs. Some people are quite critical about the newest multimedia wave because they remember the earlier waves—programmed learning, 16mm film loops, educational television—which were promoted as the solution to all educational problems. However, watching student groups accessing and using information about their assigned topic from paperback almanacs, Grolier's CD-based encyclopedia, magazines, and the World Wide Web will convince the most skeptical observer that these new formats can enhance learning experiences and allow students to be creative in many new ways. Multiple formats also allow for students and teachers to become critical selectors and users of information appropriate to their tasks.

Effective use of multimedia in the school and library media center is not an easy task. Having access to a wide range of media formats is not the same thing as being able to use these formats creatively and critically. It seems to the authors that true literacy involves the ability to read critically and to create "productions" in a number of formats. For many years library media specialists have helped children in the process of critically evaluating print materials—Is this story really true? How are stories, biographies, and history different? How are stories and illustrations created? What makes a good story? How do you write a story? Compare these two versions; which one do you like and why? Can you finish this story? What is the difference between fiction and fact?

These questions are raised in the context of having students actually create stories, biographies, family histories, factual reports, and so on. They are reinforced by visits from local and nationally famous authors, illustrators, storytellers or by videos of those individuals. All these efforts attempt to develop the students' critical media literacy.

The same process can be broadened to include a variety of computer-related media. Students need to understand how television programs are made. They need to acquire, active "behind the television camera" skills that develop their awareness of the process of creating television. They need instructional programs that enable them (at a very early age) to distinguish between reality and what television commercials say. Computer programs that allow students to create illustrated stories, utilize sound in their stories, and add video to their stories can be used in the same ways. The general rule can be stated simply: Help the students develop the necessary critical skills so that they become active, selective users and creators of all information formats, not just passive, uncritical receivers of what is presented to them.

Students Must Be Prepared
for Lifetime Learning

Traditional paradigms of education assumed that individuals could be educated once and for all for the jobs they would hold for all time. But workplaces are changing rapidly, requiring flexibility in job assignments and frequent retraining. Sullivan stresses the increasing need for flexibility in training and the workplace and lists four traditional workplace paradigms that must be challenged: (1) equating time spent at the office with productivity; (2) equating long hours with dedication or commitment; (3) equating the ability to watch employees with the ability to control their work; and (4) equating an office full of employees with teamwork.[13]

Educators need to rethink the educational experiences that students have during their stay in school. We can raise some interesting questions:

1. Are we modeling educational practices that encourage students to learn new ways of doing things and new ways of thinking?

2. Do students have opportunities to learn to work effectively in changing group settings, both in the school and in the community's workplaces?

3. Do students gain the ability to take responsibility for their learning and reporting on that learning without constantly being watched?

4. Does the educational process cultivate lifelong learning skills and a love of acquiring new skills throughout life?

As we move toward lifelong learning and away from the factory model of education, David cites Dryer and Ringstaff on the shift in teachers' beliefs and practices:

From	To
Teacher roles	
Instruction	Construction
Teacher-centered	Learner-centered
Didactic	Interactive
Fact teller	Collaborator
Always expert	Sometimes learner
Student roles	
Listener	Collaborator
Always learner	Sometimes expert
Instructional goals	
Facts	Relationships
Memorization	Inquiry and Invention
Concept of knowledge	
Accumulation of facts	Transformation of facts
Demonstration of success	
Quantity of facts	Quality of understanding
Assessment	
Norm-referenced	Criterion-referenced
Multiple-choice instruments	Portfolios and performances[14]

Every school curriculum and every library media program must be reexamined to see if those programs are pushing students toward the realization of the need for continued learning and skill development. Often the traditional testing programs in public education do not support continued learning. It is very easy for a standardized test-based school program to become a program in which teachers must teach and students must learn specific things for a specific target date—*the test!* After that date it is assumed that the learning can be dropped. When teaching in the classroom or library media center is teacher-centered, the assumption is made that the teacher knows the information essential to success and that the educational process involves transferring that information to the students and testing to see that they have learned it.

Such traditional views of education assumed that there was a discrete body of knowledge that could be learned once and then used throughout life. Jobs were assumed to require certain specific skills that could be learned and used as long as the individual worked. None of these assumptions is true. The best library media programs should raise questions in the students' minds; questions that require students to explore outside-the-school information resources—families, public libraries, government agencies, religious organizations, universities, and social agencies. Whenever possible, we should avoid the definitive answer to a student's question. It is far better to say, "Let's find out" and work with the student using some information resource so that you discover the answer (or the lack of an answer) together. Computer-related technologies and telecommunications simply extend "Let's find out" into the world. Our students should leave school with a longer list of questions to be answered than the list of questions they first brought to school. Little children are often bothersome because they keep asking "Why?" We want our students to grow in their abilities to seek out answers to "why" questions. We want them to bother higher education, their employers, and the whole society with those questions. The future "good" society demands citizens who can articulate these "why" questions to their leaders and select leaders who can give appropriate answers.

Being able to present information in a variety of formats allows for the comparative evaluation of a wide range of resources. For example, different print resources often provide different answers to the same question. How do we evaluate these different answers and select one? Many institutions and businesses provide search programs on the World Wide Web. If students search for the same information using different programs (AltaVista, Lycos, Web Crawler, Unisearch), they will come up with varied answers. Again, the question is how to evaluate the answers given. These higher order thinking skills are essential to success in the future world.

The authors know that we may be asking for the impossible and are very conscious of the extreme pressures put on teachers and media specialists by the current trend toward standardized or criterion-referenced testing. State and federal agencies are talking about tying student test results to teachers' pay. These pressures can make educators forget what they are about and be forced to prepare students for testing procedures which they will never meet again in life. These tests are used to evaluate students' current information store rather than their critical thinking and learning abilities. No adult faces standardized or criterion-referenced testing in the workplace.

Still, we believe that our students will need to learn new skills and concepts again and again throughout their lives and that our best instructional programs will prepare students who are able to assess critically their current situation, find out what they need to learn, and know where they can go to get the information they need to do that learning. These are skills that students can indeed use throughout their lives.

Computer-Based Communication Is Increasingly Important

In an article about association management in the information age, Benjamin suggests that there are nine important areas of technology that associations will need to consider and/or implement during the next several years if they want to transform their operations, better serve their members, and keep pace with competitors: (1) the Internet, (2) bulletin boards, (3) computers with more power, (4) the electronic office, (5) digital printing and imaging, (6) multimedia on the desktop, (7) interactive multimedia training, (8) telephone and satellite communication, and (9) intellectual property.[15]

Voluntary associations that survive will learn to use these technologies successfully with their clients. We can apply the same criteria to K–12 education and ask how well we are doing in utilizing these technologies as integrated parts of the school's curriculum and administration.

There is no point to computer-based technologies or any other resource in the library media center if they cannot be utilized in the instructional program of the particular school. The authors want to be completely clear about this issue: No communication system or device has any value if it cannot be used to support the instructional program of the school and the library media program in that context. We have seen too many cute technological devices that were promoted to schools and often advertised as instructional support devices go unused or be misused. Students will leave the school and emerge into a world of work where all information and communication tools are evaluated on the basis of their usefulness in the particular business or service. The same principle applies to the school: those resources we have must be effective as a part of the total curriculum.

In the midst of all this technological development, library media specialists will need to evaluate the claims of new technological offerings and understand that any new formats and processes require staff development for teachers and training for students if the formats are to be integrated into the school's instructional program. Much information is now available in digital formats, and even more information will be available in that format in the future. Teachers and students will need to be able to find, retrieve, read, reorganize, and share information in the digital format.

The library media center provides an environment in which teachers and students can learn the essential skills for working in a telecommunications-based world. Beginning with a computer-based catalog and circulation system, the library media center provides experience with manipulating a very large database of information on the basis of subject index terms, key words, formats of material, authors, and dates. The concept to finding information using different search strategies clearly applies to many work/life situations in modern business and education. Providing encyclopedic information on CD-ROMs allows teachers and students to contrast the search strategies used with the online catalog with those used in the CD-ROM product. Can we still do key word searches? Can we search for specific formats of information? What other help is given the use of the CD-ROM?

Access to databases outside the school through subscriptions to Dialog or the World Wide Web adds another learning dimension to this equation. Can we use the same search strategies here as we used with the online catalog or the CD-ROM? What information can we find at remote sites that we cannot find in our catalog or on CD-ROMS? How is information organized on the World Wide Web? Why is spelling the words correctly so important?

Teachers and students need exposure to already constructed databases of information; in part, because they need to learn how it should not be done! Once they have some experience with the ways in which other people have organized information, students and teachers should have the opportunity to construct their own database using simple "flat" database or spreadsheet software such as that which is found in Microsoft Works or Filemaker Pro. Vast numbers of freeware or shareware programs exist in almost every computer language for this purpose. Designing and implementing even a very simple database of information moves the student from user of a system toward the more critically important role of producer of a system.

An example in elementary school might be a survey of your classmates including height, favorite food, favorite color, favorite musical entertainer. Once this data is collected it can be manipulated by database or spreadsheet software. Primary grade students may be instructed on manually creating a graph of information which can then be placed in a simple graphic program. Older students can enter data in a spreadsheet and find out things like the most popular food, the number of students who like blue, the average height of the class. They could also be instructed in how to create a database with fields for each type of information and how to create simple reports on the basis of that information, as well as graphic displays in color on the computer.

Within the instructional program of the library media center, students could construct a simple database of favorite books with fields where they list the author's name, the class number, the title, the publisher, the date, and a note section where they make comments. Similar databases could be constructed around regional or state-level book award programs or in cooperative programs with the public library where a database allows for comments on the summer reading list. The point behind all of these activities is to provide experience both as a consumer of computer-based information systems and as a designer and critic of such systems. All computer-related technology learning must be active and critically aware. Again the emphasis is on moving the student from a passive receiver of information to an active participant in the creation and critique of information sources and services.

Learning Becomes Flexible
in Time and Place

The traditional concept of education and work centered around collecting the resources for work or learning at a site and then transporting the workers or learners to that site for a specified period of time. During that time, work was done and learning took place. Everyone realizes that teachers and students learn a great deal outside the regular school day and building. Equally, we know from our own experience that people take work home, on business trips, and on vacation. The traditional image of the work or learning place has remained strong. Easily accessible communications technology—cellular phones, notebook computers, high speed telecommunications, the Internet—is breaking down that traditional image in work and education.

Increasingly accessible communications means that people will work, play, and learn in a wide variety of settings and times. We see rapid changes in the workplace as many workers choose to work flexible hours by creating portable work-sites that they can use at home, on an airplane, or at the beach. Teachers and students have access to mass media and individually selected resources at home, at the mall, and in restaurants. Adults and children take courses via distance education programs in which they can see, hear, and talk with other students. Many courses are offered via the World Wide Web and are accessed not only by those who pay tuition but by anyone who has access to the home page address of the program.

It is possible to envision future educational programs that will be accessible at a particular place but will also be accessible anytime and from anyplace. Such programs would provide direct instruction, curricular materials, assignments, testing and evaluation, and background information materials via the Internet or other telecommunication channels. Students would study, discuss, ask questions, and demonstrate their learning via these systems. The Alfred P. Sloan Foundation's *Program in Learning Outside the Classroom* focuses on asynchronous delivery of education using remote resources.[16] Remote resources in this context can mean other people, library resources, or software simulations. Asynchronous means that access to any remote resource is at the student's convenience in terms of time and place.

The Sloan program uses the illustration of a student contacting a colleague or a teacher through e-mail, or engaging in discussion with a group through a conferencing system or bulletin board, collaborating interactively with other students in a team project that requires problem analysis, discussion, spreadsheet analysis or report-preparation through a commercial groupware package.

Traditional lectures could be transmitted through computers or on videotape or CD-ROM, allowing us to envisage "distributed classes" in the same way we think of in-school classes. Asynchronous computer networks have the potential to improve contact with teachers, other individuals, and community agencies. Learning has the potential of becoming self-paced: students can progress through a course of study as their learning style and time allow. For example, a motivated student could progress more rapidly; students who are motivated but find they cannot keep up the pace may be able to slow down and take longer to complete an instructional unit.

Of course, correspondence schools have operated this model for many years, often with a high degree of success by utilizing regular mail to provide students with printed and video materials for learning and a means of assessing that learning. In the last decade, a number of these programs began to provide instant access to assistance through 800 telephone numbers. More recently, they have begun to utilize voice mail systems so that students can "dial a lesson" through their telephone. As Internet access becomes more common, we are beginning to see all types of educational institutions offering educational programs through those systems. In such systems the learners select the time and place for learning and also select when they will have their learning assessed by the program. Programs may provide local face-to-face discussion groups as a part of these programs or may provide e-mail listservs for such discussions.

Earlier in this book, a strong case was made for flexible scheduling of instruction in the library media center. Indeed, a strong case is made for more flexible scheduling throughout the total school program. Such flexibility makes sense in terms of the ways in which people learn and the differences in subject areas in the curriculum. Flexible scheduling allows for adapting *time* to *people* and *subject*, rather than *people* and *subject* to *time*.

Flexibility is also important because of the ways in which the worlds of work and learning are changing. More and more institutions in our society are moving away from the rigidly scheduled work processes of the industrial age into more flexible work patterns that allow for work to be done at different locations, in different time frames, and with different groupings of people skills. A cooperative, planned, instructional program that involves classroom activities, library media center activities, and community-based activities prepares students for the emerging world of work and leisure.

Computer-related technologies make possible the creation of a library media program that is accessible at anytime from anyplace. Typically, such access begins when the online catalog of the library media program is made accessible through telecommunications. Such access can be created as a dial-in service so that teachers, students, and the public can access the online catalog from other sites, using a modem and a telecommunications software package. Some schools and school systems are now creating World Wide Web home pages and can create an access point to the library media online catalog as a part of that home page system.

The library media specialist in his/her role as instructional consultant should assist teachers in integrating computer-related technologies into the curriculum. Planning is essential here because utilizing the technology appropriately often means learning how to use it yourself, giving the teacher instructions, and assisting with the instruction with students. The library media specialist should always plan for alternatives. What are we going to do in this module if the computer stops? This massive task can sometimes be made less burdensome by using the "each one, teach one" philosophy in which a small group of students comes to work with the library media specialist on a new program package. They then bring one other person with them and offer instruction to that person, who in turn instructs another person. Here we are moving from the student as learner only to the student as learner and expert. Some schools have found that such teaching by older students is particularly helpful in the primary grades and preschool settings.

Public Agencies May
Be a Source of Equity

The equity of access issue is increasingly critical as the economic distance between the very rich and the rest of us increases. The importance of this issue was highlighted during July 1996 when the *Atlanta Journal–Constitution* devoted a full week of editorials to the implications of the growing economic gap in America which has spawned a kind of economic social Darwinism that states, "Those who have no resources for health, education, and welfare have created the situation in which they exist and deserve the consequences."

In support of equity of access, the American Library Association provided testimony during the 1996 hearings on the Telecommunications Act of 1996. On April 12, 1996, ALA President Betty Turock testified before the FCC-Joint Board on how discounted telecommunications rates for libraries and schools should be implemented and the value of telecommunications to the American public.

> The library mission is to provide the American public with access to the whole world of electronic information. . . . "Technology is changing rapidly, and many of the most interesting and useful information services are at the leading edge. Libraries need more than a telephone and modem. They need discounted access to the full range of telecommunications services.[17]

The Telecommunications Act of 1996 mandates, for the first time, that libraries and schools be considered universal service providers. In her testimony, Turock offered the following recommendations from ALA:

1. Any telecommunication service offered by a carrier should be available to libraries at a discount.

2. Core universal services for the residential consumers should be defined, at the very least, as the level of technology required for entry-level access to the Internet.

3. Any telecommunication service offered commercially should be made available to libraries at the lower of either the lowest price offered to any customer or the Total Service Long Run Incremental Cost, which covers a company's cost of offering a service and is similar to a wholesale price.

4. Carriers should be required to certify that their rate for libraries is the lowest available.

5. Libraries and schools in rural, insular, and high-cost areas should receive deeper discounts because of the special barriers to affordable connections.[18]

Seen in a global context, the differences between computer-related technology-rich nations and nations with very limited technology continue to grow. These problems have become so critical that the United Nations called a World Summit for Social Development in Copenhagen, Denmark, in March 1995. The conference officially marked the 50th anniversary of the United Nations. Its formal agenda focused on three core issues: enhanced social integration, poverty reduction (today over a billion people, one-fifth of the human race, subsist on an annual per-head income of less than U.S. $1 per day), and expanding productive employment (in sub-Saharan Africa, not one country has had single-digit unemployment since the 1970s). The summit summarized the problems and potentials in this way:

> We are witnessing in countries throughout the world the expansion of prosperity for some, unfortunately accompanied by an expansion of unspeakable poverty for others. This glaring contradiction is unacceptable and needs to be corrected through urgent actions. Globalization, which is a consequence of increased human mobility, enhanced communications, greatly increased trade and capital flows, and technological developments, opens new opportunities for sustained economic growth and development of the world economy, particularly in developing countries. Globalization also permits countries to share experiences and to learn from one another's achievements and difficulties, and promotes a cross-fertilization of ideals, cultural values and aspirations. At the same time, the rapid processes of change and adjustment have been accompanied by intensified poverty, unemployment and social disintegration. Threats to human well-being, such as environmental risks, have also been globalized.[19]

If the trend toward increasing distance between rich and poor continues, the libraries—public and school—may be the only places where millions of children and their families have access to the tools of the information society. It is probably not good social policy to force citizens into the use of public institutions like hospitals, social agencies, and schools. Freedom should mean the ability to make choices for oneself and for one's children. However, it is good social policy to suggest that parents and students who make the choice to use public schools or who must use those schools have the best possible opportunities to participate in the new ways of learning and working that are emerging in our society.

As the distance between the rich and the poor grows in our society, there is a dangerous tendency for the rich to attempt to enforce the social Darwinism view that the conditions of the less rich are the fault of those individuals, and the conditions of the rich are the reward of social selection. In 1998, Congress passed and the

President signed a welfare reform package that will ultimately abandon many poor people and their children. The current attempts to remove legal immigrants and their children from social services, health, and educational programs is yet another illustration of this trend.

Libraries of all types should contain and make available a wide variety of information resources that would otherwise be unavailable to people. In cooperation with public libraries, school library media programs need to reclaim the historic role of serving as the people's university. An increasing number of public school students will be drawn from the culturally and linguistically diverse elements of our population. Typically, these students and their parents will not have had equal employment opportunities and will be poor. Reclaiming this role will call into question a number of current practices in school library media centers. If the library media center is to be a resource for the community of people who will otherwise be left out, then we can raise the following questions:

1. *Who are our allies in this work?*
   Are there other community and educational agencies seeking to empower people's lives so that they can participate in work, leisure, and the political process? If so, what can we do to cooperate with them in this joint effort?

2. *Does the current collection development policy of the school library media center reflect this changing user population?*
   The authors have argued throughout this book that all materials and programs in the library media center must be curriculum-related. But if your service population changes to include the parents of children and the community, we may need to rethink the policy, just as we may need to rethink the curriculum of the school. Schools that take the involvement of parents and community very seriously are now faced with this gigantic rethinking task.

3. *Do the hours of operation serve our redefined user groups?*
   Library media centers have traditionally been open for use when the school was open. In other areas, such as sports, we have realized that we must provide additional time, staffing, and transportation in order to serve that population. It is probable that the changing concept of user groups will force school libraries to adjust their hours—earlier in the morning, after school, and weekends. If we adjust hours, we will be faced with adjusting staffing

and service patterns. We might even consider adjusting instruction so that parents, community, and students can participate in the instructional program at times appropriate to their lives! The authors would argue for increasing access to the library media collection through changing the hours of the school program to conform with the life patterns of our user population.

4. *Do we have the skills that are essential to work with the populations we serve?*
   Most librarians come from English-speaking, middle-class backgrounds and have limited experience of other cultures and traditions. The future will demand skills in several languages in spite of the efforts to make English the official language of the United States. Even more important, experience with and knowledge of the histories, stereotypes, and values of other cultures will become essential. The authors believe that future school library media specialists will need to develop true multicultural perspectives through staff development and preservice programs that immerse media specialists in other cultures. It is probable that library media programs will need staff members who can speak at least one other language—probably Spanish.

Censorship Increases as Access to Information Increases

The American Library Association and its Office of Intellectual Freedom have a long history of supporting the right to read against a variety of individual, religious, and governmental censors. All librarians know that censorship is not a new thing brought on by computer-related technologies. Governments, religious authorities, and parents have always wanted to protect their children and citizens from harmful influences. Some individuals have sought to use the force of government to protect everyone from harmful influences, as perceived by those individuals. They express their versions of the truth freely in public and in print. The American Library Association has long affirmed the right to read in the Library Bill of Rights:

> The American Library Association affirms that all libraries are forums for information and ideas, and that the following basic policies should guide their services.

1. Books and other library resources should be provided for the interest, information, and enlightenment of all people of the community the library serves. Materials should not be excluded because of the origin, background, or views of those contributing to their creation.

2. Libraries should provide materials and information presenting all points of view on current and historical issues. Materials should not be proscribed or removed because of partisan or doctrinal disapproval.

3. Libraries should challenge censorship in the fulfillment of their responsibility to provide information and enlightenment.

4. Libraries should cooperate with all persons and groups concerned with resisting abridgment of free expression and free access to ideas.

5. A person's right to use a library should not be denied or abridged because of origin, age, background, or views.

6. Libraries which make exhibit spaces and meeting rooms available to the public they serve should make such facilities available on an equitable basis, regardless of the beliefs or affiliations of individuals or groups requesting their use.

(Adopted June 18, 1948; amended February 2, 1961, and January 23, 1980, by the ALA Council)[20]

Sometimes the high ideal of protection has taken on the aspect of protecting individuals and groups from the truth—because that truth was too revealing, ugly, or incriminating. Sometimes those in authority have been unsure of their own grasp on the truth and have tried to strengthen their view of the truth by insisting that their truth was the only truth. Whatever the motives, censorship seems to increase as our global society provides access to more and more information containing widely diverse views of almost any topic.

The history of the Communications Decency Act further illustrates government attempts to "protect" citizens from specific types of information. The idea of the Communications Decency Act was generated by Senator Jim Exon (D-Nebraska) after he viewed a segment on "Dateline NBC" in July of 1994, which portrayed the Internet as nothing more than a dumping ground for pornographic material. Exon was unsuccessful in his first attempt to pass an amendment restricting such material on the Internet. Backed by President Clinton, Senator Patrick Leahy (D-Vermont) later attempted to convince Congress that government restrictions of the

Internet were not necessary. He proposed that the Department of Justice and the Commerce Department first study how users could self-select content before enacting vague and overly restrictive legislation. Leahy's attempt failed.

In July 1995, the Senate passed the Communications Decency Act (84 to 16), which set fines of up to $100,000 and two years in prison for violations. Internet access providers would also be held liable for offensive material on their servers posted by users. The bill was defeated in the House of Representatives and Representatives Chris Cox (R-California) and Ron Wyden (D-Oregon) proposed the Cox-Wyden Amendment, which passed in the House (420 to 4). Also known as the "Internet Freedom and Online Family Empowerment" amendment, it prohibited the Federal Communications Commission from regulating the Internet and relieved access providers from liability regarding the material their customers posted.

Though the Cox-Wyden Amendment still censored the Internet to a certain extent, it was much more specific and liberal as to what material the government considered obscene. When the amendment reached the Senate, Exon added in a few changes. The major change was switching the specific and more liberal term "harmful to minors" to "indecency," which is very vague and open to varied interpretations. The amendment passed in the Senate and was enacted on February 1, 1996, with these changes intact, becoming the Communications Decency Act of 1996. President Clinton signed the amendment February 8, 1996.

A number of organizations, including the American Library Association, filed lawsuits to have the CDA declared unconstitutional. These organizations argued that:

1. The Internet is a unique communications medium, which deserves First Amendment protections at least as broad as those afforded to print media. Individual users and parents, not the Federal Government, should determine for themselves and their children what material comes into their homes based on their tastes and values.

2. The CDA will be ineffective at protecting children from "indecent" or "patently" offensive material online.

Many of these organizations cited their own official position statements in support of the First Amendment to the Constitution of the United States. A three-judge federal panel in Philadelphia ruled that the CDA was unconstitutional on June 12, 1996. The ruling paved the way for the Supreme Court to overturn the law. The case to challenge the Communications Decency Act was brought by the Citizens Internet Empowerment Coalition and the American Civil Liberties Union. The American Library Association was a member of this coalition. The Clinton administration has pledged to continue to support the current law before the Supreme Court. At this writing, another attempt is being made in Congress to get legislation on the books that would restrict access to the Internet and provide criminal penalties.

In the final hours of the 105th Congress, Republican leaders slipped into the last mega-spending bill a measure that cyber-activists have dubbed the "Spawn of CDA." The measure, which is identical to the "Child On-Line Protection Act" (HR 3783) proposed by Representative Michael Oxley (R-Ohio), seeks to punish commercial distributors of material deemed harmful to minors but would inevitably block adults from obtaining a wide variety of online materials. The bill was signed by President Clinton despite serious constitutional concerns raised by his own Justice Department. This new version of the CDA contains many of the same constitutional defects as its predecessor, which was unanimously struck down last year by the Supreme Court in *Reno v. ACLU*. Ironically, if CDA II had been law in mid-September 1998, even news sites that published the Starr Report and carry advertising or charge for access might have been subject to criminal prosecution.[21]

Every school library media specialist should have a collection development policy statement that details (1) the process by which materials are selected for the school library program, (2) the role of the media advisory committee in this process, (3) the curriculum as the focus of the collection development program, and (4) the formal procedure through which challenges are handled by the local school and the school system. Every school district media program should have school board approved policy and procedures on handling formal and informal challenges to materials in the curriculum, in professional literature collections, and in local school media centers. In the area of censorship, the well-planned response should be in place before the censorship attempts are made. All libraries can count on being challenged about items in their collections. The American Association of School Librarians has issued a position statement concerning access to resources and services in school library media programs:

Access to Resources and Services in the School Library Media Program: An Interpretation of the Library Bill of Rights

The school library media program plays a unique role in promoting intellectual freedom. It serves as a point of voluntary access to information and ideas and as a learning laboratory for students as they acquire critical thinking and problem solving skills needed in a pluralistic society. Although the educational level and program of the school necessarily shape the resources and services of a school library media program the principles of the LIBRARY BILL OF RIGHTS apply equally to all libraries, including school library media programs.

School library media professionals assume a leadership role in promoting the principles of intellectual freedom within the school by providing resources and services that create and sustain an atmosphere of free inquiry. School library media professionals work closely with teachers to integrate instructional activities in classroom units designed to equip students to locate, evaluate, and use a broad range of ideas effectively. Through resources, programming, and educational processes, students and teachers experience the free and robust debate characteristic of a democratic society.[22]

Access to electronic information sources such as the Internet pose additional problems and require that schools adopt acceptable-use policies that offer teachers, students, and parents guidance on what instructional uses of the Internet are appropriate to the instructional goals of the school. A search of the World Wide Web reveals that most electronic network systems—educational and commercial—now have acceptable use policies. Library media specialists and media advisory committees do not need to invent their own policies statements. Sources on acceptable use policies are found at the end of this chapter.

Information Privacy Is a Critical Civil Right

Because all the new information sources are interconnected, personal information privacy—the ability to personally control information about oneself—is fast becoming one of the most important ethical issues of the information age. Information technology developments, coupled with the increasing value of information to decision makers, are causing a rising tide of concern about personal information privacy. Even in the face of the Saudi Arabian bombing of United States facilities, the TWA 800 disaster, and the Olympic Park bombing (July 1996), Congress was unable to pass an emergency terrorism bill because of concerns about expanded wiretapping and the impact of that ability on the private lives of citizens. If business and education do not choose to confront the privacy issues in their organizations, it is likely that levels of concern will continue to rise and that citizens will look to their government for relief.[23] Glastonbury and LaMendola point to a list of individuals' rights, which they claim are reasonable for all to expect in relation to computer-based data about themselves, and which include the following rights: (1) to individual autonomy, (2) to be left alone, (3) to a private life, (4) to control information about ourselves, (5) to limit accessibility, and (6) to exclusive control of access to private realms.[24]

A part of the library media program is the valuing of information privacy. Modern online circulation systems allow each teacher and student to have a user identification (usually a number). As these identification numbers are given out, the need to keep each person's number confidential should be stressed. The media advisory committee should work out policy and procedure for dealing with students who use the identification numbers of other students. Library media centers often have a policy about what happens when students have books overdue. Typically, students cannot check out other books until the overdue books are returned. Use of another person's identification is more serious than penalties for overdue books and the media advisory committee needs to consider the possibility of removing borrowing privileges for a period of time. In schools that have a student court, identification forgery should be handled as a serious offense by that tribunal.

Circulation systems that are used by teachers and student assistants should have a password required to get a listing of materials checked out by other people. No one but the library media specialist should have access to this checkout list. In fact, many states, including the authors' home state of North Carolina, have statutes protecting the library user's checkout list. Again, the reason for this policy should be publicly stated in orientations, faculty meetings, and PSTA sessions: We value the information privacy of our students, staff, and parents. Many instructional software programs like *Accelerated Reader* have testing packages that require a password. The same principle applies here. Each student has a private password which is not to be shared with other students. Violations of the privacy of teachers, students, or parents should be handled as serious breaches of the code of conduct of the school.

Summary

This chapter has presented a number of future implications for education and the library media programs in general. The authors believe that library media specialists should take leadership roles in defining what the shape and impact of the future will be on education. Much of the future discussion has focused on computer-related communications technologies and their potential; we have tried to move that future discussion toward a consideration of the human factors involved. How will people develop the skills, have the opportunities, and secure their rights in the future? Throughout this book, we have suggested a proactive stance in relation to defining the process and instruction for students. The next chapter considers the future for school library media programs, using the model of high-reliability organizations.

Acceptable Use Policies (AUP)

Allen County Public Library. *Use of Computer Resources*. Ft. Wayne: The Library, 1997. URL source: http://www.acpl.lib.in.us/about_acpl/index/library_policies.html#anchor477720.

American Library Association. *Free Access to Libraries for Minors: An Interpretation of the Library Bill of Rights*. I (Adopted 30 June 1972; amended 1 July 1981; 3 July 1991, by the ALA Council. URL source: ftp://ftp.eff.org/pub/CAF/library/access.minors.ala.

Clancy J. Wolf. *Developing a School or District "Acceptable Use Policy" for Student and Staff Access to the Internet*. Bremerton, Wash.: Olympic Educational Services District 114, 1994. URL source: gopher://inspire.ospi.wednet.edu:700/00/Accept_Use_Policies/IN_policies.txt.

Dave Kinnaman. *Critiquing Acceptable Use Policies*. 1995. URL source: http://www.io.com/~kinnaman/aupessay.html.

Houston Independent School District. *Armadillo Collection of Acceptable Use Policies*. Houston: HISD-Armadillo, n.d. URL source: http://www.rice.edu/armadillo/acceptable.html.

Internet Advocate. *Develop an "Acceptable Use Policy" (AUP) for Schools and Public Libraries*. April 1999. URL source: http://www.monroe.lib.in.us/~lchampel/netadv3.html.

Internet School Networking (ISN) Group. Internet RFC 1587, "Primary and Secondary School Internet User" Questions. URL source: http://www.cusd.claremont.edu/www/people/rmuir/rfc1578.html#qasae.

VICON Networks. *Taking Care on the Net.* State College, Pa.: VICON, 1999.. URL source: http://www.vicon.net/internetguide/takecare.htm.

Notes

1. Sandra Kerka, *Life and Work in a Technological Society; ERIC Digest No. 147* (Syracuse, N.Y.: ERIC Clearinghouse, 1994, ERIC Reproduction Service No. ED 368 892), 1.

2. Kerka, *Life and Work*, 1.

3. M. W. Green, Jr., and J. A. Fugel, "Third Wave Has Ups and Downs," *Rural Telecommunications* 15, no. 1 (January–February 1996), 10.

4. J. Shoesmith, "The Marco Polo of Cyberspace," *Computing Canada* 21, no. 6 (March 15, 1995), 15. (Ogden's theory and work are discussed here.)

5. Kathleen W. Craver, "Shaping Our Future: The Role of School Library Media Centers," *School Library Media Quarterly* 24, no. 1 (fall 1995), 13–18.

6. R. J. Marcusse, "In the Wired Age, Location Isn't Everything," *Upside (UPS)* 8, no. 5 (May 1996), 88.

7. Library Instruction Round Table of the American Library Association, *Information for a New Age: Redefining the Library* (Chicago: American Library Association, 1995, available from Libraries Unlimited, Inc., P.O. Box 6633, Englewood, CO 80155-6633).

8. Robert A. Gross and Christine L. Borgman, "The Incredible Vanishing Library," *American Libraries* 26 (October 1995), 900–902. Debora J. Shaw, "Libraries of the Future: Glimpses of a Networked, Distributed, Collaborative, Hyper, Virtual World," *Libri* 44 (September 1994), 206–23.

9. Marilyn L. Miller and Marilyn L. Shontz, "Expenditures for Resources in School Library Media Centers, FY 1991–1992," *School Library Journal* 39 (October 1993), 26–36. Marilyn L. Miller and Marilyn L. Shontz, "The Race for the School Library Dollar," *School Library Journal* 41 October 1995), 22–33.

10. Walt Crawford, "Paper Persists: Why Physical Library Collections Still Matter," *Online* 22 (January–February 1998), 42–44.

11. Walt Crawford and Michael Gorman, *Future Libraries: Dreams, Madness, and Reality* (Chicago: American Library Association, 1995).

12. Benton Foundation, *Building Books and Bytes: Libraries and Communities in the Digital Age: A Report on the Public's Opinion of Library Leaders' Visions for the Future* (Washington, D.C.: The Benton Foundation for the W. K. Kellogg Foundation, 1996, 40. URL source: http://www.benton.org/kellogg/buildings.html).

13. S. A. Sullivan, "Break Down Barriers to Flexibility," *HRMagazine* 40, no. 9 (September 1995), 166, 168.

14. D. Dryer and C. Ringstaff, *ACOT Overview* (Cupertino, Calif.: Apple Computer, Inc., 1992).

15. M. H. Benjamin, "Prospering in the Information Age," *Association Management* 47, no. 8 (August 1995), 96–206.

16. Alfred P. Sloan Foundation, *Program in Learning Outside the Classroom.* URL source: http://w3.scale.uiuc.edu/education/ALN.new.httw.

17. Betty Turock, "ALA President Betty Turock Testifies Before FCC-Joint Board on Affordable Rates for Libraries and Schools," *ALAWON* 5, no. 18 (April 12, 1996), 1. URL source: http://ncsulib2.lib.ncsu.edu/stacks/a/alawon/alawon-v5n18.txt.

18. Turock, "Turock Testifies." Same URL list of provisions.

19. World Summit for Social Development, *Copenhagen Declaration on Social Development* (Copenhagen, Denmark: World Summit, United Nations, 6–12 March 1995), 1, URL source: http://www.jsrd.or.jp/dinf_us/wssd/a—9.en.txt.

20. ALA Bill of Rights (Chicago: American Library Association, 1948). URL source: http://www.ala.org/work/freedom/lbr.html/rights.

21. American Civil Liberties Union, testimony of the American Civil Liberties Union before the United States Congress, February 10, 1998. URL source: http://aclu.org/congress/to2/098.html.

22. American Association of School Librarians, *Access to Resources and Services in the School Library Media Program: An Interpretation of the Library Bill of Rights* (Chicago: American Library Association, 1990). URL source: http://www.ala.org/aasl/positions/ PS_billofrights.html.

23. Wentworth Worldwide Media, *Acceptable Use Policies: Defining What's Allowed Online, and What's Not.* URL source: http://www.wentworth.com/classroom/aup. html, 1994–1996. Also in *Classroom Connect Newsletter*, December 1994, January 1995, with follow-up comments in October 1995. Nancy Willard, K–12 acceptable use policies. URL source: http://www.erehwon.com/Kl2AUP. She publishes acceptable use templates. School systems wishing to use these templates are assessed a $50 fee. B. J. Fishman and R. D. Pea, "The Internetworked School: A Policy for the Future," *Technos: Quarterly of Education and Technology* 3, no. 1 (1993), 22–26. Classroom Connect, *Computer Use Policies and Related Discussion: K–12 School Acceptable Use Policies* (Lancaster, Penn. URL source: http://www.classroom.net/policy.htm. Clovis Organization, *What You Need to Know About Acceptable Use Policies* (Evanston, Ill.: Northwestern University), COVIS project, n.d. URL source: http://www.covis.nwu.edu/ sinfo/. Clovis provides Web links to acceptable-use policy statements.

24. Sandra J. Milberg and Sandra J. Burke. "Values, Personal Information Privacy, and Regulatory Approaches," *Communications of the ACM* 38, no. 12 (December 1995), 65–75.

12

High Reliability Principles

Technology holds great potential for revolutionizing education. This claim has been widely heard since microcomputers first appeared well over a decade ago. Since then, technology's exponentially increasing power, decreasing costs, portability, and connectivity have surpassed the wildest dreams of the early 1980s. Yet inside classrooms across the country, there is little evidence that any kind of revolution has occurred, and remarkably little evidence of technology. The primary reason technology has failed to live up to its promise lies in the fact that it has been viewed as an answer to the wrong question. Decisions about technology purchases and uses are typically driven by the question of how to improve the effectiveness of what schools are already doing—not how to transform what schools do.[1]

Introduction

We cannot move into the future by changing programs, adding technology, and making schedule modifications so that we continue to do what we have done in the past. If school library media programs are to be successful, there must be a vision of what those schools and their media centers can become. Such a vision would include a major role for school library media programs to play among future social institutions serving our society. The authors have been attracted to the vision of the school and its library media program as "high reliability organizations." In business and government, such high reliability organizations are expected to operate trials without errors.[2]

Researchers investigating the characteristics of these systems have referred to them as high reliability organizations.[3] In the emerging information society, it is not acceptable to have any students who do

221

not learn the basic skills necessary for functioning in the society. Society cannot afford to have partial learners, nonlearners, or students who drop out. Rossi and Montgomery point out the characteristics of high reliability organizations:

1. They require clear definitions of goals.

2. They use standard operating procedures insofar as research and experience show such procedures to be effective, although they are not bound by these procedures.

3. They recruit and train extensively in order to develop skills in the use of standard operating procedures.

4. They identify standard operating procedure problems by developing early warning systems to identify surprises or problems in the system, to suggest changes that will correct those problems, and deal with these problems before they become major crises.

5. They promote and demand mutual performance evaluation (administrators and line) without a counterproductive loss of overall autonomy and confidence.

6. They are hierarchically structured, but during times of peak loads, they emphasize a second layer of behavior that emphasizes collegial decision making, regardless of rank. High reliability organizations respond to potentially disastrous situations as being far too important to trust to rules alone.

7. They are invariably valued by their supervising organizations.[4]

This chapter presents a modified version of high reliability organization characteristics and the implications of these characteristics for future library media programs.

High Reliability Principles: Clear Goals

First, high reliability organizations require clear definitions of goals and objectives. Everyone in such an organization has a strong sense of what the primary mission of the organization is. They know where they are going, and they have agreed on that goal. The National Education Goals clearly establish a mission: all students entering first grade ready to learn, reducing the high school dropout rate by over 50 percent, and raising the mathematics and science achievements of all U.S. students to very high levels. Establishing and maintaining clear goals has been one of the most frequently cited characteristics of highly effective schools.[5] Schools with low achievement scores have been found to have a lack of clear goals and often conflicts among goals within the school, the school system, the school board, and the larger community. Creating a strong set of agreed-upon goals in a school takes time, a lot of listening, and occasional firmness on the part of school leadership. No local school can do this task alone.

In the future, library media specialists cannot operate as they have done in the past. What has been usual operation will not do. The pace of change in information technology and the increasing number of options in information storage and instructional delivery systems require that the school staff and the library media specialist have a common understanding of where the instructional program is going, and what that program's targeted goals are. Every activity of the library media program must be evaluated against these goals—by the library media specialist, by the media advisory committee, by the teachers, by the students, by the supervising administration, and by the larger community. Where activities are not found to be in line with the goals, they should be modified or dropped.

The authors suggest a possible goal scenario for a school in the twenty-first century—that the school take as its overarching goal becoming a full-service school in which many different cultural, educational, health, and social services programs are available to students, families, and the larger community. Full-service public agencies in the twenty-first century will have the following characteristics:

1. *Full-service agencies are one-stop public service centers.*
   Driving around any medium-sized city, one is impressed with the number of public and private service agencies literally scattered throughout the area. Many of the people who need to use the services of these agencies must go from agency to agency, often using inadequate public transportation or taxis, in order to receive services. There have been a number of efforts to move services to the places where people live and work. We have seen satellite police stations where policemen walk around the neighborhood, public health nurses in schools, voter registration and immunization programs in branch libraries, and various other combined public service agency facilities.

The increasing diversity and poverty of our society will require a major restructuring of public and private services. All services should be available in the local neighborhood, either in person or through the use of telecommunications systems. As schools move toward becoming wired for telecommunications and use of the Internet, they become one logical choice as a center of public services activity. In North Carolina we are already beginning to see health diagnostic services offered to remote areas through the North Carolina Information Superhighway. Decentralizing services and combining the efforts of public and private agencies could mean that preventive health services, welfare services, and educational services would again become based on the neighborhood and its school.

An alternative to neighborhood-based services may be place-of-employment service centers. The number of families where all adults and many children work increases all the time. Moving services, including child care, to places of employment so that services can be secured before work, during breaks, at lunch, or after work seems to make real sense. Dryfoos describes full-service schools in which communities integrate service agencies through their local schools.[6] Among these schools are school-based health centers, youth-service centers, family-resource centers, "lighthouse" schoolhouses, and community schools. All of these models share the provision of community agency services in school buildings with the goal of creating comprehensive, one-stop educational service centers.

2. *Full-service agencies integrate public and private service agencies.*
   Many communities have service agency councils where the people responsible for various human services meet to discuss issues, needs, and policy. Such councils are a small step in the right direction. The authors believe that future human service demands combined with a decreasing public commitment to serving those less fortunate will require far more radical steps in interagency cooperation. In the authors' own community, over 75 percent of human services are offered by private or nonpublic charitable agencies. While there is fairly good communication between these multiple agencies, there is little service integration.

The authors envision a much closer integration of these agencies, requiring major changes in local and federal laws. Often agencies are serving the same clients without knowing that fact. Current regulations can prevent agencies from sharing that information. This lack of coordination presents two problems: some individuals can receive conflicting advice or services from several agencies, and others can "fall through the safety net" and not receive services at all.

3. *Full-service agencies will have increased service-consumer involvement.* Businesses have discovered that being close to the customer makes any business more profitable. They have also learned that ignoring the customer leads to disaster. Future social service agencies, including schools, must take their customers seriously. Many agencies are so overwhelmed by the volume of service requests that they tend to take the bureaucratic step of developing procedures to place their customers into more manageable groups. Demanding the filling out of complex forms, refusing to have forms in the native language of customers, treating all cases in a single way, refusing to take time to listen, offering only the services that are mandated, and treating people as numbers are all symptoms of this harried approach to the customer. Such agencies have no time to listen to what the customer really wants and needs.

As our society becomes increasingly diverse in economic status, languages, and cultures, traditional social agencies are bound to fail unless they modify their approach to their customers. Unfortunately, most social agencies, both public and private, are still legislated, managed, and evaluated by individuals who are not part of the customer group. Successful future social agencies will involve their clients in every phase of their operations—goal setting, planning, implementation, and evaluation.

Schools seem ideally structured to deal cooperatively with other social agencies. Schools have faced major problems in trying to deal with all of the demands placed on them by the social order. For some time it has seemed as if all the social problems identified were added to the school's agenda of services—often without any funding or personnel to support those services. At the same time other agencies are being overwhelmed by similar demands for services. As agencies try to cope with this overload, some school systems and social agencies are moving toward integrated, school-based social services.

Zigler discusses the school of the twenty-first century model for school-based and school-linked service provision, which has been implemented in over three hundred schools to provide high-quality services to children from birth through age twelve.[7] Jeffers and Olebe stress the fact that families and their circumstances must be seen as a part of a school's mandate to educate. They urge schools to secure their own futures and become a center for community activity by bringing together representatives of service agencies and becoming an umbrella location for the delivery of their services.[8] Readers of this book will note how closely these ideas mirror those of the Comer school movement in its attempts to involve parents and the local community in the whole educational process.

It is not easy to change organizations so that they can actively cooperate in spite of different governing structures, different sources of income, and different goals. These coordinated school-based social services may be one of the most promising aspects of current educational reform. However, moving from a policy that calls for coordinated service integration into the actual practice of providing services means resolving a host of complex, interacting issues. Specific areas that require a lot of cooperative effort include staff development, role definition, and the larger issues of turf, marketing, and financing.

Wehlage and Stone studied twenty-four schools and found that adding school-based support services to bureaucratically organized schools does not prove effective, or produce better student achievement.[9] Communally organized schools involve the whole faculty as well as the staff members of social agencies in collective responsibility for students' academic and social well-being. Social service programs must be integrated into the organization of the school to create a focused vision and sense of shared responsibility. Miller identified three distinct yet related approaches to building strong school-community relationships: (1) school as community center, in which the school becomes a resource for lifelong learning and delivers a wide range of educational, health, and social services; (2) community as curriculum, emphasizing student involvement in the study of community in all its complexity; and (3) school-based enterprise, in which students develop entrepreneurial skills by identifying service needs in the community and establishing a business to address those needs.

Important elements in sustaining partnerships over time are a strong base of community support, the engagement of teachers in related curriculum work, and long-term commitment.[10] There has been some debate in educational circles about the role of schools in providing an array of human services. Many educators, including the authors, have become convinced that the school cannot ignore the total life of the student and his/her family. Students bring the rest of their lives into the school setting. If the needs of the community, the family, and the individuals in those families are not being met, then the student has a more difficult time in learning and working with other students.

The same principle holds for other social agencies. Agencies cannot have a focus on a particular problem situation—violence, drug abuse, illness, or whatever it may be. Rather, they must take a holistic approach that seeks to serve all of the needs of the family and community. Obviously, no agency can do this job alone. In cooperation with other agencies, the school must move toward a village concept of education: It takes a whole village to raise a child. If the school takes on the goal of becoming a full-service school that collaborates with other social agencies in providing human services, the program and services of the library media center must also change.

In the first phase of developing a full-service school, there will need to be some changes in the library media program. Among them:

1. *A change in service hours to reflect the needs of the community*
   Readers will note that this suggestion has appeared several times in this book. The authors do not believe in an 8 A.M.–2:30 P.M. media center. The full-service school must make itself available when people have time to seek services. In cooperation with other agencies, a library media center schedule will be developed that will probably involve evening and weekend hours. It is probable that the school will be open anyway because of the needs of other agencies that have service staff in the facility to serve the community. These changes will require rethinking staffing needs as well as increased use of trained volunteers and student workers. Full-service library media programs will require additional staff.

2. *A modification of the professional collection to serve the needs of the different professions*
   Library media center professional collections have traditionally served the information needs of teachers and administrators. The full-service school professional collection will need to reflect the information and reference needs of all the professionals who are using the school as a base for their operations. Often these professional resources will be online through telecommunications or the Internet. As collections are modified to meet new demands, the funding structure for collection development needs to be changed so that everyone who benefits from the collection is involved in providing part of the collection development budget.

The media specialist will need to build a community–family life collection as an integral part of the library media collection.

Because community members are utilizing the school as a service agency, the library media collection should reflect this change and provide the resources that those people need. The interests, reading abilities, and format preferences of the community must be assessed as this collection development activity begins. This involvement will mean that the media advisory committee will need to be expanded to include representatives of the participating agencies, community members, and the other libraries in the area.

The traditional media advisory committee is made up of teachers and sometimes students as the primary users of the library media center. In the full-service school this committee must be expanded to reflect the information interests and needs of the total service population—both professionals and community members. This change will mean the involvement of other information agencies in the community. Some social agencies will have special libraries as a part of their operation; local branches of public libraries and community colleges will also offer information services to the community.

As the media specialist begins to build such a media advisory committee, it may become too large to be manageable. One suggestion would be to divide the committee into three groups: (a) the professional users of the library media center—teachers, professional staff of agencies housed in the school, other professional staff cooperating with the program; (b) customers of all of the services, including students, parents, and community members; and (c) librarians who are serving both of these groups. Often these different groups have very different interests and need to discuss those interests with others who share them. Coordination of these groups is possible by having each group select representatives to work with the library media specialist as a coordinating committee.

3. *Initiation of instructional programs targeting all of the customer groups*
Traditional library media programming targets students, teachers, and sometimes parents. In the full-service school, the library media specialist now must add community groups and professionals serving them to that list. Often programs already underway will serve a wide variety of groups. Some examples of such programs include:

- *Author, illustrator, or expert visits*
  Such visits are usually confined to meeting with classes, a luncheon, and an evening reception with the host group. Often experts in various aspects of child development, parenting, or instructional techniques are involved in local school staff development activities. School systems often pay to bring such experts into the local community. Parents, community members, and allied professionals would also be interested in meeting these authors, illustrators, or experts. The opportunity to get books autographed, ask questions of a expert, be introduced to books and other materials that can be used with their children and grandchildren would be valued by many people. Such visits can easily be modified to involve the large social agency group in planning, funding, and promoting them, scheduling presentations so that the community can participate, and inviting local authors, illustrators, and experts to the presentations.

- *Staff development activities*
  Often staff development activities for teachers and staff are not oriented to specific curricular areas but to the acquisition of specific skills—especially in the area of computer-related technologies, but also in the areas of specific reading skill or mathematics skill techniques. Such events are of interest to parents and the larger community, too. Think about reviewing all staff development activities and schedules and asking the question, "Is this an activity that would interest others?" Far too much library and educational history is made up of staff development activities conducted with a specific group as if other groups did not exist and were not interested. Naturally, the shoe also fits the other foot. When other agencies are having staff development activities, the school should expect to be included.

- *Reading, modeling, recovery, or renewal activities*
  A wide variety of reading encouragement and example programs are emerging as schools attempt to deal with the major reading deficits in our society. Most of these programs involve individual and/or small group activities with an adult. Involving parents, grandparents, other community members in such activities not only serves to model good reading behavior and attitude to the students, it also models the importance of these activities to the adults around the school. Incidentally, it may

also be a source for improving adult literacy in the larger community.

4. *Development of formal multitype library collaborations*
Public libraries have often developed extensive programming relationships in the larger community, including day care centers, juvenile justice programs, family literacy projects, extension services, adult centers, and so on. Community college learning resource centers are often the hub of adult literacy, GED, and other noncredit, high-interest course activities cosponsored by various community agencies and businesses. The school library media program needs to strengthen its current relations with all other types of libraries in order to tap into the network of community relations already existing elsewhere.

Such collaboration might include shared staffing of facilities; joint programs offered concurrently to children, parents, and the community; promotion of common goals such as Freedom to Read, Children's Book Week, Banned Books Exhibits, and other agreed-upon projects. The initial step in such collaboration goes back to chapter 2 of this book. It all depends on people relations. If the professional librarians in each of these agencies see full-service libraries as a common goal, if they can work together to make those goals a reality, and if they can overcome institutional inertia, the total community will benefit from improved, coordinated library services.

High Reliability Principles: Standard Operating Procedures

Standard operating procedures for schools assume that we know which procedures and processes are effective in schools. By the time of the third edition of the *Handbook of Research and Teaching*[11] there was beginning to be some consensus among researchers about these issues. Standard operating procedures can create consistency in the school setting. This higher rate of consistency on the part of teachers and staff is clearly related to the behaviors of the school principals, and is not related to the income levels of the communities being served. Some principals are already insisting on, and getting, relatively high reliability and consistency in instructional delivery. Obviously, practice in schools and library media centers has been slow to follow. Many of the recommendations for library media programs in this book are not original with the authors but are based on the emerging consensus about what makes school library media programs effective as an integral part of the instruction of students and in students' lives in a broader context.

The chapters of this book on instruction and collection development principles and on scheduling make a number of recommendations based on research concerning effective school library media programs. Although these principles are presented as recommendations, the authors do not mean to imply that library media programs can continue to do whatever the library media specialist or the administration thinks is a good idea. We are far beyond that point in the knowledge base about effective school library media programs. Education is beyond the stage of "everyone's opinions have the same weight." It is time for library media programs to be run under standard operating procedures adapted to the needs of the particular school and its students and staff. Media specialists need to make good use of the research that has already been done, and contribute to that research through planning, implementation, and evaluation of their programs on a continuing basis.

The authors now present minimum recommendations for standard operating procedures:

1. Maintain a program that focuses on people work over procedures, rules, or tradition.

2. Develop a long-range, multiyear view of instruction and collection development.

3. Review all school scheduling in light of instructional goals, moving toward flexibility in the scheduling of all instructional activities.

4. Plan and evaluate all instructional activities, all of the time involving teachers, students, administrators, parents, and communities in that evaluation process.

5. Build realistic, long-range budget proposals based on instructional goals.

6. Monitor and modify facilities to meet changing instructional needs and goals.

7. Build a full-service philosophy of broad community inclusion and governance throughout the library media program.

Our standard operating procedures goal statement might be:

> The school library media program focuses on the needs of people;
> views education as a lifetime process; plans and evaluates its schedules,
> collections, programs, and facilities to meet the instructional needs of
> a diverse community; carefully spends its budget to meet these goals;
> and seeks broad inclusion of the whole community of staff, students,
> parents, and community in its program.

Once standard operating procedures are adopted, the programs of
the library media program should be aligned with those operating
procedures.

As anyone who has gone through a curriculum alignment knows,
such alignment is not an easy task. Often the ways things are done in
the library media center have become unconscious habits. Teachers,
students, and administrators expect things to be done in a certain way
and on a certain schedule. The library function analysis suggested in
an earlier chapter gives the library media specialist a chance to review
what actually goes on in the library media center. Once we know what
is actually happening, we can move toward asking, "Is this activity
being done in the most appropriate way, considering our principles of
standard operation?" When changes in procedures are initiated, the
library media specialist needs to work closely with the media advisory
committee, the leadership team, and the PSTA to ensure that
everyone understands why the change is occurring. Changes in
library media center programming should not be seen as capricious or
based on the personal preferences of the media specialist.

High Reliability Principles: Recruitment and Training

Teachers and staff cannot be expected to follow consistent procedures and processes if they have not practiced those procedures
and seen them used by other teachers and administrators. High reliability organizations have spent a great deal of time seeking out professional and support staff who already know the standard operating
procedures or who are willing to learn. Because staff development is
a continual effort, high reliability organizations have also spent a
great deal of time and money on training—introducing theory,
modeling standard operating procedures, allowing time for practicing in a safe environment, offering feedback, encouraging experi-

mentation, building up confidence in each staff member's professional judgment, and honing skills.

Readers will note that these training principles seem "right"—that is, they have face validity. Anyone who has acquired a new skill (tennis, graphic processing, roller-blading) knows the importance of these steps in the process. In most professional disciplines these processes are incorporated into preservice and inservice training. People do not learn new procedures just by reading a book or attending an inservice session after work. They observe their colleagues, and then are themselves observed performing the new task and provided with real-time feedback.

The authors acknowledge that educational institutions have very little experience with effective staff development activities. The one-day seminar or the workshop scheduled after a full day of teaching is the more normal pattern. Coordinated, *in-class* modeling, creative mentoring, and honest, shared feedback spread throughout the year are very rare. High reliability schools will require radical restructuring of staff development activities in the schools and equally radical adjustments in preservice education for all of those who will later take on professional roles in the schools. The most critical factors in training are the interest of the trainees, their trust in the trainer, and the support of peers and supervisors. All staff development programs should be evaluated in these terms.

Both preservice and inservice education of library media specialists fall short of this high reliability characteristic. The current public discourse about the state of education, especially public education, keeps claiming that education is in a bad state.

As this final chapter was being written, a national evaluation of the educational *Goals 2000* progress was published and discussed on television. The main focus of these discussions was, "We are not doing very well at reaching our goals." Even if the statistics do not support such a negative view of education, it is still true that transforming schools into high reliability organizations will require huge efforts on the part of teacher education programs, state departments of education, and local school systems.

The pace of change discussed in chapter 1 of this book requires that individuals go through retraining throughout their adult lives. Barker suggests thinking about education as:

Education K through competence
But now we have begun to understand the real goal of education. Not eighteen and out with a mediocre education, but stay as long as you

need to, to become competent to be a citizen/worker of the twenty-first century.[12]

The authors of this book would add, "and come back as often as you need to for re-education and retraining." The concept of an educated individual who is finished with learning simply will not do. For schools, a major part of the effort will be in continual retraining of professional personnel to meet the instructional needs of students as they prepare for a lifetime of learning. Most teacher education programs prepare students for the traditional school schedule. Few preservice teachers or library media specialists have actual experience in more flexible settings. Most of the textbook materials available do not even discuss a multiyear perspective on the instructional process.

Additionally, collaborative planning, teaching, and evaluation are still rare within the teacher education classrooms; in fact, some students are educated with their peers in a particular area and have no idea what other professionals, with whom they will have to work, are experiencing in their educational process or what their roles are in education. Even at the graduate level, the training of educational specialists is rarely integrated so that reading specialists, special educators, administrators in training, library media specialists, and counselors have a common educational experience. Current professional accreditation of graduate programs in education and the requirements of state certification often make such common experiences impossible because of course requirements and practicum experience requirements in particular disciplines.

The media specialist must be involved in at least two types of continual training: (1) training and re-education for him or herself and (2) staff training programs that allow teachers and other staff members to acquire the skills they need to integrate the ever-changing forms and delivery systems of information into their instructional program. One of the purposes of stressing the evaluation of library media programs is to highlight areas where the library media specialist needs training, or where the library media collection needs improvement. Clearly, self-evaluation of training needs is not sufficient; the library media specialist should seek out teacher and administrative evaluation to supplement this self-evaluation.

With regular evaluation, the library media specialist can expect to be able to design a professional improvement program that directly addresses needs established in the evaluation process. Please notice that the authors have suggested that the main purpose of any evaluation procedure is to assist the library media specialist in improving performance, not to assist administrative personnel in performance evaluation for the purposes of merit raises or summative performance evaluation.

If the concept of a full-service school is actually implemented, both the evaluation process and the professional improvement program become much more complex. In that context, the library media specialist is not only seeking to do a better instructional job with teachers and students but to interact effectively also with parents and the larger community. Experience in schools attempting to implement this model would indicate that the realistic involvement of parents in planning, offering, and evaluating instruction will require new skills on the part of administrators, teachers, and support staff, as well as the parents. It may seem obvious, but adults are not children and they do not learn in the same ways as children. When parents and the clients and staffs of other community agencies are involved in the school, the ability to understand, work with, and teach adults becomes very important.

One major area of working with adults comes in staff development programs for the staff and parents of the school. For most teachers and parents, stress is often caused by the need for time to learn new techniques, master new technologies, and develop instructional materials within a limited amount of time. Cambone presents the time problem in this way:

> And many school staffs across the country have begun searching for ways to find time for teachers to do the important work of restructuring while they continue to teach. All kinds of methods are employed, from highly original released time schemes to buying more substitute time. However, even in those schools where time has been created, bought, borrowed, or stolen for restructuring work, among teachers there remains a feeling that it still isn't enough. Inevitably, the work quickly surpasses the time allotted. Time, adequate in quantity and rich in quality, is elusive. Yet we continue to look for more ways to get it. Somehow, if we can find more time, we seem to say, we will be able to successfully meet the task of restructuring schools.[13]

The members of the National Education Commission on Time and Learning (1994) presents as one of their recommendations: "*We recommend* that teachers be provided with the professional time and opportunities they need to do their jobs." They go on to say:

The daily working life of most teachers is one of unrelieved time pressure and isolation; they work, largely alone, in a classroom of 25–30 children or adolescents for hours every day. . . . American teachers have little time for preparation, planning, cooperation, or professional growth. The Commission believes that time for planning and professional development is urgently needed—not as a frill or an add-on, but as a major aspect of the agreement between teachers and districts. The whole question of teachers and time needs to be rethought in a serious and systematic way. The issue is not simply teachers. It is not just time. The real issue is education quality. Teachers need time to develop effective lessons. They need time to assess students in meaningful ways and discuss the results with students individually. They need time to talk to students, and listen to them, and to confer with parents and other family members. They need time to read professional journals, interact with their colleagues, and watch outstanding teachers demonstrate new strategies.[14]

In full-service schools, the library media specialist will need to be alert for opportunities for adult education in collaborative teaching, instructional development, group-based decision making, and the infusion of technology into the curriculum. He/she will keep track of staff development opportunities offered by other agencies in the community and communicate those opportunities to the professional staff. While the library media specialist is not solely responsible for these efforts, he/she should take a leadership role in discovering information resources, area and regional workshops in appropriate areas, and skills leaders who can assist in such activities.

High Reliability Principles: Early Warning Systems

Having standard operating procedures does not mean that high reliability organizations are rigid or that procedures cannot be changed. Professional judgment is valued, and finding problems or flaws by leadership, staff, and customers has high priority. As an example in education, Stringfield and Yoder present a case study of an exemplary school serving highly disadvantaged Hispanic children. That school consistently developed standard operating procedures and with equal frequency sought out methods for improving those procedures.[15] Federal law even mandates the search for flaws and their correction in education. The 1988 Hawkins-Stafford amendments to the U.S. compensatory education laws mandate a self-study and program improvement process for schools in which compensatory education students are not making adequate academic gains.[16] Thousands of schools have been identified nationwide, and in several states those schools have entered into an extended self-study with the eventual goal of school-directed improvement.[17] In most modern organizations working with the public, all staff must have adequate training and interest in the product or service provided. In beginning library science classes the authors always tell students that from the perspective of someone coming into the library, anyone they meet is the librarian and that individual's action will influence their future opinions of library services.

High reliability organizations find that small failures in remote parts of the system can quickly grow into major disasters for the whole system. Areas requiring quick response or decisions made at the place and time where the problem occurs are highlighted, and individuals within the organization are given specific responsibility and training in order to make judgments and develop strategies to deal with particular problems. Organizations often formalize the process of early warning by setting up listening posts close to customers and service outlets to catch small failures in their initial stages.

These organizations often have a zero-defects attitude about product and service and consequently produce products and services that are not defective in any way. Listening posts are made important by assigning senior staff to them on a regular basis and by giving immediate, full-force attention to reports from those posts. People who solve specific problems are celebrated by the organization through recognition and rewards.

Stringfield and Teddlie's recommended use of observers who pay attention to daily academic functioning would logically lead to quicker discovery of and response to any lapses.[18] Schools that use teaming meetings such as Philadelphia's charter schools, Coalition of Essential Schools, and many middle schools in which student progress is discussed and instructional strategies planned to deal with problems logically lead to an early warning system. In many schools serving students at risk, significant percentages of students arrive in second, third, and even fourth grade unable to read. Although students quickly learn to mask their reading difficulties, it is unlikely that previous teachers have not noticed these deficiencies. Yet it is obvious that adequate correction had not been instituted in large measure because the problems were not communicated effectively across grade level. Such programs as Success for All[19] and Reading Recovery,[20] when successfully implemented, show that these situations are not inevitable but have been allowed to happen.

High reliability schools will have procedures that give all the professionals in the school regular, informal feedback about student progress, and which allow for team-based instructional diagnosis and remediation for those students who are falling behind. Such remediation would be initiated immediately rather than at the end of nine weeks or the end of the year. Such a school would be a school in which teachers, students, staff, parents, and community members know that one of their most critical responsibilities is the early identification of potential problems. They would feel safe in bringing those problems to everyone's attention and in trying experimental solutions as the problems emerge.

It is probably safe to say that the typical teacher or library media specialist does not view him or herself as having the right or the power to change significant school and district procedures. If schools and districts are to reliably educate virtually all students, the teachers and principals must have more voice in establishing and modifying school procedures. Standard operating procedures will have to be modified to deal with local needs.

The recent emphasis on site-based management is one attempt to move standard operating procedures in education toward local school flexibility in implementation. Site-based management tries to transform schools into communities where the appropriate people participate in major decisions affecting them. Really effective site-based management requires that the school have a well-designed community structure, enabling leadership, a student and adult learning focus, and a school wide perspective.[21] Although site-based management gives teachers, principals, and communities a method for directly affecting and improving their schools, the greatest pitfall is the amount of time needed for successful implementation, which usually takes five to ten years.

A second challenge is the redefinition of roles and new roles for the school administrator and the teachers.[22] These new roles can be very demanding because principals and teachers are often given total responsibility for budgeting, selecting textbooks, scheduling, and hiring of personnel. Few teacher and administrator education programs currently prepare these individuals for such roles.

Site-based management has also had a number of critics. Black notes that site-based management is suffering from growing pains and "shop-floor realities."[23] Principals and teachers are managing schools through trial and error. Many principals are paranoid about their changing roles, and teachers are struggling with budgeting and other management responsibilities. Reitzug and Capper found that current empirical data on school-based management projects show that this process is failing to produce radical changes in school practice.[24]

Writing from an Australian perspective, Smyth has argued that site-based management appears to be primarily concerned with dismantling centralized education systems and replacing them with a free-market ideology of competition and choice. Although site-based management is often promoted as promising more democratic community involvement, more parental choice, and better managed and more effective schools, what has actually happened is that site-based management is promoted to justify less centralized support for students, teachers, and administrators, as well as to justify for the state's avoidance of its social responsibility to provide an equitable quality education for all.[25]

Although site-based management has the potential for democratizing the workplace and equitably addressing students' needs, that potential has not been reached because of the rigidity of standard operating procedures often expressed in the requirements of regulations or legislation. Still, if we want to move toward schools that take the instructional needs of students and teachers seriously, we are going to have to reform the ways in which decisions are made so that they are taken much closer to the place where the work is done—the school. We are going to have to involve the whole staff in this process.

Believing that there are multiple learning styles and intelligences, the authors advocate instructional programs that continually assess the intellectual and affective growth of students rather than programs that wait until end-of-course, nine-week, and end-of-year testing periods. Periodic evaluation processes are almost totally useless in the context of children's learning. Things change too fast; situations can become crises overnight. The learning process for all students in a vast complex of variables, all interacting at once. Schools cannot afford to wait until problems become big enough to notice. No matter how carefully crafted they are, the standard operating procedures of the school and the library media center are bound to face problems over time.

Rule-bound library media programs insist that students and teachers conform to a series of regulations that were originally designed for efficient and effective library instruction and services but are now outdated and impeding the effective instructional use of the library media center. Librarianship has many examples of rules designed for a particular time that no longer exists, yet are still practiced. In a high reliability school, the library media specialist needs to establish a series of listening posts that can provide feedback about how the library media instructional program is going.

Such listening posts include, first of all, the students themselves. Ask the students for informal, immediate feedback on any instructional activity. Second, the media advisory committee. This committee should be involved in all library media program plans, and in the evaluation of those programs soon after they are completed. Third, the school leadership team. This team engages in curriculum planning and makes major decisions about the goals and objectives of the school. It should evaluate the instructional program of the library media center as a natural part of that process. Fourth, parent or PSTA groups that focus on the program and services of the library media center, and fifth, organized educational, library, and service groups in the community. If schools move toward becoming full-service schools as suggested in this chapter, then the library media specialist will need to develop listening posts in agencies outside the school system so that the impact of the library media program on the larger community can also be evaluated.

By definition, the media advisory committee focuses on the program of the library media center; it is not necessary for the other groups to take that focus all the time. However, each group should be asked to focus on specific aspects of the library media program from time to time. Such evaluations are not reports on how well things are going in the library media program; rather, the library media specialist presents data gathered in various informal and formal ways and asks the listening post group to review and interpret those data in the light of what they know about the overall school program.

In the authors' experience, the best library media specialists always know what is going on in the local classrooms, in the school, in the school system, in the community, and in the educational and library professions, and their programs reflect this knowledge. They have utilized a whole series of early-warning listening posts. On the other hand, the poorest library media programs are often managed by individuals who do not seem to know what is going on in the classrooms, the school, the community, or their profession.

An excellent example of this dichotomy is found in the ways that library media specialists deal with censorship problems. Some specialists know what titles are under attack, by what groups, the position of the American Library Association and the Freedom to Read Foundation, and have a collection development policy that clearly defines policy and procedure for dealing with title challenges. They are in continuous contact with other library media specialists and the regional resources for dealing with censorship challenges. Other library media specialists cannot even tell you what current titles are under attack.

Librarianship is a profession with a wide array of professional activities and publications, so the best library media specialists are also involved in their local, regional, and national professional associations. They are able to list and expound on the basic instructional, service, and ethical issues facing the profession. They serve on school librarianship and technology committees at all levels, including the national association level. How do these people always know what is happening? Because they also participate in these important areas:

Leadership of the School

Throughout this book the authors have stressed that the library media specialist needs to be *involved* in the leadership operation of the school. Such involvement is both formal (membership of appropriate school committees and planning groups) and informal (being around for faculty discussions, being available before and after school for "chance" meetings in the hall). A major reason for this involvement is the need to know not just what is going on but what is going to happen in the future. If library media programs are to move beyond reacting to what happens to a more proactive, planning-based program, the library media specialist needs to establish early warning systems throughout the school. If he/she knows what is being discussed, planned, hoped for in the school's program, then the library media program can be adjusted to participate in those emerging programs.

The Planning and Evaluation Committees of the School System

Every school system has multiple committees, task forces, and ad-hoc groups dealing with school reform and the future. Most school boards are also involved in such efforts. The library media specialist needs to know about and become involved in as many of these efforts as possible. Participation in such committees has two purposes: to be sure that the impact of the committee's decisions takes into account the impact on library media programs, and to gain access to information for library media program applications. In school systems where there is a library media supervisor, such roles may be a formal function of that position; however, it is vital that the school-based library media program input be available at the system level.

Community Organizations

Participation includes the public library, community colleges, and all organizations involved in educational and library services from birth through old age. The authors are not suggesting that every library media specialist should be a member of all of these organizations. In a typical medium-sized community that would mean membership in approximately thirty to forty-five organizations! Rather, the library media specialist should be selectively involved based on personal and school interests, but always asking, Where can I best represent our school? Information about other programs can be gained from other library media specialists and teachers serving on other committees, from regular reading of the newsletters, e-mail, and Web pages.

State, Regional, and National Associations

Informed media specialists are active members of library and educational associations at all of these levels. The authors can anticipate the protests this suggestion will bring: "How can we afford the membership dues and the time such involvement takes?" Another way of looking at this problem is to ask, "How can you afford *not* to be involved as much as you can afford?" Professional associations provide us with early warning systems about pending legislation, trends in the field, colleagues to share our concerns, staff development opportunities, as well as opportunities to develop leadership and presentation skills.

Obviously, just as with community organizations, we cannot be members of all of the educational and library associations at the same time. However, we can: (1) select those organizations that seem most appropriate to our school's mission and goals; (2) be an active participant in those associations at all levels; (3) rotate our memberships among organizations over time; (4) drop those organizations that become irrelevant or whose publications you never get around to reading; and (5) be alert to new professional association possibilities. As more and more organizations make use of the Internet and the World Wide Web, such participation becomes more and more feasible.

High Reliability Principles: Mutual Evaluation

Mutual evaluation is used to identify effective people who must make judgments and implement strategies to solve problems, to reward effective staff members, and to identify those who need additional training, transfer, or termination. In American public education there is minimal evaluation of teachers by administrators or fellow teachers, and virtually no evaluation of administrators by teachers, while the school board is typically only evaluated at the ballot box.

Rumburger and Larson present a system, in the context of Chicano education, in which peers become much more aware of each other's teaching. Current discussion of team planning, teaching, and team meetings about ways to accelerate an individual student's progress all can contribute to mutual monitoring.[26] Mutual monitoring, especially across lines of authority, is difficult to achieve unless there is an intense level of trust among the professionals in the school. The readers of this book will have experienced performance evaluations done in a routine or judgmental way. Evaluating your supervisor to any good effect is typically seen as a useless exercise, something like having a suggestion box with no bottom placed over a waste basket. Even peer evaluation demands a high degree of trust among those who are evaluating and being evaluated.

High reliability organizations pay particular attention to performance evaluation to improve the effectiveness of their organizations. Feedback from coworkers is an increasingly popular human-resources device aimed at improving employees' on-the-job performance. Many companies are using feedback to accelerate the shift to teamwork and increase employee empowerment. Such mutual evaluation systems are currently called "360-degree" evaluation systems.[27]

Traditionally, companies have evaluated employee performance by relying exclusively on supervisor ratings. In 360-degree feedback, supervisors, colleagues, customers, and subordinates are given anonymous write-in questionnaires about the individual under review. The questionnaires are more concerned with personality and attitude than with on-the-job competence. The focus of the review can be on perceptions of talents, ethics, leadership, personality, habits, and even weaknesses. Such feedback offers a much broader perspective of employee job performance, evaluating job performance by an immediate supervisor as well as other individuals who have direct contract with the employee being appraised.[28]

One of the most consistent findings of the 360-degree process is that one's own perceptions of strengths and weaknesses are not the same as the perceptions of supervisors, peers, or the people being supervised. Having some idea of how one is perceived by others is helpful in developing better performance with those individuals. Such evaluation is helpful to organizations because it relies on multiple sources of data, rather than the politically charged data of supervisors alone. School organizations clearly need better methods of performance evaluation *at all levels*. Systems like the 360-degree process, used in an atmosphere of common trust and confidentiality, can move staff performance in better directions.

Some performance evaluations do occur in schools and other public institutions and many educational institutions in the United States are placing a renewed emphasis on performance-based evaluation of teachers.[29] But tenure-type regulations, union agreements, civil service regulations, the refusal of administrators to be evaluated by their staffs and their peers, and the inability or refusal of administrators to deal effectively with problem staff mean that the majority of incompetent teachers and administrators are allowed to continue to intervene in the educational lives of children. Stringfield and Teddlie reported that principals in more effective schools took teacher recruitment, development, and evaluation more seriously than did principals in less effective schools.[30]

Principals in the effective schools had counseled-out, forced the transfer, or otherwise removed one or more teachers from their staff. In high reliability schools, administrators, teachers, teacher assistants, and specialists, including the library media specialist, would be evaluated on a regular basis. Such evaluation would not be top down only, but would include peer evaluation, self evaluation, and student evaluation, as well as parent and community evaluation. Such evaluation processes do take a lot of time, but they provide information for program improvement that can be gained in no other way.

Most of us have been schooled by experience to limit the amount of external evaluation we receive. It is more pleasant to selectively receive only that feedback which tells us what we want to hear. Still, if the library media program is to be instructionally significant, the program and the library media specialist must attend to honest evaluation from a number of sources. The less we hear or accept, the more likely that the library media program will become ineffectual. It is not easy to move from a work or personal situation that has little or no feedback toward a situation in which one receives immediate, regular feedback from all sides. Knowing how difficult it is to offer constructive criticism to students and their work, it will be easy to see why this difficulty arises.

Mutual evaluation is not easy for the person being evaluated, or for the evaluator. Effective mutual evaluation can only be done in an organizational atmosphere of trust. This atmosphere of trust includes students, staff, teachers, and administrators. If anyone is outside the circle of trust, communication breakdowns occur. For such trust to begin, the staff must come to some agreements about the purposes of peer observation and feedback. The authors suggest the following goals for any mutual monitoring among school staff.

Mutual Monitoring Principles

We collaborate, observe, and share our instructional work in order to: (1) challenge the privatization of our work as teachers. We are in this thing together; (2) build community and conversation about teaching and learning by observing others and through self-assessment; (3) develop an identity as teachers and learners, to find our best teaching and learning styles; (4) become more aware of our instructional methods and to modify those methods that are not accomplishing what we set out to accomplish; (5) share ideas about teaching that go beyond the practical, mechanical, and safe—to dare to be experimental, to fail, and to pick ourselves up and start again together; and (6) identify areas of needed change in our teaching strategies, styles, and effect, and to develop together strategies for making those changes.

In many schools the mutual trust upon which mutual monitoring is based is only in a beginning stage. Sometimes a library media specialist will find that actions by administrators, fellow teachers, or former library staff have pushed mutual trust to the breaking point. The authors would contend that, as stressed in chapter 2 of this book, library media programs cannot successfully operate in isolation. In order to function effectively the library media specialist *must* develop trusting relationships with students and staff. Acknowledging that the task is very, very difficult, the authors makes these suggestions:

1. *Start the process of trust and mutual observation*
   If there is no process now, there will never be one unless someone starts it. Do not wait for administrators, teachers, or students to suggest that they would like to monitor your work. Take the initiative and ask for immediate feedback from anyone who will give it. Create easy, formal ways for teachers and students to evaluate your work (see chapter 5 of this book).

2. *Do something visible with the feedback you receive*
   There is a long history of people seeking advice and feedback and then ignoring it or making excuses about content or conduct. If the library media specialist seeks feedback, there should be a response in instructional programming, collection development, or other activity which can be easily noticed by those who give the feedback. Businesses that seek customer feedback through customer panels, suggestion boxes, or other means have found that such programs are only successful if those participating see some institutional reaction to the feedback. In one case, a grocery store maintained a suggestion box and posted responses to suggestions within twenty-four hours!

   The library media specialist can follow a similar pattern and post responses to feedback on a bulletin board—"Someone suggested that we needed more space for small group activities in the library; we are planning to rearrange things next week as illustrated in this drawing. Let me know what you think of the new arrangement."
   When new materials are ordered in response to suggestions, be sure that the person making the suggestion knows when they arrive. (Send them a note or the materials, even prior to cataloging.)
   When you change instructional modes or styles, always ask for feedback: "I'm trying out a new way of doing this unit; please help me by filling out this form or leaving me a note."

3. *Plan with teachers and administrators*
   Often, during the planning process for instruction, it is possible to suggest that "we really need to try this idea out and evaluate how it works." If the library media specialist is coteaching a unit,

suggest that we coplan a way to evaluate the outcomes of the instruction. Always see to it that your part of the evaluation is done before you evaluate anyone else.

High Reliability Principles: Collegial Decision Making

In these organizations authority patterns quickly shift from hierarchical to functional, skill-based authority, as needs arise. In contrast, most schools and school systems are rule-focused and rule-driven. In some schools and systems exceptions to the rules are almost never tolerated. Even special education, which began twenty years ago to focus on Individualized Educational Plans stressing the particular needs of the student, has become rule-bound and weighed down with an excess of paper forms and legal processes imposed by the federal government, state agencies, local education agencies, and the courts. If schools and teachers are to be responsive to the needs of students who might fall through the cracks in a rule-driven system, they must have a way to adapt the rules to the local setting and the needs of the individual child.

Madden offers examples of systems designed so that the school staff catch students who might fall behind.[31] Almost all systems that pay attention to learning styles, multiple intelligences, and individual differences of students require the flexibility of modifying the rules to deal with the problems and potentials of individual students and groups.

Professional staff in such settings are able to quickly consult with one another, make a decision, and execute that decision. Such interdependence requires a school atmosphere where there is very little blame placed on anyone who actually tries to do something, and where responsibility is shared throughout the administrative structure of the school. Such schools are exciting places; relationships are complex, coupled, and sometimes urgent. Mortimore and colleagues found that involvement of teachers in decision making and consistent teacher inservice programs both were related to school effectiveness.[32] Stringfield and Teddlie also reported that high levels of cross-classroom and cross-grade coordination were positive predictors of schools that would have more success with students.[33] Such flexibility is aided by having instructional goals that are very focused. Programs that try to be all things to all students usually create an atmosphere where everyone is so busy that they cannot afford to deal with emerging student problems because they have so many instructional topics to cover.

When the leadership team of a school, as in the case of *Success for All*,[34] focuses on one major instructional area, a much more flexible situation arises. When school systems stop adopting every new fad, especially in technology, and begin to focus budget, central staff, and instructional power on a targeted goal, the whole instructional system develops time enough to put children first. Because so many demands are placed on schools by society, the school professional staff will have to be sure that their targeted goals are clear not only to the school staff but also to parents, the school system, and the larger community.

A rule-bound organization creates professional isolation and is the enemy of any school program trying to serve students effectively. For example, in a rule-bound school, equipment maintenance and reporting of malfunctions is covered by rules and executed by forms. Equipment must be sent to the right place and signed off by the correct person beyond the local school.

Usually, such systems have a backlog in technical repairs of at least 25 percent. In more flexible school settings, equipment is maintained and kept in top working order on site. Individuals are trained to deal with the most common problems. Students and volunteers are recruited and trained to deal with routine maintenance. The responsibility for checking the operation of equipment is made by anyone using that equipment, and most routine repairs are made at the local school. The current mess related to equipment may in part be a result of many educational administrators viewing no equipment other than lights, heating, and an office telephone as deserving of their personal attention.

In times of high demand, high reliability organizations expect everyone, no matter what their specific responsibilities or level of training, to perform at a high professional level. The hierarchy gives way to effective response at the point of need. This attitude is characterized by cooperation and coordination. At these times, line staff are expected to exercise considerable discretion. Everyone on the staff receives training on how to deal with "peak" load situations and crisis situations. In public education, there does not seem to be any national effort to deal with the effects of peak time situations. A few schools have intuitively developed ways to deal with such times and provided the necessary training and incentives so that everyone on the staff functions at a professional level when the need is there.

In other schools, temporarily heavy loads become excuses for poor performance by staff members and things break down. In any organization where you can hear, "That's not part of my job!" or "That responsibility is beyond the local school," you know there will be trouble. If we are to educate all children, then there must be ways to ensure that the system does not break down, or that when breakdowns do occur, they are dealt with and corrected quickly by whomever is at hand. High reliability schools will have *competent people at all levels*. All of these people will be working toward the same goals.

In the library media center, policies and procedures keep things running on track in the direction of the goals and objectives of a particular school. The authors do not advocate ignoring or "going around" school or system-level policies and procedures. We do not need maverick library media programs. Still, the focus of the library media program needs to be on the instructional needs of students and teachers. Policies and procedures are not written by God and the paperwork that is associated with them is not written in stone. When current policies or procedures are interfering with the education of children, those directly involved in instruction need to bring that fact forcefully to the attention of the school administration. Again, communication is the key to the process. People do not change rules if they do not know the impact of those rules on people. The involvement of parents and the larger community will sometimes make this process easier for the professional staff because parents and community members can say things without risk of censure or being fired.

Everyone who works in the library media program needs to be sufficiently trained so that they can deal with routine problems as they arise. Everyone should know how to deal with the unruly child, the panic when a piece of equipment does not work, the materials that are missing. For this reason, the library media specialist will need to spend time training support staff, parent volunteers, and student workers in "how we deal with things here." Such training is critical because we will not run things in the same way that other schools do. No matter what experience people may have had elsewhere, this is a school with specific goals and objectives, and we operate the library media program to support those goals.

An example may help clarify this point. School library media collections have traditionally been thought of as isolated library collections where the library owned everything that the students and teachers would want. There is no way a library media center can own all of the information materials that students and teachers will need, especially as these programs move toward dealing with varied learning styles and multiple intelligences. Standard library response to that problem has been to say, "We do not own a copy of that item." If the library media program is to be relevant to the emerging instructional paradigm, then everyone must know a new response, "We do not own that particular item. Let's see what else we can find to fill the need on the Internet, on CD-ROM, or by accessing the public library." For teachers and students we might also add, "Sorry we didn't have that item. We'll see who has it and try to get you a copy as soon as possible." If full service is the policy, everyone needs to know what full-service appropriate responses are.

Organizations outside education that have followed the high reliability or Total Quality Management models have found that a wide range of skills is required if staff members are to take initiative, identify and solve problems, make decisions, and engage in a spectrum of tasks. The leaders of these organizations have discovered increasing demands for continual and collaborative training through the work careers of staff at all levels.[35] If we want flexible instruction, flexible scheduling, continual evaluation, and improvement in library media programs, we will have to spend a lot of time in training and retraining everyone in the organization.

Standard operating procedures of the library media center and the whole school should be continually reviewed for their impact on people. The library media center acquires materials, purchases technology, and creates access to information resources beyond the library to support the teaching and learning processes of people. Rules have no intrinsic value, so when the people problems are not being solved, everyone needs to move to solve them. When the standard operating procedure does not cover the situation, have a library media program that can adapt quickly to meet the need or problem and then modify the standard procedure to deal more effectively with the newly discovered need.

High Reliability Principles: Value in the System

In most large organizations, high reliability units are regarded as extremely valuable. They are often used as benchmarks for Total

Quality Management analysis. Organizations in serious operational trouble will spin off an operating unit, give it a specific goal, and allow it to develop into a high reliability organization that the rest of the organization can use as a model. Organizations often express their valuing of such high reliability units with pay differentials, special awards, and public relations events.

In the public sector there is very little effort to support a unit in its efforts to become more reliable in its operation and service. There may even be subtle pressure for high-performing units to lower their performance so as not to show up the rest of the organization. Staff have little incentive to move beyond standard operating procedures, even in the face of crisis. In public education there is some evidence that school districts do provide more attention and support to some schools than others, and that it is often the schools in the least advantaged neighborhoods that receive the least attention and local support.[36]

Valuing of high reliability school programs would include rewarding those schools that are doing the best jobs with their students in terms of the overall goals of the school system, allowing programs sufficient time to be successfully implemented and evaluated, terminating programs and personnel that do not function well over time, and giving public awards to teachers, support staff, students, parents, and communities who are doing outstanding high reliability work. In terms of cost/benefit analysis such valuing will not make short-term sense. Often the cost of developing a high reliability organization is rather high; it is only when it becomes fully operational and when results are measured over time ("What happens to our graduates?") that the real cost benefits become clear.

The library media specialist can create an excellent program and then wait for it to be valued; or he/she can start in the local school. The authors recommend the following proactive processes as possibilities:

1. *Begin by creating recognition of excellence and high reliability anywhere in the school.*
   Such recognitions can be initiated by the school leadership team, or by the library media specialist. When someone—teacher, student, parent, volunteer—does an excellent job dealing with a problem, understanding the real need, or helping another student, recognize the fact by a note on the library bulletin board. In fact, create an "EXCELLENT! WELL DONE!" bulletin board and put something on it every week (still better, every day). An-

nounce in faculty meetings, PSTA meetings, and other community forums the outstanding job that someone has done this week.

2. *Whenever there is an outstanding library media program, let everyone know about it.*
Use the public relations channels of the school system; promote programs on local television talk shows; create opportunities for teachers, students, and parents to write letters to the editor of the local newspaper; create a local school library media World Wide Web page, and promote your outstanding programs on it.

3. *While promoting your own library media program, remember that the best promotion comes from other people.*
Have such a good program that teachers, students, parents, and community agencies are willing to boast about the program in other places. Attend school board meetings to make statements. Ask questions in county government budget hearings. Your best public relations will always be done by others.

4. *Publish what you know and can find out about library media program options, problems, and opportunities in the library literature.*
The authors know that you are too busy to sit down and write . . . so are we. Now that excuse is out of the way, school library media specialists need to share their experiences, failures, successes, and wisdom with each other. There are multiple outlets, including the Internet and all of the divisional publications of the American Library Association, as well as opportunities for presentations at conferences. Having taken the time to gain wisdom, share it with others.

Summary

The authors are not in favor of abandoning any segment of our society in the future. We are excited about the future of the library media programs. We have urged that schools and their library media programs become high reliability organizations. We have stressed that library media specialists and the rest of the administrative and instructional staff must develop a philosophy of broad community inclusion and governance in the instructional program of the school. That inclusion involves teachers, students, administrators, parents, the community, and other agencies seeking to define and fulfill a common goal: To make available the best life possible for all of the people in the community, utilizing whatever technologies are appropriate. All agencies combine their efforts so that information essential to living, understanding, and enjoying life is available all of the time in all of the places possible.

Reaching such a goal is possible, but enormous changes have to take place in the bureaucracies of schools and other community agencies. The ways in which schools and other agencies are funded by the federal, state, and local government must change so that agencies that do move toward collaborative high reliability are rewarded, and agencies that do not change will be prodded to change by loss of revenue. Most of all, attitudes among the varied professionals must move from distrust of cooperation and parental involvement toward full, open collaboration among all the segments of a united community.

Notes

1. Jane L. David, "Realizing the Promise of Technology: The Need for Systemic Education Reform," in *Systemic Reform: Perspectives on Personalizing Education—September 1994*, ed. Ronald J. Anson (San Francisco: SRI International, Bay Area Research Group, 1994), 1.

2. Todd LaPorte and Paula Consolini, "Working in Practice But Not in Theory: Theoretical Challenges of High-Reliability Organizations," *Journal of Public Administration Research and Theory* 1, no. 1 (1991), 19–48. Quote is from p. 20.

3. Karlene H. Roberts, "Some Characteristics of High Reliability Organizations," *Organizational Science* 1, no. 2 (1990), 1–17.

4. Robert J. Rossi and Alesia Montgomery, eds., *Educational Reforms and Students at Risk: A Review of the Current State of the Art* (Washington, D.C.: Department of Education, produced by the American Institute for Research under contract, 1994), chap. 11.

5. Thomas L. Good and Jere Brophy, *School Effects, Occasional Paper No. 77* (East Lansing, Mich.: Institute for Research on Teaching, Michigan State University, 1985, ERIC Document Reproduction No. ED 264 211). Daniel U. Levine and Lawrence W. Lezotte, *Unusually Effective Schools* (Madison, Wis.: National Center for Effective Schools Research & Development, 1990, ERIC Document Reproduction Service No. ED 330 032).

6. Joy G. Dryfoos, *Full-Service Schools: Schools and Community-Based Organizations Finally Get Together to Address the Crisis in Disadvantaged Communities*, paper presented at the annual meeting of the American Educational Research Association, San Francisco, April 18–22, 1995 (ERIC Document Reproduction Service No. ED 385 899).

7. Edward F. Zigler, "Child Day Care in the Schools: The School of the 21st Century," *Child Welfare* 74, no. 6 (November–December 1995), 1301–26.

8. George J. Jeffers and Margaret Olebe, "One-Stop Family Service Center: The Community School," *Community Education Journal* 21, no. 3 (spring 1994), 4–7.

9. Gary G. Wehlage and Calvin R. Stone, *School-Based Student Support Services: Community and Bureaucracy* (Madison, Wis.: Center on Organization and Restructuring of Schools, 1995, ERIC Document Reproduction Service No. ED 387 926).

10. Bruce A. Miller, *The Role of Rural Schools in Rural Community Development. ERIC Digest* (Charleston, W.V.: ERIC Clearinghouse on Rural Education and Small Schools, 1995, ERIC Document Reproduction Service No. ED 384 479).

11. Melvin C. Wittrock, ed., *Handbook of Research on Teaching* (New York: Macmillan, 1986).

12. Joel A. Barker, *Paradigms: The Business of Discovering the Future* (New York: HarperBusiness, 1992).

13. Joseph Cambone, "Time for Teachers in School Restructuring," in *Systemic Reform: Perspectives on Personalizing Education—September 1994*, ed. R. J. Anson (Washington, D.C.: U.S. Department of Education, 1992), 179–80.

14. The National Education Commission on Time and Learning, *Prisoners of Time* (Washington, D.C.: U.S. Department of Education, 1994, Recommendations, No. 5, ERIC Document Reproduction Service No. 378 686).

15. Samuel C. Stringfield and Nancy Yoder, "Toward a Model of Elementary Grades Chapter 1 Effectiveness," in *Students at Risk in At-Risk Schools*, ed. J. Waxman et al. (Newbury Park, Calif.: Sage Publications, 1992), 203–21.

16. Mary J. LeTendre, "The Continuing Evolution of a Federal Role in Compensatory Education," *Educational Evaluation and Policy Analysis* 13 (1991), 328–34.

17. Samuel C. Stringfield, "Implementing a Research-Based Model of Chapter 1 Program Improvement," *Phi Delta Kappan* 72, no. 8 (April 1991), 600–05.

18. Samuel C. Stringfield and Charles Teddlie, "Observers as Predictors of Schools Multiyear Outlier Status," *Elementary School Journal* 91, no. 4 (March 1991), 357–76.

19. Robert E. Slavin et al., *Success for All: A Relentless Approach to Prevention and Early Intervention in Elementary Schools*, ERS Monograph (Arlington, Va.: Educational Research Service, 1992, ERIC Document Reproduction Service No. ED 373 863).

20. Gay S. Pinnell, *Success of Children at Risk in a Program That Combines Writing and Reading, Technical Report No. 417* (Urbana: Bolt, Beranek and Newman, Illinois Center for the Study of Reading, 1988, ERIC Reproduction Service No. ED 292 061).

21. Jane L. David, "The Who, What, and Why of Site-Based Management," *Educational Leadership* 53, no. 4 (December–January, 1996), 4–9.

22. Charlene O. Meriwether, *Site-Based Management in Secondary Schools* (Reston, Va.: National Association of Secondary School Principals, 1996, ERIC Document Reproduction Service No. ED 392 163).

23. Susan Black, "Share the Power," *Executive Educator* 18, no. 2 (February 1996), 24–26.

24. Ulrich C. Reitzug and Colleen A. Capper, "Deconstructing Site-Based Management: Possibilities for Emancipation and Alternative Means of Control," *International Journal of Educational Reform* 5, no. 1 (January 1996), 56–59.

25. John Smyth, ed., *A Socially Critical View of the "Self Managing School"* (Bristol, Pa.: Falmer Press, 1993).

26. Russell W. Rumburger and Katherine A. Larson, *Keeping High-Risk Chicano Students in School: Lessons from a Los Angeles Middle School Dropout Prevention Program* (1992, ERIC Document Reproduction Service No. ED 368 582).

27. Mark R. Edwards, *360-Degree Feedback: The Powerful New Model for Employee Assessment and Performance Improvement* (New York: AMACOM, 1996).

28. Jay Klagge, "360-Degree Sociometric Feedback for Individual and Organizational Change," *Public Administration Quarterly* 19, no. 3 (fall 1995), 352–66. Mark C. Marchese, "Industry: The Power of the 360-Degree Feedback," *Pennsylvania CPA Journal* 66, no. 6 (December 1995), 19, 47.

29. Jason Millman, ed., *Handbook of Teacher Evaluation* (Beverly Hills, Calif.: Sage Publications, 1989).

30. Stringfield and Teddlie, "Observers as Predictors," 362–63.

31. Nancy A. Madden et al., *Success for All: Multi-Year Effects of a Schoolwide Elementary Restructuring Program, Report No. 18* (Baltimore, Md.: Johns Hopkins University, Center for Research on Effective Schooling for Disadvantaged Students, 1991). Idem, "Success for All: Longitudinal Effects of a Restructuring Program for Inner-City Elementary Schools," *American Educational Research Journal* 30, no. 1 (spring 1993), 123–48.

32. P. Mortimore et al., *School Matters* (Somerset, England: Open Books, 1988).

33. Stringfield and Teddlie, "Observers as Predictors," 358.

34. Slavin et al., *Success for All*, 4–5.

35. Susan Imel, *Workplace Literacy: Its Role in High Performance Organizations, ERIC Digest No. 158* (Columbus, Ohio: ERIC Clearinghouse on Adult, Career, and Vocational Education, 1995, ERIC Document Reproduction Service No. ED 383 858).

36. Robert K. Wimpelberg et al., "Sensitivity to Context: The Past and Future of Effective Schools Research," *Educational Administration Quarterly* 25, no. 1 (February 1989), 82–107.

Appendix

National Educational Organizations
Engaged in School Reform

Accelerated Schools Project
Stanford University, CERAS Building
Stanford, CA 94305-3084
(415) 725-1676
This project, developed by Henry Levin and colleagues at the Stanford's Center for Education Research, emphasizes improving the academic performance of disadvantaged students by acceleration rather than remediation. It proposes to eliminate achievement gaps by changing curriculum, instruction, and school organization. The Accelerated Schools Project was piloted in elementary schools in California in 1986 and is now in operation in Missouri, California, Illinois, Connecticut, and other states.

Coalition of Essential Schools
Brown University
Box 1969
Providence, RI 02912
(401) 863-3384
Founded by Theodore Sizer in 1984, the Coalition of Essential Schools supports secondary schools, districts, and states in their efforts to focus on the school's primary purpose: to improve student learning. The coalition asks practitioners to work from a set of ideas—the nine Common Principles—to restructure their own schools based on the particular needs of their community. It publishes a newsletter, HORACE, that covers activities underway at coalition schools.

League of Schools Reaching Out
Boston University
605 Commonwealth Avenue
Boston, MA 02215
(617) 353-3309
The League of Schools Reaching Out is a project of the Institute for Responsive Education, a nonprofit public-interest organization that promotes parent and

citizen involvement in education, with a special emphasis on equity issues. It is an international network of about ninety schools with partnerships involving families and communities. The Institute provides facilitators in some schools to help coordinate three key components: a parent center, parent outreach workers, and teacher researcher teams.

National Center for Restructuring Education, Schools, and Teaching
Teachers College, Columbia University
Box 110
New York, NY 10027
(212) 678-3434
This membership organization is intended to connect individuals and organizations working to build learner-centered schools. It offers publications, conferences, workshops, and technical assistance. Linda Darling-Hammond and Ann Lieberman are codirectors. Write or call for membership information and a publications list.

National Diffusion Network (NDN)
U.S. Department of Education
555 New Jersey Avenue NW
Washington, DC 20208-5645
(202) 219-2134
Supported by the U.S. Department of Education's Office of Educational Research and Improvement, the National Diffusion Network helps inform educators about excellent education programs that have proven to be highly effective in other schools and districts. These programs are validated, or examined for proof of effectiveness, by a Program Effectiveness Panel. Program information is compiled in annual editions of a catalog, Educational Programs That Work. State facilitators in every state, the District of Columbia, and the territories are available to help local school districts identify programs that meet their needs and obtain the assistance they need to implement the programs successfully. Developers of successful programs are available to train teachers in the adopting schools.

National Network for Educational Renewal
University of Washington, 313 Miller Hall
Seattle, WA 98195
(206) 543-5319
This network comprises school–university partnerships committed to the simultaneous renewal of schooling and of the education of educators. John Goodlad's Center for Educational Renewal serves as the hub of the network. Approximately twenty-five colleges and universities, one hundred school districts, and two hundred fifty partner schools in fourteen states are linked to the National Network for Educational Renewal. The network emphasizes forming partnerships, strengthening liberal arts and professional curricula, and developing a system of rewards and incentives for faculty members.

New American Schools Development Corporation
1000 Wilson Boulevard, Suite 2710
Arlington, VA 22209
(703) 908-9500
NASDC, a private, bipartisan, nonprofit organization headed by former Deputy Secretary of Education David Kearns, was founded in 1991 by corporate and foundation leaders to support the design and creation of outstanding public schools. NASDC selected eleven design and development teams from a pool of nearly seven hundred proposals and now supports nine teams in the implementation of their designs. Teams include ATLAS Communities, Audrey Cohen College, Community Learning Centers, Co-NECT Schools, Expeditionary Learning/Outward Bound, Los Angeles Learning Centers, Modern Red Schoolhouse, National Alliance for Restructuring Education, and Roots and Wings. The teams currently work with one hundred forty schools in nineteen states. Following refinement of their designs, they will aid other interested communities in adapting and implementing their prototypes for school reform. Contact NASDC for a brochure on the design teams.

School Development Program
Yale Child Study Center
230 South Frontage Road, P.O. Box 3333
New Haven, CT 06510
This program, founded in 1968 by James Comer, is designed to improve the academic performance and school success of low-income minority students by building supportive bonds among children, parents, and school staff to promote a positive school climate. The Comer Process emphasizes a no-fault atmosphere, collaborative working relationships, and decision making by consensus. Each school in this program establishes the following teams: a school planning and management team that includes parents, teachers, administrators and support staff; a mental health team that addresses children's developmental needs; and a parents' group that strengthens the bond between home and school.

Success for All
Center for Social Organization of Schools
The Johns Hopkins University
3505 N. Charles Street
Baltimore, MD 21218
(410) 516-0370
This program of the Center for Research on Effective Schooling for Disadvantaged Students emphasizes restructuring elementary schools and reconfiguring the uses of Chapter 1 and special education funds to emphasize prevention and early intervention rather than remediation. Under the direction of Robert Slavin, "Success for All" has expanded beyond Baltimore to about eighty-five schools in nineteen states. Its principal features include reading tutors, direct instruction and flexible grouping in reading, frequent assessment, enriched preschool and kindergarten programs, and family support teams.

Index

About the Authors

Kieth C. Wright is chair of the Department of Library and Information Studies at the University of North Carolina at Greensboro, where he has been a faculty member for the last twenty years. He has taught, conducted workshops, and written about the use of computer-related technologies in libraries and has co-authored books and articles about library services to persons with disabilities with his wife, Judith F. Davie.

Judith F. Davie is the librarian at Hampton Year Round School in the Guilford County School systsem, where she has served for the past six years. Prior to that time she served as a library supervisor for the Greensboro City Schools. She has been a faculty member at Appalachian State University and the University of North Carolina at Greensboro, where she taught school library media services, supervised practicums, and taught children's literature. She is the co-author of several books on library services to persons with disabilities with her husband Kieth.